VERTICAL LIVING

VERTICAL LIVING

FIND YOUR INNER GURU
BE A HIGH PERFORMER WITH PURPOSE

VIDYANGI

PARTRIDGE

ISBN: Hardcover   978-1-4828-7549-2
             Softcover   978-1-4828-7548-5
             eBook   978-1-4828-7547-8

Print information available on the last page.

To order additional copies of this book, contact
Partridge India
000 800 10062 62
orders.india@partridgepublishing.com

www.partridgepublishing.com/india

Contents

When problems get hard and the existing framework of thinking fails,
it helps to change perspective. Here I talk about how an individual
can be empowered beyond imagination, to solve great problems,
effect great changes, just by being creative in looking at life.

A view of the change that is coming, and how best
we can brace ourselves to welcome the future.

I dedicate my book to **the super power** in you.
Namaste: I bow to that super power in you!

Author's Address and Contact Information

Author's e-mail: patilvidya@gmail.com
Book's web address: http://awakenyour.guru/vertical-living/
Author's Blog: http://awakenyour.guru/blog/
Author's LinkedIn profile: https://www.linkedin.com/in/vidyaangipatil
Facebook Page: https://www.facebook.com/livingvertically/
twitter handle: https://twitter.com/vidyaangi

Disclaimer

Other Creative Information and ISBN

Cover/Title page art and illustration: Megha Vishwanath
Image credits for Dedication page: Ron Chapple www.dreamstime.com
Partial Image credits for charts: Maksym Leshchenko www.dreamstime.com
Editors: Arya Hebbar, Linda Jay
Developmental Editors: Jyoti Paintel, Arya Hebbar
ASIN: B01E0PGUKE

How the Book Evolved and How to Use It

This book started off as a collection of some of my most popular blogs and speeches. It is by no means a self-help or a feel-good book. It is abstract in many ways. The ideas in the book will evolve organically with you, every time you read them, because some of the ideas that I share with you are timeless; for instance, the miraculous effects of deep breathing, or the philosophy and power of love. I get my ideas to compose a speech or a blog in the wee hours of the morning, or when I am daydreaming, dancing, when I am in the shower, or when I go off on a long drive and I am in quiet and solitude. I let these ideas marinate inside me for many days and weeks and feel these ideas seep into my perception of reality. These ideas then take over my world and haunt me till I pen them down as blogs and speeches. Writing is like that, it is a flow that cannot be stopped, even if you have to interrupt a meal or forget about sleep. The thoughts absolutely must collide with paper!

This book is my way of looking at the world, but I am also playing conduit to some of the greatest thinkers and people who have landscaped the field of medicine, art, philosophy, mathematics, and physics. I hope you like my view of the world as I stand on the shoulders of these stalwarts and share my visions with you. But feel free to disagree with me and go off on your own journey of creative ideas. My efforts will be victorious if, after reading my book, you make a shift in ideas in your life towards progress, towards expanding your reach towards the impossible; they call it moonshot thinking. I call it living in an awakened state. Once you complete reading the book you will realise both these references somehow intersect. Believe me, this realization will feel like a blooming, a rising, and an awakening that was long waiting to happen.

I introduce terms like vertical living, inner guru, higher intelligence, and high performer; and redefine them the way I see them. When you read through Chapters 1, 3, and 7, you will be able to grasp these dimensions of my world.

Every chapter can be read as a standalone; however, it is of prime importance to understand the concepts of *vertical living, inner guru, high performer, and higher intelligence*. They are central to the theme of the book. They need to be understood just as they have been explained in the book, because I use these terms differently—the way I see them! There is no other reference to these terms as defined here, outside of this book. For the rest of the terms, use the book's glossary or Google the references supplied.

This book was seeded in me, waiting to be expressed, for a long time now. Even as a child, I had always strongly sensed that there was a burning need for realization of creativity, happiness and fulfillment, waiting to be addressed. As an adult, I watched the world evolve into a materialistic and technology-driven society, and I realised that this need was growing day by day, by leaps and bounds. I felt a lack of compassion, genuineness, energy, and awakening in most people I met. I loathed myself for being half asleep and not seeing the grandeur and largesse that life had to offer. I detested the way I had half-lived my life all the time without enjoying the subtleties in beauty, love, and compassion that life exudes. With this book, I have tried to tackle this sleepy and limited view of the world and cajole my readers into living a much awakened, vibrant, fulfilled life; to persuade them to conceive and realise grand ideas, in taking a shot at the moon, if you will!

Preface

SETTING THE STAGE

What makes people think differently and find success in realizing their innate potential? How did men and women who changed the face of physics, art, mobile communication or space travel, muster the courage to stand behind their path breaking ideas? Why did the world's youngest billionaire choose his enterprise over formal schooling? What does it take to realise the unthinkable and make it a reality? Of all the brilliant people with great academic backgrounds, multiple degrees and certificates adorning their resume, what sets the game changers apart? I have asked myself these questions all my life. When I posed them to educated people I know, their responses reflected a multitude of different perspectives.

I finally decided that I would figure it out myself. I went on a break from a predictable lifestyle, of being a busy working mom with a 9-to-5 job and a secure paycheck, and became a full-time writer. I had previously done a lot of blogging and public speaking as an amateur, and discovered I was good at it and loved doing it. I had managed to create a loyal following which liked to hear me speak and loved what I wrote. They had tried to cajole me into writing a book many times in the past. While authoring a book had been on my wish list for a few years, to go all out and pursue my dream required me to overcome my inner fear of exploring the unknown.

A few friends who heard about my hiatus from work life questioned my credibility as a full-time writer. I stuck to my gut feeling and did not go back on my decision. All my doubts disappeared when a mentor I look up to and consider a role model showed confidence in my enterprise. I went ahead with the idea of writing this book and have not looked back since. Here I bring to you my firsthand experience in starting off my adventure without a paycheck and following my inner calling to write, how I experimented with my own theories, and saw successful results. This, for me is the greatest testimony that my theories work!

I couldn't get enough of this new life! My whole being was bitten by the energy bug; miracles were always just around the corner. I felt an intense creative energy and sparkle in my eyes. I thought about writing the book and sharing its message all the time. I dealt with exciting people every day, flipped through the unwritten pages of life, and worked on the script as best as I could. It got hard at times and I often felt I was going uphill, with lots of challenges and uncertainty.

However, there was one distinct advantage to all this madness. I was, in many ways, able to relate to people who changed the course of history. They chose a life of uncertainty because they were true to their inner calling. At this point, I feel the same way. In this chapter, I talk about myself, the book, and my motivation and inner calling to write it.

A LITTLE ABOUT ME

I was born and raised in Bengaluru, the city now regarded as the Silicon Valley of India. When I was growing up, Bengaluru was a melting pot of diverse cultures, languages, and traditions. It was home to the birth of many new tech companies. I was part of a large joint family; my home buzzed with friends and family members moving in and out all the time. Charity in education, as well as sharing and donating resources such as food, was a way of life for my sister and me. Both my parents are doctors; they own a hospital in the northern part of the city. During most of the time that I lived with them, I was involved in discussions about strategies in managing teams at work and at home. My sister and I spent summer vacations in yoga camps (on Siddha Samadhi Yoga, for example) and workshops conducted by the Ramakrishna Mission and the Institute of Human Potential and Development (run by Dr Bharat Chandra, an international success coach). As a consequence, our discussions at lunch and dinner frequently centered on concepts in attitude, personality, and altered states of the conscious mind for effectively dealing with changes in our personal and professional lives.

My mom constantly talked about techniques that involved combining energy-healing and alternative medicine in conjunction with allopathic medicine. Not a day went by where we did not discuss the power of prayer, meditation, or the meaning of Karma, as explained in ancient Indian philosophy. These were the very concepts that were later reiterated by thinkers such as Edgar Cayce and Dr Brian Weiss in the Western world. I attended a Christian missionary school for my elementary and middle schooling, and I started seeing very early that self-realization is a theme common to Eastern and Western philosophies. I have come to understand that every religion in the world talks about the path of self-realization. It was interesting to see that my parents were able to apply those very concepts of self-realization to the journey of entrepreneurship. This was second nature to them, because they began their careers intending to be entrepreneurs.

My parents worked round-the-clock for most of the year, and as far as I can recall, seldom had a predictable routine. They were always on the go, and to them, their work itself was a way of life. They were savvy about good business practices, but daily they willingly served free of charge people who had limited means of income. I will never forget the times when my mom fasted and prayed for her patients to come out of critical illnesses and how she would help ameliorate their pain during childbirth by using techniques from Pranic healing.

My life and ideas are deeply rooted at the intersection of self-realization and entrepreneurship, the two pillars of my upbringing. I clearly see the underlying principles common to Eastern and Western philosophies and religions, and find peace in the principles that guide nature and life itself—principles of the heart, or what I call the 'inner calling'. I will talk about these throughout this book.

WATCHING MY DAD AS AN ENTREPRENEUR WAS HARD, BUT FUN!

The challenges of thriving in an entrepreneurial ecosystem are not new to me. Very early in my journey, I frequently crossed paths with innovators and entrepreneurs. I grew up watching my dad navigate the highs and lows of being an entrepreneur. The ideas in this book have been waiting to see the light of day ever since I was a child, and witnessed him putting his life on the line to make his vision a reality.

My dad, a self-made man, is one of eight siblings born to a lower-middle-class family. He hails from a small village in South India where education was treated as a luxury. Having my father as my closest guide and mentor, and listening to stories of how he realised his dreams in Bengaluru, has made me relate to entrepreneurship as a way of life. The greatest lesson he has taught me is to stay alert and aware at all times, and not let the past get in the way of the present or the future. He had taken huge risks, turning down opportunities that promised safety and comfort in order to start off on his entrepreneurial career. He balanced his risk-taking ability with a high degree of intuition, teamwork, calm rationale, thorough planning, hard work, and unmatched dedication to the task at hand. He has inspired me in many ways to realise my true potential, and to be effective as an entrepreneur. I will share these lessons with you as I take you through the journey of my book.

WHAT WAS IT LIKE BRING RAISED IN BENGALURU, THE SILICON VALLEY OF INDIA?

Image courtesy: Vishwa Kiran www.dreamstime.com

The city of Bengaluru has been a fertile ground for nurturing companies that are focused on research and development in the physical sciences, life sciences, and information technology. The city I remember as a child was home to people from diverse backgrounds, languages, countries, food preferences, and lifestyles. The open mindset in Bengaluru fostered the growth and evolution of a culture of constant innovation, which is also a defining characteristic of Silicon Valley, California.

Throughout my childhood and formative years, I was frequently thrust into the epicenter of groundbreaking inventions that turned the tide of social psyche in the age of the Internet. I distinctly recall how the dot-com boom, the bubble, and the recession that followed, affected my job search and influenced the trends in career and education in my peer group.

Image courtesy: Noppasin Wongchum www.dreamstime.com

For me, the digital era redefined technology, the meaning of relationships and values, and changed my perception of life itself. The world transitioned from an age of exclusive and limited access to resources, to a powerful and fast age of digital communication with endless possibilities for everyone. *This digital world was also shallow, because it was in many ways, only a world of virtual realities.* I saw the emergence of communities for dating, friendships, and matrimony across nationalities. Budding entrepreneurs of the Internet era had access to large amounts of data and an unprecedentedly large audience, all just a click or a swipe away. In *Vertical Living*, I draw from this experience of transition to reiterate the vital importance of being connected with oneself amidst the unlimited opportunities and rewards offered by the Internet age. The ability to stay rooted, connected, and true to one's nature is rooted in self-realization.

WHY TALK ABOUT SELF-REALIZATION?

Self-realization means realizing your true inner potential; in other words, knowing and accepting yourself with all your strengths and weaknesses. Religions tend to prescribe a lifestyle or a set of practices that will lead you to self-realization or maximizing your human potential. For example, in Hinduism, there is a practice of chanting a 'mantra' during prayer [109]. This is a way of meditation because it aligns and focuses the mind with the act of saying something repeatedly and with reverence; there is a sense of purity and devotion while chanting. Many people do not follow a religion. But they go about their daily activities with the same degree of devotion and purity as what is recommended during chanting. Their personal potential is maximised in their daily activities, just as it would be for a person who chants during prayer or meditation.

Everything you have ever felt or experienced is through your body and mind. If you do not understand how they are constantly changing, you will not be able to assess your strengths and weaknesses completely. If you do not fully understand your strengths and weaknesses, you will not be able to set reasonable goals for yourself and will end up chasing unreasonable goals—and life is too precious to be wasted in such pursuits. You want to experience life fully, every single moment, all the way! You start by knowing yourself completely through self-realization. I call this kind of lifestyle *vertical living*. I urge my readers to follow their inner calling, and adopt *vertical living* as a lifestyle in order to maximise their inner human potential. I will talk more about vertical living, which I also refer to as the lifestyle of an awakened person, in Chapter 1 *What is Vertical Living?*

WHY VERTICAL LIVING AS A LIFESTYLE?

My upbringing in India was accentuated by a lifestyle of self-realization. Emigrating from India to the US almost reset my entire framework of thinking. Having moved out of my parents' home to attend graduate school, I found myself searching for my inner voice. I was longing to reinvent myself. All my attempts have taken me back to the roots of self-realization. That is why I recommend such a lifestyle as a path to maximizing our human potential.

After moving to the US in 2004, I spent much time exploring the philosophy of interpersonal dynamics, creativity, and meditation. I am a member of Toastmasters International, a well-known nonprofit organization that helps people develop public speaking and leadership skills. I have used this forum as a ground for experimenting with communication, leadership, and mental and physical state management. I explored literature about self-help in the works of Eckhart Tolle, Tony Robbins, Paulo Coelho, Napoleon Hill, Stephen Covey, and Deepak Chopra; and soon started to see a parallel between self-realization and self-help. I explored the literary works of J. Krishnamurthy, Osho, Sadhguru Jaggi

Vasudev, and the Brahmakumari Spiritual University. I studied the practices of Buddhism as well as the philosophy of the Upanishads or Vedanta. In time, I began to realise that all my role models and mentors, both inside and outside the corporate world, display traits consistent with those on a path to self-realization. These traits have helped them become high achievers and game changers in their own rights. I set out to ascertain this fact by studying the biographies of game changers from history, and interviewing my mentors from everyday life.

Much of my writing has been influenced by my life in Silicon Valley over the last eight years. A constant pursuit of wealth, power, and happiness is a way of life in this valley of the modern-day gold rush. The hectic pace of change in technology and the need to stay ahead in the game have ushered in the biggest breakthroughs in advancing human capacity. For instance, think about riding in a driverless car that shows you traffic updates and news headlines, as well as statistics from the heater and water sprinkler in your home, while you are working on your laptop or participating in a conference call as part of a business meeting. Quite often, I have felt the unbelievable excitement of living in the middle of such an aggressive, smart, hectic, and ambitious lifestyle. Believe me, it is fun; but can eventually tip us out of balance from a healthy and fulfilling lifestyle.

VERTICAL LIVING HELPS YOU STRIKE THAT BALANCE!

If you need to stay abreast of advancements in technology while being rooted in human nature, there must be a consistent and effective way to do so. In *Vertical Living*, I try to help you achieve this by tapping into your mind, body, and sensory abilities. This way you can elevate your inner human potential.

Is there a way of life that can unleash supra-human abilities to create, sustain, and elevate human capacity? My book talks about vertical living as such a lifestyle. It is a term I introduce in this book, in the context of human potential.

Vertical living is elevated living, i.e., elevated in your ability to be aware of yourself in body, mind, and emotions; and being compassionate about your surroundings. It is a way of living life in depth, harnessing intuition, imagination, creativity, and connecting with the true purpose of your life, i.e., the path shown by your inner compass, inner guide or intuition.

INTUITION AND IMAGINATION: WHAT'S THE BIG DEAL?

Imagination and intuition are integral parts of vertical living as a lifestyle. I iterate these ideas time and again throughout the book. These factors clearly form the building blocks that shaped the thinking behind Silicon Valley. I will tell you more about it in Chapter 2, *The Secret of Game Changers*.

I am deeply inspired by the culture of entrepreneurship and innovation in Silicon Valley. It leads the way in path breaking innovations, a hallmark of some of the world's largest tech corporations as well as smaller startups that call this place home.

What I admire most about the people who have guided the course of technology is their innate ability to follow their inner calling, to foresee the future through intuition, and courage to realise their imagination. To name a few such game changers of silicon valley: Robert Noyce, nicknamed *the Mayor of Silicon Valley*, was one of the pioneers of the semiconductor industry; Steve Jobs, who ushered in the age of the personal computer with the Apple Macintosh; Bill Gates, though not primarily associated with Silicon Valley, is nonetheless a visionary who transformed computer software into the industry that it is today; Facebook, led by its founder Mark Zuckerberg, who connects billions of users online and encourages an open culture of learning and sharing; Elon Musk, who not only set off a new age revolution within the automobile industry as cofounder of Tesla, but is also leading the drive to redefine the boundaries of human potential, bringing scientific fiction to the very brink of reality. What was their innate ability indeed, which caused them to landscape the face of technology in shaping Silicon Valley itself?

Using their combined power of intuition and foresight, these revolutionary thinkers have been able to model the future in their imagination and transform it into reality with resounding success.

Silicon Valley has been the birthplace of such creative minds, and has nurtured them to become entrepreneurs of the highest calibre. In such a spectacular environment for innovation and enterprise, every so often I see my peers, childhood friends, and acquaintances emerge as entrepreneurs. Their journeys have allowed me to closely witness the intricacies and triumphs of a chaotic, high-energy, and performance-driven lifestyle.

Image courtesy: Rolffimages www.dreamstime.com

From Leonardo da Vinci to the pioneers of the semiconductor industry, from Bruce Lee to Steve Jobs, every game changer displayed vertical living as a lifestyle. Following your inner guide raises your human capacity. When you raise your human capacity, the natural tendency for you will be to become creative and successful in your business, social life, and personal endeavors. My book covers this whole process from striving to attain elevated or vertical living to achieving success in personal and professional life.

As a human being, each of us is intelligent and sensitive to emotional, physical, psychological, intuitive, and spiritual inputs. In the last few years, on my journey through self-realization, self-discovery, and motherhood, I have found that my overall personality and ability to perform is a sum total of my inner mental health, physical health, and inputs from my surroundings. I also found that such ability is at an optimum when one lives in awareness, is guided by intuition, maintains health, and pursues happiness as a way of life. I call this lifestyle vertical living.

I propose that by adopting vertical living as your lifestyle, you will start accessing your inner voice or inner compass, and start realizing your true elevated inner potential. Vertical living as a lifestyle is the guiding light of high performers, overachievers, creative thinkers who challenge the conventional mindset, entrepreneurs, and people who believe in experiencing excellence in their lives. In the chapter *Vertical Living*, I talk about the ability to exist in meditative states in everyday life in order to heighten creativity, decision-making, and the perception of any given situation [1].

CAN YOU REALLY MAINTAIN THE NATURAL RHYTHM OF IMAGINATION AND INTUITION AMIDST CHAOS?

Is your life driven by a constant focus on deadlines, profitability, and performance? Do you spend long hours commuting and constantly interacting with devices like the phone and the tablet? How often do you feel sleep-deprived? Do you have irregular eating habits? Do you depend on your addiction to caffeine to overcome jet lag, or keep up with co-workers in time zones spread across the globe? Is participating in social media a cause of tremendous peer pressure? Do you miss the warmth and touch of a fellow human being? To meet the demands of an entrepreneurial lifestyle, our behavioral patterns have deviated from their natural rhythms.

These unnatural patterns are affecting us negatively more than ever before, sapping our human potential. These patterns and the factors influencing them have been a focus of my study for many years now. In this book, I write about my observations and expertise to help heal these unnatural patterns and create high performers who can nonetheless maintain a balanced lifestyle. I recommend vertical living as the lifestyle to create such a balance.

In this day and age of digital media and virtual experiences, there is a great desire to talk about true happiness and fulfillment. I myself need quiet time to reflect on the factors that are affecting me constantly so that I can continue to stay grounded, happy and connected to myself, and keep that wonder of creativity alive. <u>Being yourself is the best way to maximise your potential and meet the</u> <u>demands of a fast-paced, dynamic, and performance-driven lifestyle.</u> The stories and experiences that I share in the book more than substantiate this fact.

THE BASIS FOR THE CONTENT IN MY BOOK

The content of my book has been assembled from my personal experiences, and my interviews with experts in technology, medicine, leadership and communication; I also draw inspiration from the biographies and accounts of philosophers, scientists, and inventors with unprecedented abilities in the fields of science, art, medicine, technology, etc. I not only refer to the strategies they used to achieve successful results, but also suggest modifying some of their specific approaches. My suggestions emphasise the *health and happiness* aspect of vertical living.

TIPS TO THE READER

As you read through this book, you will find tips for developing a vertical lifestyle for yourself, such as the one shown here. These tips can become points of transformation in your life. I specifically urge you to focus on the content in and around each tip.

WHO WOULD BENEFIT BY READING MY BOOK?

If you aspire to be an entrepreneur or a consistent high performer, then you would benefit from reading this book. I discuss not only how to be a high performer but also how to maintain consistency in your performance.

If you are shy about public speaking or live in fear of taking risks, I discuss overcoming fears and limitations that we set upon ourselves by using the concepts of *Beginner's Mind, Ego,* and *Icebreaker*. I will show you real-life examples of how people have successfully overcome their fears. Some of the examples are from my own experience, with a direct account of my state of mind, body, and emotions.

If you find it hard to manage and prioritise multiple tasks, and to focus on the task at hand, I can help you with some tips. In the chapter *High Performers,*

I cover various strategies for managing your priorities, which can help you see a task through to completion.

If you find it hard to create a plan and stick to it, I can help show you why you are failing. In Chapter 8, *On Goal Setting and More*, I provide valuable insights through excerpts from my interviews with people who have met tall orders by building high performing teams.

If you ever wonder how companies like Apple, Google, Facebook, and Tesla stay motivated to innovate constantly, turn your attention to the **Tips** I provide in Chapter 7, *The Heart of the Matter*. I explain the concepts of Higher Intelligence and Beginner's Mind, and take you straight into the hearts of the risk-takers and innovators who built these great companies. I also capture similar accounts of historical figures like Aristotle, Ptolemy, Leonardo da Vinci, Tesla, Ramanujan, and Einstein, who were early practitioners of such a culture of innovation and creativity.

If you think you are doing well in life but you do not love what you do, you will benefit from reading *Vertical Living*. I show you how a purposeful person who realises what he or she was born to accomplish lives and acts. Refer to the sections in and around the *Tips* mentioned throughout the book.

PHILADELPHIA: THE CITY WHERE THE IDEAS FOR THIS BOOK WERE BORN

Through the formative years of my life in Bengaluru, and later in Silicon Valley, I witnessed the power and glamor of 'making it big' as an innovator and entrepreneur. Besides the excitement and exhilaration that comes with such success, I was also aware of emerging patterns of loneliness and unhealthy living habits.

> The power of digital communication, which is breeding a higher number of entrepreneurs today, has unfortunately disconnected us from our true inner potential, and caused havoc in our personal relationships and ideas about what happiness and fulfillment are.

This thought led me to wonder if happiness, health, and fulfillment can become constant companions to the successful innovator, overachiever, or entrepreneur. Let me pose this as a question.

> How can entrepreneurs and people in high-pressure jobs stay happy, fulfilled, and focused throughout the highs and lows of their careers? What can we do to make happiness and fulfillment constant factors in a performance-driven lifestyle?

I arrived at the question above based on a specific experience in my life. After completing my master's degree in Biomedical Engineering from Drexel University, Philadelphia, I decided to get married. We moved to California's famed Bay Area. After living there for a couple of years, it was clear to me that I was living in Silicon Valley's tech bubble. Then came the recession of 2008, which took me back in time to the dot-com bubble that I had witnessed during my college days in Bengaluru.

My pursuit of a job then took me back east, to Lansdale, Pennsylvania. I moved there at the beginning of one of the harshest winters. There I was, in an unfamiliar neighborhood, living away from family, with plenty of time on my hands in the evenings after work. I hung out in downtown Philadelphia with colleagues, or friends from college, and explored the city quite a bit. But my curiosity about life required me to have a different, more meaningful experience. I was aware of the fact that this time away from my family came to me at a price, so I decided to use this time effectively to understand myself better.

In my quest for a purpose in life, I continued to interact with people of diverse lifestyles and persisted with my interviews, but none of these efforts yielded results that seemed promising. Determined to find a guru who could reveal to me the secret of a happy and fulfilled life, I joined a group of shamans and Buddhists at a meditation group in Lansdale. <u>I hoped that they would help answer my question: Can a happy and balanced life also be fast-paced, and encourage entrepreneurship and high performance?</u> I dedicated myself to exploring literature, attending workshops, and associating with people from varied cultural and professional backgrounds in the shaman and Buddhist community. I longed to find my guru.

I met many masters in shamanism, some of them women, and I learned from them in intense group sessions. Their ability to look at life creatively, in terms of energy and balance, stirred my imagination. It was such a refreshing outlook, very different from my upbringing in India and my experiences of living in Silicon Valley. They spoke about the principles of nature as applied to business and entrepreneurship. I talk more about this in the book, in all chapters referencing meditation and a few of my blogs.

I kept learning from the masters and absorbing valuable lessons. I kept experimenting with my life until I figured that I had to work on my body too to balance the intellectual path to self-realization that I had been pursuing. I had been devouring one or two books a day after work, plus attending workshops relentlessly. I developed a severe back problem from unhealthy eating habits and bad posture, thanks to my habit of reading books into the wee hours of the morning. I felt lethargic and was unable to get into fitness routine. All this took a toll on my health. I dealt with the pain over the next four years, and was able to overcome it only after I made core-strengthening exercises a part of my daily routine.

I had begun to understand the theory of self-realization, when it dawned on me that unless I was fit in my body as much as I was in my mind, there was no point to my intellectual pursuits in understanding human potential. As Swami Vivekananda said, 'The sign of vigor, the sign of life, the sign of hope, the sign of health, the sign of everything that is good, is strength. As long as the body lives, there must be strength in the body, strength in the mind, [and strength] in the hand.' [11]

SELF-REALIZATION HELPS IN BUILDING ENTREPRENEURIAL TRAITS

My experiences during the quest for happiness and fulfillment pointed me to the path of self-realization, which is the realization of your true inner human potential. For example, if you love art and are curious about it, or if you love technology and it fills you with wonder, then pursue that interest passionately. While in the process, remember to also take good care of yourself, the environment, and the family, team, or social circle to which you belong.

> 'The sign of vigor, the sign of life, the sign of hope, the sign of health, the sign of everything that is good, is strength. As long as the body lives, there must be strength in the body, strength in the mind, [and strength] in the hand.' -SWAMI VIVEKANANDA

There are many paths to choose from when you begin the journey toward self-realization. Meditating regularly, practicing yoga, maintaining a healthy diet, attaining mastery in your trade or profession, and staying positive as a way of life, are a few of the practices that will eventually lead you to this goal. I chose to pursue my interests because self-realization helps to realise your true strengths and express your abilities as marketable skills. By the time I had completed several workshops in shamanism, I had learned to get into a meditative state at will.

I tried to understand self-realization by performing daily activities in meditative states, similar to the practice of Vipassana [6]. I learned about self-realization from experts in the fields of shamanism, Vedanta, and Buddhism. I participated in discussions and prayer meetings, and attended talks by people who have switched careers. I took up activities like yoga, dancing, swimming, personal training, meditation, public speaking, and writing—all the time reinventing myself by way of changing my lifestyle and practicing healing.

My participation in these activities helped me understand myself even better. Life started to appear more and more like a jigsaw puzzle. The more I worked on the small steps toward self-realization, the more the bigger picture revealed itself, leading me eventually to the point where I could understand who I truly am and how I fit into the ecosystem around me. *In other words, as a result of all my efforts, I had realised how to maximise my true inner potential.*

Engage in different forms of creativity and challenge yourself regularly by learning something new and different from what you have tried before.
This is a lifestyle tip in vertical living.

My journey on this quest for self-realization has strongly indicated the following to be true.

1. The more I learn about myself and what I can do with my inner potential, the better is the quality of my life. For example, if my innate potential as a bird were to fly, I would be wasting my life in water trying to swim like a fish. If I can understand my innate ability, I can lead a happy life by choosing to fly in the sky instead of living miserably competing with the fish in water. A good friend of mine quit her day job and became a diving instructor because she disliked working in an enclosed space all day, and because she loved swimming. Her happiness and energy are simply contagious after she made the switch. The more I learn about myself, the more room there is for happiness and fulfillment in my life. This leads to a greater balance in my family, work, and social life.

2. The *techniques of self-realization are effective in bringing out the traits of successful entrepreneurs, overachievers, good communicators, leaders, and innovators in each one of us.* The traits that I refer to are: better time management, a higher degree of focus on the task at hand, calm and emotionally balanced dispositions, productive/profitable decision-making skills, a high emotional quotient, and the ability to build high performing teams. By adopting the path to self-realization or self-discovery, we become more creative and productive at our jobs and enterprise. I find this increasingly true from my interactions with friends, mentors and peers, as well as from reading a huge body of literature on self-help and self-realization.

3. There are many ways to achieve self-realization. It is a journey, unique to every human being. Although a guru or mentor can inspire you with the techniques of self-realization, the real journey of finding your true inner potential is yours alone.

4. On your journey to self-realization, you will meet many mentors or coaches who will lead you to achieve a specific goal; for example, someone who teaches or counsels you to be a good student or parent. You will also find role models—people who have attained self-realization

by using a method that worked for them. <u>*No one else but you can find your inner guru, inner guide, or inner calling.*</u>

Most people who changed the face of history or technology listened to their inner calling and realised the purpose of their lives. They were able to maximise their inner potential, become high performers, and find fulfillment in their creativity. They focused on that one purpose and gave it their all. Many people waste their lives trying to figure out where they need to spend their time and energy. This is where the inner calling or inner guru helps you out. All you need to do is just tune in to it and trust it!

HOW ABOUT AN ENTREPRENEURIAL APPROACH TO SELF-REALIZATION? DOES IT SOUND BETTER?

Until now we have talked about self-realization as a strategy to maximise our inner potential, to become an overachiever or an entrepreneur. Since we are all too familiar with the creed of entrepreneurs and their startups in this digital era of quick progress and fast money, I wondered *if self-realization could be achieved by using an entrepreneurial strategy.* I started thinking about this approach when I found that many of the people I interact with regularly, including my family and close circle of friends, do not believe in self-realization by using spiritual techniques. They respond better to terminology associated with entrepreneurship, like processes, practices, lifecycles, branding, marketing, pricing, selling, etc. I have previously mentioned that techniques for self-realization can help bring out the traits of successful entrepreneurs in each one of us. Naturally, I started to build my thoughts around a new, entrepreneurial approach to self-realization, or maximizing inner human potential.

Think about self-realization using an entrepreneurial approach. When that goal is reached, you create value for yourself and the world to which you belong. You build a product to address a specific market segment and to serve a purpose. You then sell the product that you have built by presenting it well and creating a good brand. This approach can be used to realise your talents and gifts in life, or achieve self-realization. An entrepreneur works with his product; a self-realised person works with his life as his product. In that sense, *a self-realised person is no different from a successful entrepreneur; they are both driven by their inner guide or inner guru towards an end product that creates value in society.*

Entrepreneurs sense the void or the desire for a product in the market, and address that need by building the product or a portfolio, effectively elevating human capacity. In doing so, they wear multiple hats—that of a designer, tester, marketer, salesperson, and even as a user of their own product. Think about Steve Jobs, who was involved in every step of the way building, designing, marketing, and selling Apple products. He was Apple brand himself! An entrepreneur literally oversees a product from concept to reality, through the entire lifecycle [2].

As a parallel to entrepreneurs who are building unique commercial products, those who are on the path to self-realization are rediscovering, building, and refining specific traits and skills in themselves to serve society—their need being to discover and unravel their true inner gifts or talents.

At this point of brief hiatus from a full-time job, I would like to share my experience using an entrepreneurial approach to self-realization as a writer and a speaker. I had to play make-believe with myself to be an entrepreneur [3] because I am always on the go; I work with a mobile office—I carry my laptop, books, and recording devices to a different location every day; I am networking all the time; and I started off on my own, with a small budget. I work for myself and I am rolling out a few products that are inspired in me by my inner calling [4]. I believe in my message and I intend to do my very best to serve people with my gifts that I have discovered.

WHAT IS IT LIKE, THINKING LIKE AN ENTREPRENEUR?

In this section I talk about my experiments as a writer and a speaker, using the entrepreneurial approach to self-realization. I knew I had it in me to become a writer and a speaker, even as a child. Throughout my life, I have enjoyed many opportunities to write and speak—in high school, college, and graduate school; in meditation workshops and job fairs; and during my stints in engineering and business schools. After eight years of serious, process-oriented, feedback-driven, disciplined, and persistent writing and speaking practice, I was able to start thinking of myself as a writer and a speaker. It took a lot of commitment, self-discipline, dedication, and hard work to develop skills that require lifecycle management, i.e., embracing the fact that I must have a vision of the end product, breaking that vision down into requirements, designing the product, and then building, marketing, and selling it to the right audience. For me, lifecycle management translated to envisioning, crafting, building and delivering good speeches and writing purposeful articles for my book, from which people can benefit and find genuine value from.

WHAT VALUE DO I BRING AS A SPEAKER AND A WRITER, AS I PURSUE MY INNER CALLING? IN OTHERS WORDS, WHAT'S NEW?

The basic question I had to ask myself before I started off was: Is there a need for a writer or speaker like me in current times? Am I creative enough to bring something new to serve and improve society? I had to find out for myself. What I discovered in this pursuit was that I enjoy developing both skills, but I need to balance my natural speaking and writing styles with the current needs of the audience. I needed to ask myself: What kind of speaking and writing do I enjoy the most? How best can I tailor my speeches and writings regarding personality development, entrepreneurship, high performance, creativity, and maximizing human potential, to my audience? I made these assessments over the last decade by participating in public speaking forums, networking events, workshops, and writing forums. My intention was to be constantly open to feedback, so I could 'fail fast' early on and quickly refine the skills I was trying to build.

> While using an entrepreneurial approach to self-realization, think of your life as your product.
> What are the skills you bring, and services you can offer to society to achieve physical, psychological, economic, and spiritual growth in your life and best realise it in this world?
> Give yourself and the world the true worth of your life and *become self-realised!*

I spent much time honing my inner calling and my inner voice, which are expressions of my intuition. My audiences have, on several occasions, sensed the purpose driving my work, and asked me: 'Where does this wonderful message come from?'. I realised that my *speeches and writings* can inspire people who need guidance to *hone their own skills*. This indeed is my true motivation!

GOING AGILE: FAILING FAST, WAS FUN! BUT VERY DEMANDING . . .

I went through several iterations of designing speeches and getting input on beta versions of my book; to better help people find their goals and inner calling. This process of constantly refining a product by being open to feedback early on, and failing fast, is referred to as *Agile methodology* in entrepreneurial or corporate language [5]. I had started marketing the message in my book, researched pricing, experimented with creating audiobook samples, and dabbled with different ways of selling the content, much before I had completed writing the first draft. I revised and improved my writing style and presentation, based on constant feedback from my core team of reviewers, editors, publishers, narrator, as well as my interviewees.

Now, do you see striking similarities between realizing a product and self-realization? To illustrate this idea, I will draw a parallel between the typical phases of a product life cycle in the corporate world, and the steps toward self-realization as I experienced them.

When I started writing this book, my goal was to share my experiences on my journey of self-realization with my readers. I then constantly refined the goals and objectives of the articles in the book as well as my speeches, to harmonise the message from my inner voice with what my audience wants to hear and read. This is the combined phase of requirement gathering in defining specific chapters and speeches, and developing or constructing them iteratively. In corporate terms, this is called as implementing a *feature* based on requirements.

The *feature* that I implemented in this phase, is my message of self-realization, i.e., realization of my speaking and writing abilities, which enabled my end products—my articles (in this book) and speeches (in speaking clubs)—to come to fruition. The end product is a small step in my journey towards self-realization.

I invested time in marketing my message and selling it to the intended audience, even as I worked on the final draft of the book. This corresponds to the marketing phase of the product life cycle.

Realizing my inner potential, to me, means translating my skills into a significant and marketable product that can be useful to people. You can extend the concept to managing teams as well. If you are the leader of a team in a corporate setup or you are coaching your team for a game for a sport, and feel that your team members are not realizing their inner human potential, helping each member align their potential to your entrepreneurial strategy would be beneficial. I will talk more about this in *Chapter 7* in the section *Leading without Managing*.

SEEKING HELP FROM THE LEAN THINKER!

I sought to get insights from someone who could relate personally to the entrepreneurial approach to being a speaker and a writer that I just described. I had to approach an entrepreneur from the tech world—who is also a speaker—as part of his professional duties and has authored a book as well.

I approached Amit Rathore, CEO of Quintype Inc. Rathore, a serial entrepreneur and investor, the author of *Clojure in Action*—a programming guide and reference that aims to help developers discover the power of Lisp (programming language). He says: 'I'm a believer of Alan Kay's vision that the real computer revolution hasn't happened yet. I believe we can do better as an industry, and the new design renaissance is just a tiny step forward. We have to make computers actually *do* more.' His latest start-up, Quintype, provides a data-driven publishing platform, rich with features for content management and collaboration, easily accessible from mobile devices as well as desktop workstations.

Rathore is a zealous proponent of the Lean philosophy of management [12], which he adheres to in his entrepreneurial ventures. In regards to applying the same principles to writing, publishing, and selling my book, he had the following three tips to share:

1. **While building your team**, always choose people with whom you can match frequencies. You have to be able to gel with your team intuitively. Nonverbal communication is a good first indicator of whether someone will be a good fit for the team. If you do not find a good fit, it is wise to move on.

2. Harness the power of Lean thinking **to leverage resources effectively.** 'Everything boils down to leveraging, when it comes to building great products and businesses,' says Rathore. He talked about leveraging elegant and sophisticated programming languages to transform an online shopping experience. Drawing from this example, I was able to successfully leverage online tools and the diverse expertise of my core team members to refine my writing style, and clear roadblocks in the process of publishing this book.

3. **Elegance** in the approach to building good products comes from **clarity in thinking and clarity of purpose.**

In the previous section, *Entrepreneurial approach to self-realization,* I talked about how I used *Agile methodology* to iteratively define the content for this book, to market it, and to delegate tasks and work with my team members across different geographic locations. It enabled me to 'fail fast' and improve quickly. I now show you how I used *Lean Thinking,* and *the theory of constraints,* as proposed by Rathore, in developing the content of the book.

ADOPTING LEAN THINKING IN ACHIEVING MY GOALS

The Lean philosophy in management was made popular by its use at the Toyota Production System [1001]. It shook the fundamentals of production management, as it delivered legendary results at the lowest costs. Toyota used a Japanese style of over-the-shoulder management, where a *sensei* (an elderly learned person) constantly alerts his team to remain in heightened states of awareness, to comprehend problems and constraints quickly. The *theory of constraints* [1001] helps you to identify constraints that need to be resolved immediately to meet your goals.

I encourage you to use the Lean Thinking used in mass production for developing your human potential at an individual level. It can help you harness your inner calling and intuition, and enable you to make key decisions when you hit bottlenecks and need to resolve constraints in the path to maximizing your human potential. The most difficult constraint I had to resolve while writing this book was the lack of approval from my reviewers, because it didn't appeal to them enough. I had to get it past the reviewers in order to proceed with publishing. I used the principles of the *theory of constraints* to resolve those bottlenecks in my path to realizing my creative potential as a speaker and writer. Ask the questions below, and constantly challenge the assumptions made by the market or the operating rules of your profession, for the sake of your own flexibility:

a. *What needs to change?* For example, I had to ask myself what changes had to be made to the initial drafts of my speeches and writings, in order to get my reviewers' and editors' approval for publishing.

b. *What should it be changed to?* I identified the distinguishing traits that made particular speeches and writings popular and appealing to my reviewers, and incorporated them after suitably modifying the content of my writing.

c. *What actions will bring about the change?* I revised every draft with a whole new perspective. Before I started on a new draft, I went on several writing retreats to clear my thinking. I started brainstorming in the wee hours of the morning when it was absolutely quiet, so I could focus better and think differently. This approach worked for me every time.

THE CENTRAL THEME:

In summary, what is the common thread between entrepreneurship and self-realization? Both pathways of effort help you maximise the intrinsic human potential, as they did, in game changers in history. Most high-achievers that I interviewed for the book, benefited by techniques in entrepreneurship and self-realization. Both entrepreneurship and self-realization require you to be a purpose-driven high performer. In leading your life using an entrepreneurial approach, you realise the importance of being a self-starter, a team player, a leader, and a good communicator.

> As you start realizing your true inner potential, you tend to become a high performer with purpose. Like Pythagoras, Leonardo da Vinci, Benjamin Franklin, Mahatma Gandhi, Nelson Mandela, Steve Jobs—and many other high achievers—who spent as much time on self-realization and self-discovery, as they did on innovations in philosophy, art, science, socio-political leadership, technology, and entrepreneurship.

The more you would like to accomplish in the material world, the more you should know yourself in the nonmaterial or spiritual world. Being self-realised means connecting with your true self or your inner guide; there is no single prescribed way to connect with your inner being; steadfastly pursue a way that works for you.

> *If you have started off on your journey toward self-realization*
> *or entrepreneurship, you are very likely to see yourself become*
> *a high performer driven by a strong and unwavering inner*
> *purpose, like the purpose that drove me to write this book.*
> *It was a Herculean and uphill task, but a fulfilling one!*

At this point, in my next section, I would like to suggest a couple of ways of looking at self-realization using the entrepreneurial approach. Again, every individual who adopts this approach may not end up being an entrepreneur. However, this approach will always keep you on your toes in terms of exploring your hidden potential and experimenting with it.

Self-realization: Using an entrepreneurial strategy to maximise your inner potential

I have represented self-realization, i.e., maximizing your human potential, using the entrepreneurial approach **linearly, i.e., a step-by-step approach;** and also using a **non-linear approach, i.e., a cyclic representation** of the components that drive this effort. I personally like the non-linear or cyclic approach where a small change in any one part of the whole process, affects all other parts in your life. For example, once you meet your inner calling of buying your dream home, you may want to re-evaluate your finances and look at how you can sustain this acquisition, by making practical adjustments to your expenses in pursuing an expensive hobby, without giving up on it. Your home may be essential for satiating your needs in surviving, giving you fulfillment and happiness besides maintaining your image or status quo in the society. Your hobby may help energise your creative juices and improve your overall productivity. In the cyclic or non-linear representation of the chart, I intend to say that changing any one aspect of life, affects all other aspects of life and one should be open, accepting, and flexible to this idea.

When I ran both linear and cyclic approaches by my peers, I felt about nearly half of them endorsed the linear and modular approach to self-realization. For example, these peers believed in working on each skill mentioned in every stage of the whole process in a step-by-step manner, i.e., based on the linear chart. This way they could stay focused and predictable in how they plan their time and efforts in accomplishing a particular stage in self-realization. So I have laid both approaches visually. There is also an explanation for the terms used in the charts so you can look up the terms involved; this way you will get a feel for what I had in mind when I created these charts. I will use both charts all throughout the book, so that you can better capture the process of self-realization in your mind.

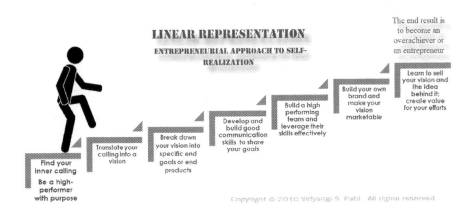

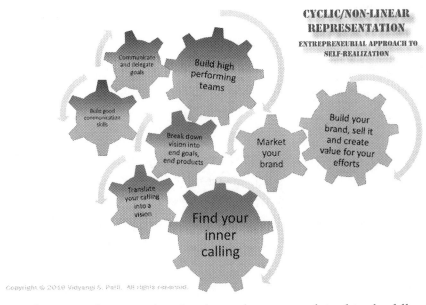

The terminologies used in the charts above are explained in the following section:

FIND YOUR INNER CALLING

It is the process in which you realise the purpose in your life. For example: I found my calling to spread the message about awakened living when I was involved in networking and public speaking events, time and again, backed by a strong urge in me to follow this calling. You can find your calling if you are awake, as in alert in your five senses. It happens intuitively, in a state of compassion, when connected with your surroundings and people around you very deeply, at the heart level. For such an insight to occur, you have to have a longing to better yourself all the time; you have to be open and seeking always.

TRANSLATE YOUR CALLING INTO A VISION

It is the process in which you realise your intuition about what you would like to do with your human potential as a major goal in your life. For example: I envisioned a book with a central thesis. This intuition and premonition occurred to me several times, very strongly, since 2007, before I finally got to commit to this vision.

BREAK DOWN YOUR VISION INTO SPECIFIC END GOALS OR END PRODUCTS

It is the process in which you realise your ability to train your intuition strategically and develop clarity in your vision. For example: I had to break down the book into specific chapters and outline speeches around it so I could understand my reader's needs, i.e., use the content of my speeches for beta testing with audience, much before I drafted the chapters in the book.

DEVELOP AND BUILD GOOD COMMUNICATION SKILLS

It is the process in which you realise your ability to translate your vision into specific negotiable goals, tasks, and inspire your team to work with you. For example: I have been raised in an environment centered around entrepreneurship and team management by my parents; I also trained for many years in writing, and in public speaking specifically last year, by affiliating with Toastmasters, to meet my inner calling of spreading the message in the book. My upbringing, training in a corporate set up, and in Toastmasters, helped me in conceptualizing content for my book, building a team, and delegating tasks to them. All this was a part of my efforts in drafting the book and creating a platform for my blogs, speeches and videos, and in spreading the word about my book.

BUILD A HIGH PERFORMING TEAM AND LEVERAGE THEIR SKILLS EFFECTIVELY

It is the process in which you realise the ability to strategise the dynamics of a team and set goals. For example: After many iterations of working with different teams, I finally chose a core team of people who brought in multiple skill set in building and marketing the content of the book.

BUILD YOUR BRAND

It is the process in which you streamline your efforts in reaching your target audience and customizing the product to reach your market segment. For example: I put in conscious efforts to create a portfolio of my speaking and writing projects to build my brand as a speaker and a writer.

LEARN TO SELL YOUR PRODUCT AND THE IDEA BEHIND IT

It is the process in which you realise your ability to create value for the public in harnessing your inner potential. For example: I have built strategies to sell my book and speeches, and experimented with live audience countless of times. I have documented both failed and successful strategies in selling my idea. I guess I will wait for the strategies to take effect. I have been successful in my demo presentations so far. I will quantify the result and make it available in the succeeding editions.

Chapter 1: What Is Vertical Living?

-Chapter begins-

Image courtesy: Erwin D'Souza

In this chapter, I elaborate on the concept of *vertical living*. I coined this term for this book to describe the lifestyle of an awakened human being. There is no other reference to the term *vertical living* in the realm of human potential. Vertical living in common terms means living in a tall, multistorey building. But the term here talks about a lifestyle that elevates human potential. It is a lifestyle centered on gratitude and human compassion in which you are hyper-aware of yourself and your surroundings. A high degree of awareness entails accessing a greater percentage of your brain, which is a marked trait of compassion-centric and a gratitude-centric life as well. Such a state involves openness to the creation and reinforcement of new pathways in your brain that enable the elevation of intrinsic human potential to the next level. I will explain more as I take you through this chapter and others.

Vertical living, as a lifestyle, thrives on the notion that the brain can change itself constantly [100]. In living this idea, you will be able to break free of your fears and inhibitions and challenge the limits of your human potential. I have seen artists, mountaineers, sportspersons, leaders of large corporations, and entrepreneurs, demonstrate this. I have seen them express supra-human abilities, i.e., exhibit a high degree of physical and mental tenacity, drive big decisions, and influence difficult circumstances and people through compelling ideas backed by sheer gut feeling. These role models have been able to counter huge challenges by thinking creatively, under situations involving tremendous pressure and financial accountability.

In situations that question the survival of the organization itself, these people have been able to create something new, by effectively tapping into their intuition and awareness. This particular state of existence where creativity and human potential are maximised is called the *flow [114]*. For instance, there have been mountaineers who have climbed the tallest mountains, defying the predictions of experts in mountaineering and succeeding in the face of intense snowstorms and adverse conditions because they are in a state of *flow* [114]. Dean Potter, a well-known rock climber and Alpinist, talks about his experience in climbing the tallest mountain in Patagonia and setting many records as a mountaineer. He mentions about listening to an inner voice that guided him through the perils of a seemingly impossible climb. In the book, *The Rise of Superman*, he quotes, 'Right before I have to make a move, the Voice tells me what to do. And it's never wrong. When the Voice tells you to do something, you do it: right then, don't think, no questions asked. Not listening to the Voice is what'll get you killed. I learned that really early in my climbing career.' Carl Jung calls this Voice '*perception via the unconscious.*' I refer to it as manifestation of the *inner calling* and heightened states of *intuition* in the book [101].

Sportspersons who engage in extreme sports are noted to have trained their neural pathways to surpass the physical limitations posed by space and altitude, at a certain phase in their sporting experience. This numbs them to the fear of failure and allows them to risk trying unprecedented feats. There is a whole body of science dedicated to understanding the science of flow [114] in extreme sports and examples of accomplishments that invoke superhuman performance [101].

It was almost unbelievable to me that naturally occurring altered states of consciousness and intuition can provide guidance through challenging circumstances, until I felt the glimpses of such intuitive states in my life. That is why I am convinced that inculcating the states of hyper-awareness, compassion, and *flow* [114] in creativity can become a lifestyle; I choose to call such a lifestyle *vertical living*. I will talk about these experiences in this chapter. I call a lifestyle that can maximise such states of flow *vertical living*.

Vertical living as a lifestyle can be observed in the historical accounts of the lives of Leonardo da Vinci, Albert Einstein, Bruce Lee, Steve Jobs, and Mahatma Gandhi. The CEOs and heads of large business divisions in multinational corporations that I interacted with also displayed consistent traits like compassion, empathy, hyper-awareness, and intuition as part of their lifestyle. It is interesting to know that these people displayed learning mechanisms preached in the education systems of the ancient Greeks, Egyptians, Indians, and the Chinese. It is a system of learning centered on self-realization, i.e., learning a skill or body of knowledge starting from knowing your true strengths and weaknesses, in following your inner calling, and feeling deeply connected with your environment. I talk more about this in the chapter '*The Secrets of Game Changers.*'

Most game changers in history were driven by a noble and genuine calling to solve a problem, or meet a higher purpose in elevating and serving humanity. The power and effectiveness of a gratitude and compassion-centric life has been acknowledged by scientists, psychiatrists, coaches of the Olympic teams, etc. [204]. These examples and experiences have more than convinced me that vertical living as a lifestyle is a great foundation for elevating human capacity and human potential. Let us now get to the core concepts in vertical living.

What is Vertical Living?

Vertical living is a lifestyle that emphasises that the present is the only truth to think about, a simple formula used by many game changers in history, and also by many successful high performers that I interviewed for this book.

> *Vertical living is a lifestyle that emphasises that the present is the only truth to think about, a simple formula used by many game changers in history, and many of the successful high performers that I interviewed for this book.*

The term *vertical* implies elevating your senses, elevating your perception and awareness of your surroundings in the present moment. In elevating your human potential, you isolate yourself from factors that drain your energy, and instead focus on the current situation. A compassion and gratitude-centric state makes it easier to reduce negative feelings that get in the way of the maximum and optimal expression of human potential.

In vertical living as a lifestyle, the forces that drain your focus don't seem to affect you anymore. I consider being inhibited by inner fears, or being rushed by time, as a few of those factors that affect human potential from being expressed fully in the current moment. The idea of vertical living rests on being able to focus completely on the here and now. If you are eating, while in a state of vertical living, you would be completely focused on the food you are eating, and aligned with the act of tasting the food. In states of vertical living, you will feel compassionate and even grateful for the food you are tasting. So you will handle the morsels of food with a lot of care and grace. In this process, you are also aware of your surroundings, i.e., the people around you, the conversations at dinner or lunch; but your focus is on assimilating the food. You are also aware of the time allotted for lunch or dinner, but it does not get in the way of being able to enjoy your food.

Time is usually perceived in the horizontal, or x-axis, in the Cartesian co-ordinate system, and living independently of the horizontal axis of time, when focusing on the task at hand (i.e., being completely vertical in your perception of the task or application of human potential), may also be perceived as vertical living. In vertical living as a lifestyle, you are aware of the factor called time, because it is a lifestyle with an elevated awareness of your surroundings; but time does not deter your creativity or rush you.

There are other factors that can cause energy drain and get in the way of your realizing your true potential. For example, being affected by peer pressure, or having thoughts which drain your human potential, like inner fears of being able to take on or accomplish a particular task, or insecurity, or jealousy. These are the side effects of deviating from vertical living as a lifestyle. They are detractors which prevent you from achieving your peak performance, or reduce your levels of awareness, i.e., utilizing your time and energy effectively for the task at hand.

It is quite natural to wander off and relax in your thinking in the effort to rejuvenate yourself, explore creativity and connect different worlds—you may conceive ideas in Art while solving problems in Math; you may solve a technical problem and discover a philosophy of life in the process, etc. Such a state of wandering was practiced by creative thinkers like Albert Einstein, Isaac Newton, or Rabindranath Tagore (Nobel Laureate and polymath from India). But even the wandering off in thought can be done elegantly and in a vertical state, without being rushed by the factor of time or detracted by negative thinking.

For instance, Albert Einstein dreamed up several path-breaking ideas in his bathtub when he was playing with bubbles. Einstein's personal life was riddled with tragedy and his professional path was quite uphill. In spite of that, he had a way of maintaining vertical states of living as often as possible and harnessing these states to support his research. If you read his biography, you will realise that Einstein got into a state of flow [114] regularly by playing his violin. It was an outlet for his emotions, and playing Mozart was the core of his creative life.

> *In vertical living as a lifestyle, you are aware of the factor called time, because it is a lifestyle elevated in awareness, but the factor of time does not deter your creativity or rush you into doing something in haste.*

Playing music is the most common way to empty the mind. If you have ever played music, you know that once you learn how to play a piece, you play by sensing the instrument and by intuition. Your mind is completely present *in the moment*. I have played the keyboard, guitar, and veena without much formal training, and almost always by intuition. I can speak for myself and most musicians that after enough practice in mastering a composition, the feeling of being present in the moment is heightened while playing.

> Dissecting all that has happened in the past or what might happen in the future is a common habit, but it takes you out of the states of vertical living because you are then no longer in the present.

The challenge is to manage the current moment and accept it without questioning yourself. Once you learn to do this, you will start unleashing the potential of your intuition. I will tell you shortly why it is important to listen to intuition. But for now, we can make the assumption that to be a high performer or a game changer in history, harnessing the power of intuition is vital.

Vertical living as a lifestyle incorporates using a high degree of awareness and intuition in daily life by living deeply in the current moment. A person who is present and aware in the current moment is aware of his inner bodily environment and surrounding ecosystem. He tends to be more compassionate in sensing his surroundings. Such compassion is the effect of heightened states of awareness in anybody. For example, once you start becoming aware of the quality of food you eat, the air you breathe in, the effect of usage of your words on others in a conversation, the way you present yourself to the outside world, etc., you tend to start caring about yourself and the people around you. In other words, you have developed a deeper sense of compassion about life. You will start working on improving the overall quality of your life. Such an awareness and progressive mindset often leads you to create something new or become creative. This is the typical trait of a person who has adopted vertical living as a lifestyle. Such a person is usually deeply connected to his inner calling and purpose in life and is very present, alert, and powerful in the current moment.

Let us look into the example of Steve Jobs to better understand vertical living as a lifestyle in play. Jobs was fascinated with the quality and nature of food and how it affected him; he followed a strict vegan diet and had hired a chef who could understand his ability to sense food very subtly. Jobs was also known for being highly intuitive and insightful about precision in product design. He was unmatched in his ability to put together great user interfaces that in turn became the defining quality of Apple products as a brand.

Jobs' genius lay in his ability to be aware of finer details, be it the food he ate or the product he designed. Such awareness is a trait that occurs in people who adopt an awakened lifestyle, or practice vertical living. The word 'awakened' here refers to an overall awareness of one's internal, i.e., bodily and external surrounding environments. Such an awareness and awakened state is a precursor to heightened levels of intuition in decision making. Once you start harnessing intuition in decision making in your daily life, you will start gravitating towards your purpose in life. As I kept interacting with gifted artists, sportspersons, speakers, serial entrepreneurs and visionaries in the field of medicine, I realised that they were all very sensitive to finer details and subtleties in life, and deeply connected to their purpose in life. They reiterated on and off that they were guided by a strong sense of inner calling or a sense of intuition or insight about a higher purpose in life.

A higher purpose is a goal that can help you express your human potential to the maximum. Human beings are one of those rare species who can rewire their brains, overcome their fears, and transform their bodies and beings to suit the love of their life. If you don't believe me, ask a boy who gave up drinking and hit the gym just to impress his date. In the book *The Brain That Changes Itself* by Norman Doige, you will find interesting facts about the way neural pathways in the brain are reinforced when you are in love or when situations demand you to acquire new tastes. For instance, you may have never tasted French food all your life but you could learn to get used to French food by necessity. The necessity could be for example: if you have taken up a job or a curriculum in France for extended periods of time and you may not have many options in your cuisine available in that specific part of France. I have known many friends and acquaintances that have consciously developed a taste for specific cuisines and lifestyles, to suit the needs of their jobs, which require heavy traveling.

Most people believe that they are born with certain abilities, tastes and predispositions, which cannot be changed during the course of their life. Vertical Living systematically explains the mechanisms of looking at problems and situations positively. This way you can elevate your intrinsic capabilities as a human being.

It is difficult to exist in vertical states all the time, but let's make a start! Begin as a habit and perfect that habit into a lifestyle. Once it becomes a lifestyle, it will be very powerful. Most importantly, I will give you examples of success stories that make compelling evidence as to the effectiveness of this approach. It is up to you to dissect, debate, question, and convince yourself whether this approach works for you.

> Another concept that is closely associated with living vertically is *mindfulness [8,200],* which is preached in Buddhism, as a conscious and nonjudgmental way of viewing our emotions, thoughts, and sensations in the present. **But mindfulness is only the first step in vertical living.** Having your <u>mind and intuition aligned while inherently acting with empathy, compassion and mindfulness,</u> is vertical living.

What does it mean to have your mind and intuition aligned, while inherently acting with empathy, compassion and mindfulness? For example, some *simple actions that bring you to a vertical state* include sitting with an erect posture, communicating so that you are fully aware of the impact of your speech on others. A few other examples could be for instance, when eating, savoring every flavor of the food, being aware of the right foods for your body, and eating only when you are hungry. These are a few ways to maintain vertical states of living. *What could be one possible benefit of doing simple actions in daily life, out of mindfulness, in achieving vertical states of living?*

Being conscious and mindful of your body's movements during your daily activities as part of vertical living helps you achieve gracefulness in your demeanor.

Vertical Living can be experienced at various levels. There are five distinct levels that I have identified, based on my experience in interviewing people in real life, observing myself very deeply, and also studying the accounts of geniuses and polymaths throughout history. There can be more levels in vertical living as a lifestyle, but I have identified five, keeping in mind my target audience for the book. I will tell you how to get to these levels, as we proceed. The basic idea driving vertical living as a lifestyle is the ability to focus on the current moment and to be aware of your surroundings unconditionally. The end goal of vertical living is to find and realise your inner calling.

Level 1: Feeling Alive

Getting to various levels in vertical living starts with living in the here and now. What does this mean? Living in vertical states means you are focusing on your subtle impulses. So start listening to your body and the world around you without much pre-conditioning. Pay attention to the reality of the situation you are in. Stop feeling bored and start becoming curious about the things around you, without any bias. Become more aware of your surroundings and how you fit into them. This is Level 1 in vertical living.

The most important trait of people in this level of vertical living is that they are attuned to the present, and this indeed is a rare trait to spot. Most people are usually fragmented in their thoughts and abilities to experience what the moment has to offer. What does it mean to be attuned to the present? From my personal experience, I feel such an attunement after a workout session, writing assignments, or after completing a dance routine. When I come out of these activities, I feel more alert and attuned to the next activity I get involved in. For instance, I can more easily discern the bass notes of a musical composition after my workout session at the gym.

The first step in vertical living is eliminating all the clutter in your mind and body that prevents you from experiencing the present moment effectively. If you have a clear mind but your body is in pain, there is a huge block in your experience of the current moment. At Level 1 of vertical living, your focus should be to clear that block by focusing on relieving your body of that pain. Either you should condition your body to be tolerant to pain or you should work on getting rid of pain by healing your body. Once this is done, you are completely receptive to the present moment, and are better able to sense your intuitive abilities.

The following Toastmasters I have met in-person are classic examples of people who have clearly mastered Level 1 in vertical living.

a. **Kirubakaran Periyannan** was competing at the International Speech contest at Toastmasters International when he did a phone interview with me. He was so alive in his conversation that at the end of a crazy day, I felt completely energised when I got on the call with him. He reiterated the importance of facing his inner fears to be able to compete in the contest. He later came to our local Toastmasters club to practice his speech. I had not seen his photograph before, but he had such an aura that I felt drawn to step up to him, introduce myself, and acknowledge his presence.

b. **Karthik Kalpat** is another veteran Toastmaster whose list of accomplishments is matched by his humility and grounded nature. He has held various senior executive-level positions in the Toastmasters community. During our interview, I recall that he was able to think like an entry-level engineer as well as the director of a business unit in transcending different levels in communication. He was so alive and present in the interview that I almost felt like he had effectively donned different corporate roles, as if in a play. I am not surprised that Karthik has great skills in people management and team leadership. His personal power, so uncluttered and influencing, could effectively drive people to meet deadlines and help realise measured goals and targets, successfully.

c. **Joseph Fernandez** is another veteran Toastmaster who has been lauded for his legendary skills in goal setting, building rock star Toastmaster chapters in record-breaking time, and meeting membership goals very quickly. When he got into the *flow* [114] in explaining his findings in optimizing goal setting, my moods were elevated and I felt very alive. I was motivated by the power in his speech. His energy and enthusiasm in experiencing every aspect of life in terms of goal-setting, transitioned me into rethinking inefficiencies in many small aspects of my life, e.g., time spent ineffectively in my day job, time allocated for daily workout, time allotted for my reading, speaking and writing projects, etc. Fernandez was able to quickly grasp situations where goal setting can be rethought and reworked in my life. I just kept flowing with his vision. His enthusiasm made me feel alert and alive, and I could perceive the reality of my life with greater depth and perception.

d. **Michael Chojnaki** is an executive coach and the President of Aikiway Professional Services. He has a novel coaching style and uses the cross application of the principles of Aikido, a form of modern Japanese martial art, to solve problems in interpersonal dynamics. He is by far the most effective teacher in exemplifying communication by way of intuition. His whole understanding of communication and interpersonal dynamics stems from the fact that he is very perceptive about his body and his surroundings. I once went to his talk on powerful presentation skills. His eyes were so powerful and alive that he was able to use minimal bodily movements to emote and express his ideas effectively.

I felt a certain ease and comfort when interacting with all of the above individuals the very first time. Their speech was timeless, and their interpersonal exchange was very intuitive. They were able to predict my next question even before I asked it, were open to critical feedback, and had very calm dispositions. Many successful top-tier company executives I've met in-person have mastered this Level 1 in vertical living.

Here is another real-life example of people practicing Level 1 skills: My colleagues who travel across various time zones for their jobs, speak multiple languages, learn about and appreciate varied cuisines and cultural diversities, are alert and aware of their surroundings; they are mindful of what they eat, how they dress, and how they speak. This means they make attempts to modulate their behavior, appearance, and speech to suit the demands of the situation.

I have lived with people who constantly travel on the job and have figured out a way to organise their life, very naturally and intuitively. Being alert, mindful, organised, and sophisticated in your lifestyle, and also being civilised in the way you treat fellow human beings, are consistent traits of achieving Level 1 in vertical living.

How to attain Level 1 in vertical living:

1. If you find it hard to stay tuned in to the moment, start with noticing the number of thoughts in your head per second. They should reduce in number to one thought at a time. Keep practicing this till you are able to narrow down your thoughts to one at a time.

2. If the above technique does not work, you need to break your routine and do something different, for example, a workout, a run, a brisk walk, a dance routine, a shopping session or a music break. Observe the number of thoughts running in your head after a recreational activity. Get back to your work and try observing the number of thoughts running in your head every second.

3. If you love your work, try observing the number of thoughts running in your mind when you are involved in it. You will observe that the number of thoughts then is very minimal, perhaps one thought per second.

4. Try enrolling in the Vipassana meditation retreat Inner Engineering Program by Isha Foundation; take a pilgrimage to a place of your choice, or any other kind of retreat that can give you time for detoxifying your mind and body. It will help you get through Level 1 in vertical living very easily.

5. Finding a way to detoxify your mind of negative thoughts and your body of toxic elements is of prime importance in this level in vertical living. If your day job and surrounding environment rejuvenate you regularly, you don't need to find specific practices, but it is always good to make a conscious attempt at keeping your mental and emotional states detoxified.

Once you find such practices, for example, meditating, breathing exercises, hiking, biking, etc., make them a part of your lifestyle. The winning formula lies in incorporating these healthy practices that detox your mind and body regularly in your lifestyle.

Level 2: Being Perceptive and Intuitive

If you have reduced the number of thoughts running in your mind at any time to one thought or nearly one, you are moving toward Level 2 in vertical living. Such a state is attained when your mind and body are conditioned for strength and focus. Your senses become sharper, i.e., you start seeing visuals in better depth, your sense of smell and your ability to refine taste and music become sharper, and your intuition about people and situations becomes more accurate. You will start reading people and situations faster.

In Level 2 in vertical living, your response rate to any kind of input shows improvement in most areas of life. You will come up with solutions to problems at work in a shorter time, or you will be better in your physical responses, for instance, handling a ball in a basketball game. You will feel closer to your true nature and inner calling.

You will start recognizing environments where you can or cannot blend in harmoniously, e.g., if you are not a party lover, you will know how to graciously exit from parties or party invitations or, if in the worst case you have to attend a party, you will feel completely at home in your own company. You will learn ways to fit in or move on to an ecosystem or workplace that better fits you. It becomes clearer to you that you have to do justice to the purpose of your life. This is an indication that you are in Level 2.

Here is someone who had mastered Level 2: Steve Jobs was a vegan and very picky about the food he ate. He was turned off by disharmonious or bad designs. He was being true to his nature when he rejected environments and situations that did not support his understanding of simplicity, symmetry, and aesthetics. Even during the last days of his life, when he was being treated for cancer, he refused to wear a badly designed mask, though it would have been a lifesaver for him [105]. There was something about his Zen-like lifestyle that enhanced his forward-thinking ideas. I call this ability to be physiologically, aesthetically, and psychologically aligning with the current moment, a vertical state of living.

Even as a child, Albert Einstein knew very well how to create an environment for himself to support his learning style. He was very aware of his true nature and the environments that supported his learning abilities; so much so, that as a child he threw a chair at his music teacher because he did not do well with the authoritarian style of teaching [111]. This behavior is not exemplary; however, the point is that Einstein had a heightened perception of how to foster his creativity, even in the choice of his teacher and his learning style. This is a classic feature of reaching Level 2 in vertical living.

Another feature of Level 2 is a heightened sense of sensory perception. Most top-tier management professionals of multinational corporations that I interacted with during job fairs, professional meetups, code camps, and cultural events are hyper-aware of their senses.

They have a sharp vision, stellar listening and comprehension skills, and a great understanding of style, symmetry and design in their choice of clothes, gadgets, and even food. Many have a great sense of smell and can recognise a cheap perfume from an expensive one; they have a sophisticated palette and can tell low-quality chocolates from good ones. Such finesse comes from being completely present in the moment (mastery of Level 1) and expanding your perception using your five senses: taste, smell, hearing, vision, and feeling. Such hyper-awareness comes from being attentive and receptive to your senses and also by practicing self-control. Once you know how to control your senses, you will become sharper at using them. For instance, if you know how to control your craving for coffee, you will tend to have a higher degree of alertness and awareness when you sip your coffee after a stint of keeping consciously away from coffee. You will enjoy that first sip very deeply and be more intelligent in your grasp of the taste of coffee itself.

From my personal observations, individuals in Level 2 display a high degree of self-control during most situations in life, by staying calm. However, by practicing daily habits like eating healthy, staying fit, spending time out in the open air, drinking sufficient amounts of water to support a healthy metabolism, speaking with forethought and insight, avoiding conversations that do not carry good intentions, and working on improving your strengths and minimizing your weaknesses, you can develop abilities in Level 2 in vertical living as a conscious choice. Such mastery of the five physical senses will lead you to heighten your sixth sense, intuition.

People who have sharpened their five senses have naturally progressed into a stage where they have a heightened sixth sense, intuition [113]. When that sixth sense is alive, it is easier to listen to your inner calling or perceive your true inner nature, i.e.: Would I be happy in a certain relationship? Would a traveling job suit me? Would I benefit by taking a part-time job over missing out on a work-out session at the gym? etc. Intuition has been best used by high achievers in choosing their profession, which indeed takes up a major chunk of our lives.

To be a high performer or a game changer in history, being able to harness your power of intuition is vital.

Dr Devi Shetty, a leading cardiac surgeon, a philanthropist and a game changer in providing low-cost and world-class health care in India, talks about knowing the purpose of his life intuitively. He said he *knew* he wanted to be a cardiac surgeon very early on, even before he understood that he had to be a doctor first in order to be a surgeon. Suhas Gopinath, one of the youngest entrepreneurs and millionaires in the world, started his company at the age of 14, and says he *knew* as early as when he was in elementary school that he wanted to be an entrepreneur and even flaunted a business card with his name on it. This whole business of *knowing* stems from intuition, your sure-shot inner guide to finding your true purpose in life.

How to attain Level 2 in vertical living

1. You need to practice self-control and self-discipline in your daily activities, such as waking up early, working out regularly, and abstaining from stimulants. This approach may not work for everyone, but it is worth trying out, as it will instill a sense of self-discipline.

2. Choose the right foods, try to stand up straight and adhere to the ergonomics of posture as much as you can, and pay attention to the clothes you wear and how they fit you. Care about everything associated with yourself, including what you say and how people perceive it. Improve your standards iteratively. Keep at it continuously.

3. When you have flashes of intuition, encourage them, and pat yourself on the back about those experiences.

4. Enroll in courses like psychology, psychotherapy, human anthropology, neuro-linguistic programming, or practices that allow you to focus on energy flow, like Tai Chi, Yoga or Aikido. These arts can help you plumb the depths of human nature and help you heighten your intuition and perception.

5. Pat yourself on the back for making astute and subtle observations, and if you are at this level, you will be making many such observations. For example, you may be able to foresee non-productive conversations and avoid them, even though they may be on your schedule. You may be able to identify a problem in your business processes by thinking beyond a rigid set of process guidelines. Oh, trust me, there will be many such instances!

6. Try to communicate with people without using words but through respectful nonverbal gestures.

Level 3: Being Creative

If you start practicing vertical living as a lifestyle and reach Level 3, you will become more creative and confident. Working hard will come to you naturally because you will figure out the rules of your trade or your environment and manage the resources within and around you with minimal effort. You will see that your intuition leads you to make effective, productive decisions. For example, if you are trying to build a six pack to strengthen your core, doing 50 push-ups as part of your daily workout routine will come to you naturally and will not feel like hard work at all. If you are at Level 3, you will become open to new ideas and will foray into unknown territories unafraid because you have started following your inner guidance more often.

This is the hardest level to get to, because you have started following your inner-guide or Inner-Guru. It is like letting go of logic and pre-programming from past experiences. Many people I know have gotten to this level after attending the vipassana [112] retreat because they continue to follow the practices prescribed in vipassana in their daily life. Many religions prescribe deep breathing and yoga-like poses as part of an ideal lifestyle. Practicing these techniques routinely will ensure that they become a part of your lifestyle. This will help heighten the levels of your intuition and the connection to your inner calling.

You will observe in yourself a few other developments as part of evolving into Level 3 in vertical living. Living with intuition slows your physical movements and also the number of thoughts-per-second; this comes from opening your mind and body to a plane of intuition and a higher degree of perception or intelligence. If you are at this level in vertical living, you will **naturally** find time and space to sit still or contemplate or be quiet. Finding quiet time for yourself will become an organic need for you, like finding food, or finding suitable shelter, etc.

Quiet time in seclusion or the ability to quiet the mind even in a crowded room, is of vital importance to people who make high-impact decisions. In the boardroom, in that moment of decision making, people who make billion-dollar investments are totally quiet, probably not even aware of their bodies or surroundings. After all the number-crunching and back-and-forth in decision-making, they are completely still and intuitive before they make that final call! It is almost considered to be a healthy business practice now, to go with your intuition, after all the hard work, when you make important corporate decisions [601].

Such a high degree of intuition also helps one to delve into different disciplines with confidence. You will become *creative very easily, as you start seeing the different possibilities for a given situation.* This is a side effect of developing intuition, because intuition declutters the mind and opens you up to the reality of the situation, free of any bias. Level 3 is all about harnessing your intuition to act creatively.

Steve Jobs and Leonardo da Vinci mastered this level as they swam across oceans of art and technology, mathematics, and science like fish in water. They saw a distinct rationale in the intersection of and transition across disparate fields, which to others seemed irrational. Jobs' ideas in style and design were deeply influenced by the philosophy of Zen, even though Zen and technology are completely disconnected fields. He took an interest in calligraphy even while he was at school and he was inspired by it when he designed computer fonts. Calligraphy is considered to put people in meditative states [104]. Meditation, again, heightens states of *intuition and helps refine and enhance creativity.*

Creativity emerges when the mind is calm; a state quite often achieved when one is in meditation or is in a meditative state about something, like professional work or amidst an artistic endeavor. When the Walt Disney Co. was at a creative crossroads, Walt Disney's Imagineers, the company's goofily named creative design and development arm, took an unusual step in inviting a therapist and meditation teacher named Ron Alexander. He says [1003], 'Over two years, I did a series of seminars on creativity, reengineering, and re-visioning, so that individuals in the division could begin to access new creative directions,' he says. The Imagineers were inspired enough to start Tokyo Disney, Disneyland Paris, and Hong Kong Disneyland, and are adorned with patents in areas like 3D virtual-reality displays and animatronic, even to this day.

I would like to quote another example from my personal experience on how intuition enhances perception. A top executive at a multi-national firm I worked for was very adept at engaging his audience. I adored his insights and always wanted to be at his talks. I longed to listen to his insights as much as I could, because he had the ability to simplify complicated concepts in management by using a minimum number of words.

I distinctly recall that once I was late for one of his talks and I was stopped by the guard at the gate, as the auditorium was full. The executive asked the guard to let me in. He did so amidst an ongoing speech, which was quite unusual for the decorum of that place. The executive could read my body language and knew how keen I was to listen to him. I also had a strong impulse to ask him a very specific question about a strategy the company had chosen to proceed with, but I did not. To my surprise, the answered my question as part of his presentation by adding, 'Here is another passing thought I would like to capture and share.' I was taken aback by how he was able to read my thought. It could have been a coincidence, but I cannot overlook the fact that he made prolonged eye contact with me when he talked about this idea. He did not look at me after that during the rest of the speech. From what I heard about him, he is very creative in his brainstorming sessions, but conservative in the way he affirms his decisions.

Such intuitive and creative thinking can act as a valuable tool to improvise a sales presentation. Such tools help in reading a customer's requirements ahead of time; this way the sales professional can increase the possibility of a successful bid.

I have had this experience with many top-tier management professionals thereafter. I have seen a consistent pattern in their ability to size up a person before they even have a conversation; they can sense positive or negative outcomes of interacting with someone ahead of time or even when far away from that person. Such professionals, from my observations, are highly intuitive and do not use words in communicating because talking slows them down. They are able to leverage their intuition for simple daily activities, which helps them conserve their time and energy for higher goals they are usually focused on.

In other words, if they have a calorie reserve or energy just enough to accomplish three difficult tasks and four easy tasks per day, their intuition, creativity, and inner calling would guide them in choosing and prioritizing those tasks. People in Level 3 usually surpass the delay caused by framing words and sentences, and cut through the whole process through intuitive and quick insights. For instance, they may use very subtle gestures in communicating their agreement or disagreement about something in a meeting, which can bring in more value to the outcome of the meeting, by cutting short lengthy energy draining arguments without an end result. For many years, I felt such quickness could be attributed to garnering experience in a specific domain. When I started understanding the workings of business processes more deeply, I realised that many of the difficult and *creative approaches* to problems in the corporate world came from people who kept their intuition alive under formidable circumstances like recession, weakening currency, and falling stock prices.

Most top-tier management professionals that I am referring to here were *creative in the way they spotted and hired talent as well.* We all know of high school dropouts who have changed the face of personal computers and turned out to be business magnates. Such businessmen also leveraged their intuition in planning and launching products, and in marketing effectively, because they were creative and almost radical in their vision for the company. Being accountable to stakeholders can be very stressful when you are running a large organization with tens of thousands of employees and shareholders who get affected by your decisions for a particular fiscal year. *But creative thinkers are confident of embracing new ideas, and are ready to play the mad scientist, even under the tremendous pressure of dealing with unknown market forces.*

I recall a lady who headed a major biomedical research division at my university. She could tell why I was going to meet her, even before I introduced myself to her. I believe it is an ability that people develop, by the systematic practice of focus and self-discipline demanded by their lifestyle. She was almost legendary in terms of her creative approaches in driving new initiatives with upper management, collaborating with cutting-edge talent and accommodating the vision of her business unit to the changing economic climate. She maintained an erect posture, was mindful of her eating habits and also her choice of words. She was probably the most organised and punctual person I had met at the university. I can distinctly recall that she had a powerful, steady gaze and was very focused in the here-and-now during our conversation; she was known for her ability to intuit questions before they were verbalised.

If I look back now, I can see that she had mastered Levels 1, 2, and 3 in vertical living. Most people that I referred to in Level 3 in vertical living loved planning their time well in advance and worked very hard. They practiced self-control, self-discipline, and embraced the idea of living in the here-and-now almost by reflex.

How to attain Level 3 in vertical living:

1. You need to be consciously open-minded, and perceptive about and receptive to your surrounding environment. It is a training of the mind that you need to put yourself through.
2. If you have practiced Levels 1 and 2 religiously, Level 3 should occur as an organic, evolutionary outcome. When people learn to use their intelligence efficiently, they move from the plane of intelligence to the plane of intuition in their perception.
3. Once you are in the plane of intuition, you will have learned to stay away from any form of cluttering that causes you to defocus; you will naturally move toward creativity in every aspect of your life.
4. Creativity in your daily routine and in problem solving is a sure outcome of Level 3 in vertical living.

Level 4: Miracles

Be prepared for miracles in Level 4 in vertical living. All aspects of your life start improving with creativity and fulfillment. Your self-confidence is infectious because you are in your skin and have figured out what your true calling is. You will become a better communicator and a better leader in most areas of your life. You will have developed better immunity to diseases. You will become healthier, calmer, and happier in your disposition. Mental and physical health come as points of priority in your daily routine, and you will work toward eating healthy, living a natural lifestyle, and being easily able to connect with anyone. *Once you start using your intuition and reach Level 4 in vertical living, you will develop a certain sense of refinement and sophistication in your approach to creativity.*

Most people in this stage are very productive. You develop more stamina to stay focused on a task and are able to manage mundane tasks very well. I focused on getting to this level when I resumed a normal work routine, post-pregnancy. I focused on strengthening my core muscles, and chose activities that put me in meditative or vertical states of living. I sensed intuitively the people and situations that put me in energy-draining situations. I recall distinctly that the whole time I experienced Level 4, if I thought about someone, they would pass right by my cubicle at work. If I thought about certain family members, they would come by my home that evening. Out of the blue, I would get a call from an old friend I had not spoken to in a long time.

This is a common experience most people in Level 4 seem to have. They feel telepathically connected to someone who then calls them or shows up. These experiences occur, when your entire physiology is aligned with Level 4 in vertical living. The results of an experiment that prove the idea of telepathy have been published by a team from a Barcelona-based research institute, Axilum Robotics, and from Harvard Medical School [110]. *It is high time that we acknowledge the roles that intuition and telepathy might play in leveraging human potential.*

The more deeply you tap into your five senses and the reality of the situation you are in, the higher is the degree of intuition and telepathy that you experience. You experience premonitions and visions in this level. Such a deep sense of perception by way of intuition coupled with intellectual reasoning can be used in building and realizing great visions. These visions could be about a career, about a life partner, about the culture of a company or workplace, about a refreshing lifestyle, or visions of trends in technology and social infrastructure.

This was probably the case with most game changers in history who were able to foresee the future before anyone else could. If you read the biography of Elon Musk, most of his concerns and thoughts lie in the future of artificial intelligence, which is a vision he is creating and living in his head all the time. He dreamed about interplanetary escape when he was 14 years old [232]. It is very clear that even in his childhood he was preparing for his future and living in the future. His efforts are constantly aligned to actualise those futuristic visions, but again, in the here and now. He is said to constantly motivate his team to work hard by sharing with them a vision of the far future where the company is earning millions of dollars in revenue every day.

Such confidence, I can vouch for, is hugely backed by Musk's ability to learn and grasp ideas faster than most people of his generation—an ability that comes with the decluttering of the mind. In such a heightened state of intuition and alignment with inner calling, you can apply learned or theoretical concepts to solving real-life problems. Such an awakened and focused intelligence can realise visions, which to the common man, appear to be miracles.

How to attain Level 4 in vertical living:

1. Once you master the lower three levels in vertical living, you will become confident in your creative endeavors. In order to sustain progress and attain Level 4, you will need to don the hat of a mad scientist. Choose a creative idea and make it happen. For example, if you like to go running regularly, aim to complete Ironman triathlon by coupling running with swimming and cycling. Plan the logistics of all the training that is involved and make it happen.

2. Try a makeover and carry it off with grace. Change your style of dressing by exploring a new line of designers. Make those purchases, put those garments together and carry off that look.

3. Try to hang out with people who have varied interests that do not intersect with yours and try befriending them.

4. The trick in Level 4 is to be creative without losing touch with Levels 1, 2, and 3. The first three levels ensure health, happiness, and an inner sense of calm. Once these elements are in place, it is time to follow your passions and creative endeavors and see that they do not take a toll on a lifestyle that ensures health, happiness and fulfillment. What I mean to say is, do not go overboard or ruthless in your approach in trying to become creative.

Level 5: The Game Changer

This is a level in vertical living where you are a master in control of your senses. You can figure out the natural principles behind most disciplines. You will be able to pick up most subjects easily. <u>Such a state is attainable if you are well aware of your inner calling and most of your activities are aimed at answering it.</u>

Very few people I've met have been able to get to this level. They usually have mastery over a certain discipline of art or science or craft or trade. They are humble and open to learning all about their trade or craft all the time. It is a lifestyle of the highest degree of focus. If you are a person with such a high degree of focus, that one purpose in life can drive most activities during your day. You would also choose to be in a relationship or not, in order to support this focus or cause. Your focus in life will determine the kind of people you interact with, the kind of food you eat, and the nature of sleep patterns that allow you to focus on this purpose. You will experience a certain degree of detachment from worldly pleasures, because such a detachment gives you more focus on that one purpose in your life.

A few chosen people actually experience such a degree of focus on multiple objectives through their life. Nikola Tesla slept very little, as he spent most of his time dedicated to his work. He was never married because he could not make time for a relationship amidst his research activities. Marie Curie was married to Pierre Curie, who understood her longing to change the course of radiation physics and the plight of women researchers all over the world. Her personal and professional lives revolved around her work. Artists like Leonardo da Vinci, who have been game changers in history, have displayed similar focus in their personal and professional lives.

In Level 5 you will find yourself in a state of *flow* most often, and it almost always makes you unafraid of experimenting with new ideas [125, 301]. Just like Leonardo da Vinci, who was well-versed in painting, science, geology, astronomy, physiology, anatomy, cartography, mathematics, and engineering, you will be driven by a strong purpose because you have learned to listen to your inner calling fearlessly, and made this voice a part of your lifestyle.

> *'If you always put limits on everything you do, physical or anything else, it will spread into your work and into your life. There are no limits. There are only plateaus, and you must not stay there, you must go beyond them.'*
> -Bruce Lee

Take Bruce Lee, for instance; he was not only one of the most influential martial artist of all times, but also an excellent tap dancer, a poet, and a philosopher. He was able to connect different forms of martial arts with yoga very creatively and effectively. He devised a new martial art called Jeet Kune Do and authored a book [102], *Chinese Gung-Fu: The Philosophical Art of Self-Defense.* He viewed martial arts not only as a way of self-defense but also as an art and a philosophy.

Being a game changer in any discipline will become second nature to you, because you will become hyper-aware; you will learn to connect deeply with everything around you, including the fundamentals of a new field or a discipline. You will start feeling accountable to and empathetic with your surroundings, so much so that you will take the initiative in driving and spearheading changes.

When I read this quote by Bruce Lee, I had no doubt about the level in vertical living he had attained [103]: 'If you always put limits on everything you do, physical or anything else, it will spread into your work and into your life. There are no limits. There are only plateaus, and you must not stay there, you must go beyond them.'

He was definitely a level 5 in vertical living, because he had not only mastered the art of creativity but also perfected his creativity by starting newer disciplines of martial arts and creating an iconic image in Hollywood. Personal achievements of this degree were rare in his cultural and social background at that time. If he meant to raise the limits in his life in a specific domain, he did so with a lot of self-discipline and training, because he was a level 5 in vertical living.

If you persist in level 5 in vertical living, you can advance to higher stages in vertical living. However, they are not in the scope of this book. When persisting in level 5 in vertical living, it is important to stay conditioned in lower four levels in vertical living, which is indeed a lifestyle change. That is why, when I conceptualised the idea of awakened states for this book, it culminated into the idea of a lifestyle, which I choose to call as vertical living. I would like to explain this idea by quoting a hypothetical scenario: if your life is dedicated to building the next generation hardware and software artificial intelligence, then it is imperative that you take good care of yourself and be awake and mindful of your mental and physical health, as you try to realise your vision.

In conclusion, vertical living is a lifestyle. If you would like to maximise your performance or change the course of events in a domain of your choice, you need to change your lifestyle to align with vertical living. It is an overhaul of lifestyle. It is a conscious change in the framework of your thinking, to become deeply aware of yourself and your surroundings, and is a lifestyle where you are driven by your inner calling. It is a lifestyle filled with love and compassion for yourself and the world around you.

How to attain Level 5 in vertical living:

1. Persist in finding your inner calling, and when you do, it is a very intuitive feeling; and a strong one. You cannot miss it!
2. Translate your calling into a vision or ambition.
3. Break down your vision into short-term and long-term goals.
4. Communicate your goals to your family, friends, and team members associated with realizing your vision.
5. Build your own brand as you start working on your vision.
6. Learn to sell the idea behind it and create value to the outside world as you realise your calling or vision. Refer to the chart in the section *Entrepreneurial approach to self-realization.*

How to Practice Vertical Living as a Lifestyle

I have introduced vertical living lifestyle tips throughout the book. The tips describe various facets of vertical living that you can recall easily. Here is a handy list of those tips and a few additional ones.

Vertical Living Lifestyle Tip 1	Be kind and compassionate with yourself. Only in such a fulfilled state can you transmit love and compassion to serve your surroundings. It is in accepting and loving yourself that you begin the process of self-realization. If you are in love with yourself, you will take good care of your mind, body, and soul.
Vertical Living Lifestyle Tip 2	Engage in different forms of creativity, and challenge yourself regularly by learning something new and different.
Vertical Living Lifestyle Tip 3	Spend time with yourself and in knowing your purpose in life; pick and choose challenges that satisfy your human potential. This way you will have a lot of energy to create and build a great portfolio of accomplishments. For example, train for that 26-mile marathon, take that course in finance, or learn a new language.
Vertical Living Lifestyle Tip 4	Perceive time in a way that brings out the best in you. The feeling of not being bound by time happens to you when you do things you love. It relieves the mind of the stress caused by time.
Vertical Living Lifestyle Tip 5	Create something new when you are feeling lost and if it helps you relax, continue to do it. What you create may or may not be useful, however, it will align and activate the energy centers in your body and give you a new perspective on existing situations in life. For example, going for a run or a swim helps me keep away from negative thoughts. Public speaking and writing improves blood circulation in my spine and legs. I tend to get into a state of *flow* when I am speaking and it helps me energise my lower back and leg muscles.
Vertical Living Lifestyle Tip 6	Practice purposeful movements driven by intuition and empathy to realise the purpose of your life and know yourself. For example, purposeful speech in an executive meeting, purposeful suggestions for a family get-together, purposeful deeds to cheer up a friend who is going through a difficult time.

Vertical Living Lifestyle Tip 7	Give yourself quiet time regularly to invoke intuition and a better perception of situations and connect with the purpose of your life.
Vertical Living Lifestyle Tip 8	Live life thoroughly. If you are stuck in a job or relationship where your resonant frequencies are not realised or released, you are probably not living life fully; take a hint and move on.
Vertical Living Lifestyle Tip 9	Let your decisions be guided by your inner sense of purpose and priority, so you can be productive in a given time frame.
Vertical Living Lifestyle Tip 10	Plan your calendar based on a purpose and be assertive in saying no to appointments that do not meet that purpose.
Vertical Living Lifestyle Tip 11	Think of your actions as a flow of movements in a dance routine and they will start feeling like movement therapy. Eating slowly becomes enjoyable, talking slowly becomes enjoyable, even sitting becomes enjoyable; your whole life develops a certain degree of grace. I call this *living in meditation.*
Vertical Living Lifestyle Tip 12	When you practice slow movements, it becomes a precursor to a *heightened state of intuition.* You can train your body to get into intuitive states regularly. This can be achieved by exercising, dancing, singing, hiking, running or pursuing any other hobby regularly.
Vertical Living Lifestyle Tip 13	Meditate before you apply yourself to a task to get rid of the inner chatter of the mind. For example, meditate before you speak to an audience. Clear your head of all the negative thinking that gets in the way of your focusing on the message in your speech.
Vertical Living Lifestyle Tip 14	Sweat it out! Completely apply yourself on your path to self-realization and beat your fears, one at a time. Beat all those fears that belittled you, by mastering the skill that takes you to a point of no fear! Hard work is the magic mantra to self-realization.
Vertical Living Lifestyle Tip 15	Ask yourself the following questions before taking on a job or challenge: Why am I doing it? What might the results be? Will I be successful? The task represented by 'it' could be, for instance, learning a new language or skill, or making that first difficult conversation in sorting out a relationship issue, or starting your own business. The task representing 'it' is closely influenced by your inner rudder or intuition.

Vertical Living Lifestyle Tip 16	*Empty your mind of the chatter that causes you a fear of failure* and holds you back from embracing newer opportunities in life, for example, taking up the role of a manager or director of a new business unit, or asking someone out on a date. If you are training yourself to get rid of one fear at a time, e.g., the fear of speaking to an audience, fear of heights, fear of meeting new people, then you are essentially dissolving negative parts of your ego by emptying your mind of the negative chatter.
Vertical Living Lifestyle Tip 17	*Belittle the part of your ego that resides in you as fear.* Train yourself to belittle your fears by overcoming your fears again and again. If you are afraid of public speaking, grab every opportunity to address large gatherings. Pat yourself on the back for all the things you did better every time.
Vertical Living Lifestyle Tip 18	*Outgrow your fears by strict discipline and practice.* Persist in your efforts till you master your fears. If you fear deep sea diving, educate yourself about it and attempt to learn the skill of deep sea diving. Engage in regular practice and do not be demotivated if you are unable to perfect the skill. Understand your learning style, and work with a teacher who can help you understand yourself well.
Vertical Living Lifestyle Tip 19	*Approach your fears by considering yourself to be a leader.* If you want to become a team leader, able to influence a large number of people, start with being a leader of your own human potential, i.e., knowing yourself and your strengths and weaknesses.
Vertical Living Lifestyle Tip 20	Use effective pauses in your daily activities so your mind is allowed to be empty. This is a great way to pace yourself to conserve your energy; you can connect with your intuition so you can accomplish more in less time. This way your actions are guided by purpose, and you are able to realise your maximum potential.
Vertical Living Lifestyle Tip 21	Leave that negative thought or conversation alone, even if it means you will lose the battle, because the ultimate victory is in the balance of empathy and logic. By leaving that negative thought incomplete and not empowering it, you can succeed in emptying your mind to focus on the current moment for realizing success and happiness.
Vertical Living Lifestyle Tip 22	Recognise that a life of 'higher intelligence' is a life filled with wisdom to accept and care for life and its resources.

- End Chapter -

Chapter 2: The Secrets of Game Changers

-Chapter begins–

The Inner Guru

Game changers and successful entrepreneurs have a fundamentally different way of looking at life. I choose to use the word *fundamentally*, because the successful entrepreneurs and high performers I interviewed were amused at the

Image courtesy: Erwin D'Souza

questions I asked; they were also surprised that they were not considered conventional thinkers. They are simply used to asking different questions in their minds all the time. Here are a few examples: How does one make at least 65 per cent profit on a deal? So what if I am a beginner in rock climbing, why can't I attempt a difficult climb by being strategic, careful and in the company of experts in rock climbing? Why can't I start my own company, even though I am new to the computer industry; since I am bold, creative, hands-on and willing to work hard in seeking advice from the experts and veterans in the domain?

Here's what Walt Disney had to say about recession: 'I've heard there's going to be a recession. I've decided not to participate'. Here is another refreshing and energizing perspective on recession by Walt Disney: 'Recession doesn't deserve the right to exist. There are just too many things to be done in science and engineering to be bogged down by temporary economic dislocations.' The point I am trying to make with these examples is that, game changers like Disney, had a fundamentally positive and creative approach to problems in life.

I distinctly recall that in my interview with a serial entrepreneur from Stanford University, I talked about the concept of following one's inner calling in becoming a high performer. He responded by saying, 'Isn't that how you should be leading your life, by following your inner calling, doing what you love, because that would be the easiest way to bring out the best in you?'

Being a game changer requires unconventional thinking, taking lots of risks and being headstrong about your vision. It may not be a way of life for everyone. But it is fascinating to learn what made the game changers in history successful in changing the course of events. If you feel underutilised or unrealised, then walking in the shoes of one of these game changers for a while may change the game of your life! It certainly has for me, and for many people that I know of.

Here are a few questions I ask myself to overcome my fear of public speaking: 'How did Bruce Lee, who was severely myopic and whose left leg was an inch shorter than his right leg, become the greatest martial artist in history? How did Agatha Christie, a dyslexic with spelling and writing problems, become one of the greatest writers in history?' If they could overcome their limitations, I very well can start dealing with my fear.

The game changers in history were savvy about marketing their considerable talent; but that was also true for their contemporaries. So what was the one trait that ensured the success of the game changers?

In this chapter, I will lay out this simple truth: Each of us has an *inner guru*; we just need to find that voice. Once we accept this truth about the inner guru, whom I also call the *inner rudder*, we will be shown the path to realizing the purpose of our lives. By focusing on that single purpose, we can best express our talent, love, and potential; we can then become high performers and overachievers. This is precisely what the game changers in history did.

I consider game changers in history my role models, because they had a way of seeing past the limitations that society imposed on them. I look up to them because they undoubtedly utilised their time and resources effectively. Their journey was always onward and upward, despite failures and hardships. They knew what they were meant to do and kept at it, despite temporary setbacks.

For instance, back in the 1500s, Galileo was tried in a court of law for proposing the fact that the sun is at the center of our planetary system. Until then, the earth was said to be at the orbital center of all celestial bodies. Galileo knew his math and astronomy well, and persisted in his proposition until others started seeing the truth of his theory. He kept proving his concepts in astronomy, kinematics, and the strength of materials as part of his natural inner propensity for and intuition about science and the scientific method [200]. This alienated him from the very society he belonged to, but he did not waver in his courage or imagination to follow his inner calling [201, 202].

Mother Teresa referred to such a calling as an insight or an epiphany. Bruce Lee had an epiphany before he started a new discipline of martial art while training with his instructor. Called Jeet Kun Do, it was based on Lee's perception of the nature of water [106]. The writers of science fiction called such epiphanies their *visions*. I call them the calling of the inner guru.

Who or what is a Guru?

Image courtesy: Anastasiia Mishchenko www.dreamstime.com

In this chapter, I lay out a simple truth: Each one of us has an inner guru in our life; we just need to find that voice.

The word *guru* has the connotation of an expert in a certain field, or a mentor. In my book, the term *inner guru* refers to your inner calling, your mentor. Your inner guru guides you through your journey and helps you realise your purpose. A guru is someone who shows you the path to self-realization; in other words, the path to maximizing your true inner potential.

You can listen to your inner guru or inner calling in heightened states of intuition. Inner calling is known by empirical reasoning; it is a realization by knowing without much logical reasoning to it. This feeling resides in the heart and sometimes in the gut. I don't think many people would disagree if I stated that a gut feeling or intuition is almost always right. Most people don't know how to invoke intuition in their life. Intuition and insights come alive in meditative states, which happen by coincidence and are not preprogrammed to occur. Vertical living as a lifestyle is centered on invoking meditative states during most daily activities.

As Steve Jobs put it [9,108], 'Have the courage to follow your heart and intuition. They somehow already know what you truly want to become. Everything else is secondary.' I call this kind of lifestyle, which is dominant in meditative states and intuition, *vertical living* [10]. This is the lifestyle I recommend to all my readers, as I take them through the different chapters in the book.

So what are game changers in history like?

They have mastered survival skills

As much as game changers love to create something new and thrive on their instinct in questioning the status quo, they almost always have great survival skills. Elon Musk, in his college days at University of Pennsylvania, rented a cheap 10-bedroom house and converted it into a night club, to pay his rent. Later on, he showed similar survival skills when it came to collecting money and garnering patrons and partners for most of his entrepreneurial ventures.

Dr John R. Adler is one of the top 20 innovators in the field of surgery in the world today. He has been hailed as the father of image-guided irradiation and awarded the Dorothy and Thye King Chan Professorship for his array of accomplishments in the field of neurosurgery. Dr Adler says 'There is a great elegance and sheer joy to thriving and surviving. Creation comes from survival, from mere existence. I know it is not about surviving as a mere lump of flesh, but surviving with will and creativity which makes it a higher level of survival. However, the ability to endure in the face of failure adds more dimensions to your persona. Just like for a wrestler, endurance in wrestling provides him with a better understanding of his persona and his muscles.'

Wrestling was Adler's favorite sport in school and, as he fondly mentions, it has been his defining style in life as well; he talks about his style of winning as surviving and outlasting the opponent. It has also made him a survivor in his challenges in steering the course of neurosurgery to unimaginable heights as an inventor and an entrepreneur. He has been instrumental in driving many changes in the field of neurosurgery and is now busy reinventing the platform for medical publishing by way of his latest venture, Cureus.com. The platform enables authors in medical science and biotechnology to publish smartly, quickly, without hassle or delay. In his interview for the book, Adler talked about his vision of being open and allowing for expression of ideas, both good and bad ones. Cureus.com is his step toward actualizing this vision.

Dr Devi Shetty is a famed cardiac surgeon and philanthropist who has singlehandedly affected policies in providing affordable healthcare; for example, he founded Yeshasvini, the world's cheapest comprehensive health insurance scheme, at Rs. 10 (20 cents) for the poor farmers in the state of Karnataka in South India. Dr Shetty has been moving towards his vision of affordable healthcare not only for everyone in India but also all over the world.

Dr Shetty understands the need for strong survival skills in building sustainable business models for his ever-expanding work in healthcare. This is his take charity and free service: 'I don't believe in charity for free. All charitable work should have a sustainable business model. Even if the wealthiest man on earth funds heart surgeries for free, he will be bankrupt in a few years.' He said that it is important to care about money because money is like oxygen for survival, but it should not become the end goal of survival.

In his inspiring interview, Dr Shetty talks about an egalitarian vision of a civilised society where healthcare is made affordable and is provided to one and all with dignity. His infrastructure provided close to 14,000 surgeries last year and he has been hailed as the *Henry Ford of cardiac surgery* by the *Wall Street Journal*. He is a game changer in the field of cardiac surgery, and understands the formula for sustainable business models. He has been able to apply this formula to his charitable work by collaborating with governments and working with private businesses to deliver affordable healthcare. Harvard and Wharton Business Schools have based a case study on the Narayana Hrudayalaya Group, acknowledging its unique affordable healthcare business model [151, 152].

They picked one purpose at a time

In my interview with Dr Adler, he was very clear about the secret of his success. He said that he would pick one purpose worth his aptitude and time, and focus his entire attention on it. I once spoke to one of America's top public speakers at a conference, and she told me that she started her career as a hairdresser, even though communication was her inner calling. She eventually developed her speaking skills by seeing parallels in the art of hairdressing and the art of communication, i.e., cleaning up the speech with finishing touches, just as she would clean up a haircut with a final touch up. She became focused on speaking as her primary purpose in life. Today, she is a top-rated public speaker at the National Speakers Association and Toastmasters International [205]. Her name is Patricia Fripp.

This is the truth about most game changers in history, like Steve Jobs, Leonardo Da Vinci, Bruce Lee, Bill Gates, Elon Musk, Mahatma Gandhi, Mother Teresa, Rabindranath Tagore, and Nelson Mandela. Their decisions appeared to be irrational many a time, but they all have indicated that at some point, they were driven by that one strong purpose or inner calling and they focused all their energies in pursuing that one purpose or calling. Such a strong drive to pursue one purpose can be called a *gut feeling* or the *call of the inner guide*—I call it *inner guru*.

They were high performers who leveraged their expertise very well.

'By failing to prepare, you are preparing to fail.'
-Benjamin Franklin

I believe that people who changed the course of history were *high performers* because they were driven by a strong *purpose*, and were great team players and taskmasters. This made them open to learning, and inspired them to collaborate with people, and master tasks and challenges that required them to acquire multiple talents to meet their purpose. They picked up skills based on the need of the hour, be it in business or technology or the art of managing teams; that is why I call them high performers.

They created great value because of the unique combination of skills they acquired as part of realizing their purpose in life. They lived very intensely, as if there was no tomorrow to fulfill their dreams.

Let us take a look at an example: Benjamin Franklin, the greatest American statesman, was also known as the Founding Father of America [206]. A postmaster by profession, he is also credited with inventions such as bifocals, the lightning rod, the flexible urinary catheter, and the odometer [207]. Franklin was interested in studying population demographics. His eclectic background in the arts and sciences was vital in helping him shape the image of America in the outside world. The most outstanding trait of Benjamin Franklin was that he could leverage his skills in one domain and apply them in another. He was not only a scientist but also a diplomat and statesman. He understood the value of creating a society open to the culture of innovation, as he was an inventor himself. He leveraged his expertise by laying the foundation for one of the most powerful nations in the world.

Benjamin Franklin retired at age 42, after which he taught himself five languages; he was extremely unconventional for his time, considering the variety of professions that he pursued. His inventions earned him degrees from Harvard and Yale.

High performers like Benjamin Franklin were very good at managing their time and prioritizing tasks in life. He once said, 'By failing to prepare, you are preparing to fail.' He was a master strategist of his time, forging timely alliances with European forces, and charming people all over the world into supporting the American dream with his slogan in 1765: 'Join or die.' It was a vision that drove the idea of a *United States of America* [206] by motivating the divided colonies to join hands together.

His ability to envision the most powerful economy in the world, and realise his vision of America as it is today, makes him a high performer and a game changer in the history of the world. Franklin was known for his systematic and planned efforts in helping to write the American Constitution. He could foresee the power of creating a social framework that could sustain modern developments. As he helped shape the nascent American society, he also inspired other societies engaged in rebuilding themselves after wars and catastrophes. Franklin gave hope to many nations engaged in developing the human capacity of their population.

He proved by setting an example that by forging resources of the people within a nation and by strategic collaboration with other nations, it is possible to build a powerful economy. America in its divided form was not economically strong enough to counter the colonizing forces, but he set the course right by spreading his slogan, 'Join or die' [206]. He also carefully and systematically steered specific efforts in developing the social infrastructure and political framework of the United States of America, which helped transform America into one of the most powerful economies of the world.

High performers like Benjamin Franklin were backed by a strong sense of inner calling or *inner guru*, which acted as a source of support to their *intuitive, seemingly irrational and bold* decisions. The activities in their life were woven around that one burning purpose. Such a degree of focus aided their decision-making skills, and helped them realise seemingly impossible goals.

I talk about this in *Level 5 of vertical living as a lifestyle* in Chapter 1: 'What is vertical living?'

The game changers in history walked the fine line
between perseverance and stupidity

Steve Jobs talks about persistence. 'I'm convinced that about half of what separates the successful entrepreneurs from the unsuccessful ones is pure perseverance. Unless you have a lot of passion about this, you're not going to survive. You're going to give up. So you've got to have an idea, or a problem, or a wrong that you want to right that you're passionate about; otherwise, you're not going to have the perseverance to stick it through.' Steve Jobs was known for his reality distortion field, with which he could seduce the best talent into seeing his vision and working towards it. As Walter Isaacson documents in the book *Steve Jobs*, Jobs delayed several product launches unexpectedly; he did not mind going over the details, over and over again and changing them to an extent of embracing strategies which he had initially rejected as incompetent. He displayed tremendous perseverance, persistence and flair for perfection and elegance in Apple products. Such unexpected delays announced by Jobs, caused unrest in his team members. However, Jobs did not mind walking the fine line between perseverance, perfection, and insanity.

Albert Einstein talks about perseverance and persistence. 'Insanity: doing the same thing again and again and expecting different results.'

Sam Walton, the founder of Wal-Mart, is quoted in his biography, *Sam Walton: Made In America*, 'Mother must have been a pretty special motivator, because I took her seriously when she told me I should always try to be the best I could at whatever I took on. So, I have always pursued everything I was interested in with a true passion—some would say obsession—to win. I've always held the bar pretty high for myself: I've set extremely high personal goals.' [208].

Bill Gates says that people favored his ideas on graphical user interface because he was very persistent and fanatic about realizing his ideas. His supporters often said that he worked so hard and was so persistent with his ideas, so even if he was wrong, he could eventually turn the course of events and change the game in his favor. He also acknowledges that he was quite fanatic and persistent about his vision; he recalls that he did not believe in taking a break on weekends or using any vacations when he was getting Microsoft up and running [209].

My stint in the domain of medical devices and radiation therapy brought me the great fortune of being able to talk to Dr John R. Adler, the neurosurgeon credited with revolutionizing the field of radiosurgery. He talks about his style of wrestling, his favorite sport, which is his defining style in life as well. 'What defines a great wrestler is their unmitigated resistance to pain and discomfort. That was kind of my style as a wrestler. If I am going to win, it is simply because I am going to outlast you. The battle here is most likely in your head; the opponent is in your head as much as anywhere else. The goal in wrestling is not as much to be artful as it is to outlast your opponent. It is actually my defining style; I never give up. I find something I believe in, which is worth my time, my effort, and energy, and never give up . . . Is that a good thing? I don't know. Sometimes you could pursue a fool's mission, which could be a waste of your time and your energy. This basic philosophy has served me well, and I don't think I've wasted my life.'

Dr Adler certainly was not on a fool's errand; we would have missed out on some of the greatest inventions in the medical device industry if he had not persisted! From what I surmised, he has been driven by a strong purpose all his life; his intellect and intuition have always guided him to choose his professional goals. He is a classic example of employing vertical living as a lifestyle.

'What defines a great wrestler is their unmitigated resistance to pain and discomfort. That was kind of my style as a wrestler. If I am going to win, it is simply because I am going to outlast you.
The battle here is most likely in your head; the opponent is in your head as much as anywhere else.
The battle in wrestling is not as much to be artful as it is to outlast your opponent.
It is kind of my defining style in life; I never give up. I find something I believe in, which is worth my time, my effort and energy, and never give up.'
Dr John R. Adler
Dorothy & TK Chan Professor, Emeritus, Stanford University
Inventor, Cyberknife

The game changers in history retained a beginner's mind in their approach

---

'In the beginner's mind there are many possibilities; in the expert's mind there are few.' is a very popular quote used by Zen teachers [210]. Beginner's mind is about staying free of preconceptions in learning, even though you may be a learner at the advanced level. If you would like to apply beginner's mind in your life, you will be starting at basics, and examining concepts in first principles. It is a method of questioning everything until you seek an answer yourself; you do not make any empirical assumptions. It is the philosophy behind the work culture at Google as referred to in the book, *How Google Works* by Eric Schmidt and Jonathan Rosenberg.

Elon Musk is a great proponent of questioning concepts in first principles or by questioning truths using Socratic methods. In an interview with Kevin Rose, this is what Elon Musk had to say:

'*I think it's important to reason from first principles rather than by analogy. The normal way we conduct our lives is we reason by analogy. [With analogy] we are doing this because it's like something else that was done, or it is like what other people are doing. [With first principles] you boil things down to the most fundamental truths . . . and then reason up from there.*'

If he has been able to build a SpaceX rocket at a competitive price, it is because he was able to break up the rocket into its raw materials and then figure out how much it would cost to build the machine from scratch. He could have very well drawn from the pricing suggested by the products in the market, but instead, he chose the beginner's mind approach; he came up with a cost-effective solution to building the SpaceX rocket [211] by questioning the status quo in building and then assembling the rocket. This was an unprecedented move in the history of space engineering, which has been dominated by NASA for many decades now.

Steve Jobs was forced to exit from Apple Inc., the very company that he had conceptualised and built, in 1985. However, he went back to Apple Inc., to rescue and reinstate its glory and image in 1997 and rebuilt the company into one of the largest and most powerful corporations in the world. The fact that Jobs was able to go back to the company whose executives had conspired against him, shows that he was very adept at retaining a beginner's mind towards setbacks and failures.

The game changers in history were unafraid of standing alone

Galileo Galilei, an Italian scientist and polymath, is most well known for having invented the telescope. He was imprisoned for supporting the heliocentric theory, i.e., a theory that talks about the sun being at the center of solar system versus geocentricism [212], where the earth is considered to be the center of all celestial bodies. He was placed under house arrest indefinitely, but he produced some of his best work in *Two New Sciences* [213] during this period. The book talks about kinematics and the strength of materials. He was not afraid of standing up for his beliefs even though it meant that he had to stand alone or face imprisonment.

Albert Einstein received the Nobel Prize for Physics in 1922 for his discovery of the Law of Photoelectric effect, even though he had deserved a Nobel Prize much earlier for his discovery of the Theory of Relativity in 1905. He spent a great deal of his life dealing with the unfair treatment from the academic ecosystem of his time. In one of his quotes, Einstein says, 'Great spirits have always encountered violent opposition from mediocre minds. The mediocre mind is incapable of understanding the man who refuses to bow blindly to conventional prejudices and chooses instead to express his opinions courageously and honestly.'

One of the biggest distinguishing traits of becoming a game changer is to be able to look beyond the conventional mindset and be honest about it [214]. Elon Musk has held his stand about clean energy and habitation in the interplanetary ecosystem. The story of what went into the making of Tesla is only a testimony to the fact that game changers in history are not afraid of standing alone; they are unafraid of accepting the struggle, and the pain that comes with it; most game changers have almost always known how to keep themselves motivated.

The game changers in history are unafraid of taking risks

Robert Noyce, co-founder of Intel and nicknamed the *Mayor of Silicon Valley*, was able to see the potential in transistors and semi-conductors at an age when it was a very novel concept to even imagine portable electronics. Elon Musk, who will go beyond Tesla, Solar City, and SpaceX as he forays into future technologies, has also proposed Vertical Take-Off and Landing vehicles and Hyperloop for high-speed transportation.

The founders of Google said no to traditional work culture, and chose simple management strategies over glamorous textbook management styles proposed by the best talents in the industry. Steve Jobs, the co-founder of Apple Inc., revolutionised the cell phone, computer, music, and movie industries by his concepts of usability, connectivity, and quality.

They are all game changers in the history of the tech industry because they raised human abilities in computation, connectivity, and perception of information to a whole new level. We are almost at a point where machines can read our thoughts and predict our daily schedules; for example, Google Now predicts traffic updates based on the location of a meeting scheduled on Google Calendar.

Steve Jobs once said, 'People who change the world are the ones who are crazy enough to think they can.' He predicted the advances in cloud computing and the Internet at a time when computers were formidable and clumsy. His ideas seemed unbelievable, but they have come true.

I believe that the rationale for game changers' crazy ideas stems from the guidance provided by their vivid inner calling. Even if Elon Musk runs out of a budget for pursuing his plans to make human beings an interplanetary species, he will nonetheless be spurred on by a strong vision for the future, backed by high risk-taking ability and a great degree of intuition.

Game changers followed their calling by harnessing intuition and altered states consciousness in daily life

---

Be it Steve Jobs or Jeff Bezos or Elon Musk, the game changers of Silicon Valley were not afraid of being different and did not hesitate to follow the untrodden path. *Their ability to work hard and be experts in their domain was not unique. What made them unique was their ability to be focused on their original visions and be guided by their inner compass to achieve their goals.*

These game changers lived in meditative states, i.e., *states that heightened their intuition (knowingly or unknowingly).* Intuition comes alive when you pursue any task with singular focus or give yourself quiet time and your mind is thought-free; a state most commonly achieved during meditation, running, listening to music—again, with a singular focus. Tuning into intuitive states helped these high achievers to adopt difficult, demanding, controversial, and game changing decisions or strategies. Heightened intuition or being guided by a strong sense of inner purpose or inner calling has been recognised as a common result of the practice of meditation [203, 204]. Such states are natural to people who read voraciously or apply themselves to tasks that require constant and rigorous learning. They are able to adapt to new schools of thought and adapt to changing circumstances by being fast learners.

Most people who serve in high pressure jobs in the government, presidents, CEOs, and top executives of large multinational corporations who travel across countries for business, or professors in academia who are guiding cutting edge research, are thrust into situations that demand them to adapt their analytical skills, cultural sensitivities, and emotional quotient, to changing circumstances. They adapt quickly to changing situations by trusting their intuition *inherently*. I can vouch for this fact from firsthand experience working in both industry and academia for the past 11 years.

Many years ago, when I was in conversation with the founder of a multinational corporation in India, I recall him mentioning that he hired people by intuition, by reading their nonverbal cues in the first ten minutes of the interview. A professor in Bio-engineering, who guided me in course work and thesis, told me that he did all the groundwork before he started off on a research grant proposal, but almost always knew by gut feeling when things were going to fail or when his choices were not appropriate.

An expert in martial arts, or any kind of art, will probably tell you that they now work intuitively after many years of rigorous practice [215]. Anticipating the opponent's move before the opponent even strikes is the secret to the master martial artist's strategy. What I am trying to say is that in intense and focused activity, and dedicated application of oneself to a task, and by repetitive practice, we can get into intuitive states that allow us to solve complex problems. Intuition can help us be perceptive about situations, and is a guide to courageous decision-making. Mother Teresa, for instance, mentioned that while traveling by train to the Loreto convent in Darjeeling, she had a sudden intuitive insight. 'I was to leave the convent and help the poor while living among them. It was an order. To fail would have been to break the faith.' [216] This was a turning point in her life that started her off on her journey to found the Missionaries of Charity.

Most decisions based on intuition are powerful, since they give direction to the intellect that is involved in decision-making. Saar Bitner, VP of Marketing at Sisense, a business analytics software company, quotes from *A Fortune Knowledge Group study: Only Human: The emotional logic of business decisions*, 'that 62 per cent of executives feel it is often necessary to rely on *gut feelings* and soft factors when making big decisions on partnerships and proposals.'

Srinivasa Ramanujan, one of India's greatest mathematical geniuses, is known to have credited his mathematical findings to the Goddess of Namagiri. She appeared in his visions, proposing mathematical formulae, which Ramanujan would then have to prove later on. He quotes one such event as follows:

'While asleep, I had an unusual experience. There was a red screen formed by flowing blood, as it were. I was observing it. Suddenly, a hand began to write on the screen. I became all attention. That hand wrote a number of elliptic integrals. They stuck to my mind. As soon as I woke up, I committed them to writing.' [217] Furthermore, in a dream, Ramanujan's mother received permission from Namagiri Amman for Ramanujan to go to England [218].

Albert Einstein has been one of the most powerful influences on the philosophy of science. He was the founding father of the general theory of relativity and established the relationship between mass and energy in one of the most famous equations in physics, i.e., $E=mc^2$. He had no qualms about highlighting the limitations of Newtonian mechanics, even though it meant that he had to confront the academic ecosystem of his time. Einstein had, time and again, emphasised the importance of play and creativity in the advancement of scientific research. Creative ideas have long been associated with meditative states, e.g., Sanyama, an ancient yogic attentional technique that provides a neuropsychological explanation for extraordinary creativity [219].

In one of his quotes on philosophy, Einstein states, 'There is neither evolution nor destiny, only being.' *Being* is considered as the core of existing in a meditative state or the central theme of living in the moment; I call it being tuned into the moment, the core and foundation of vertical living as a lifestyle.

Game changers use their mind and body effectively to live in awakened states

---

Think about people like Mother Teresa, Mahatma Gandhi or Nelson Mandela. They had to encounter fierce opposition all their lives to stick to their vision. If you read their autobiographies and quotes, it is clear that they trusted their gut feelings or awakened states as much as they relied on their constant efforts to succeed in their endeavors. In his sleep or in dreams, Gandhi received creative ideas to conduct campaigns in nonviolence in order to rally support from the public. Mahatma Gandhi's idea of Dandi March came to him in a dream [220].

Mother Teresa spent much time in prayer and meditation as part of her disciplined lifestyle. Nelson Mandela found his peace in reading and self-pursuit. His life in prison was tough and he was denied the basic amenities, but he followed his inner calling and tapped into his higher human abilities by using poetry and literature as his sources of personal power. The people I refer to here were all extremely strong and persistent in effecting social changes of mammoth proportions; they had learned to tap into supra-human dimensions that gave them tremendous staying power amidst crisis and opposition.

When you observe their personal lives, it is clear that these game changers used their mind and body effectively to exist in awakened, adaptive, self-realised, and highly perceptive states of being—almost by habit.

Engage in different forms of creativity and challenge yourself regularly by learning something new and different.

This is a lifestyle tip in vertical living.

Mahatma Gandhi and Mother Teresa were known to have practiced rigorous self-discipline in their speech, lifestyle, and ethics. This awakened and elevated their body and their being into awakened or meditative states. This state is also achieved by obstacle racers—people who run 26-mile marathons—and climbers, who choose precarious hiking trails. Such a state is achieved by the ability of the human brain to work with newer neural pathways and reinforce them by the power of human will. This is the core of Hatha Yoga, a form of self-realization proposed by Hindu philosophy. In Bhakti Yoga, dedication and devotion to God or a particular superior or higher purpose or cause, becomes a way of life and unleashes tremendous power in devotees of a certain philosophy.

In Patanjali's eight limbs of yoga, he mentions Pratyahara as a stage where practicing self-control, self-discipline, and self-denial makes human beings alert and acutely aware of their senses. Practicing yoga as a way of life heightens the likelihood of being able to achieve meditative states. All forms of yoga need to be adopted with supervision and guidance from a learned person in that particular discipline. For now, we can learn how meditative states and intuition have helped game changers develop specific abilities. Let us look at a few leaders in history who developed stellar reading capabilities.

How game changers in history used intuitive states to read books

Let us start by trying out an exercise in reading. To become a fast reader, pick up your favorite book; choose an easy paragraph. Try using your index finger to run along the text when you are reading the paragraph. Try to couple this reading style with fine-tuning your eye movements and avoid random movements. This will help you focus better. Fine-tune all your movements to keep increasing your speed of reading; persist with this habit for 10 minutes every day. At one point, you will start reading and sensing a paragraph by intuition. You could even skim through a book in a few minutes. Game changers in history have apparently accomplished this!

Theodore Roosevelt, American statesman, author, and reformer, read one or two books a day. John F. Kennedy read 1,200 words a minute. Reading was an intuitive exercise; they could skim through huge chunks of text in a very short time. As former presidents of the fastest growing economy in the world, Teddy Roosevelt and John F. Kennedy were extremely busy and productive in their personal, professional, and social lives. Their ability to skim through a book amidst a hectic workday helped them gain great insights into better decision-making. They were able to effect many bold changes in society because they were extremely well read, and well informed.

Inner calling and intuition inspired the writers of Sci-Fi

I look at authors of science fiction like H. G. Wells, Isaac Asimov, and Arthur C. Clarke, as game changers who pushed the frontiers of technology. They have inspired many physicists and visionaries to examine concepts in space travel, artificial intelligence, robots, and time travel; and have inspired the entrepreneurs of today to attempt to colonise distant planets. Many authors of science fiction dreamt of the unusual content for their books in their sleep or while daydreaming. Such states are very close to altered states of consciousness, which can be acquired during meditation [7]. They displayed uninhibited creativity in writing about inventions such as spaceships and space travel, and wrote about these subjects when there weren't many motorised modes of transportation. These great visionaries had to publish their concepts as fiction because their ideas were rejected by the scientific and research community at the time.

Inner calling and intuition—the Greeks and Egyptians believed in it

For Archimedes, Pythagoras, Leonardo da Vinci, and Aristotle, being a polymath was a way of life. Leonardo da Vinci was considered one of the greatest painters of all time. He was also well versed in sculpting, architecture, music, mathematics, science, engineering, literature, anatomy, geology, astronomy, botany, writing, history, and cartography. He has been called the father of paleontology, ichnology, and architecture [221]. Aristotle was another notable polymath in ancient Greece, who contributed by way of his writings to physics, biology, zoology, metaphysics, logic, ethics, aesthetics, poetry, theater, music, rhetoric, linguistics, and politics [222]. Being a polymath allowed for unlimited sessions of creativity and enterprise in the lives of these great visionaries, and enabled them to stay focused on pioneering changes in art, mathematics, natural, and pure sciences.

Great emphasis was laid on meditation in the Academy, which was started by Plato [223, 224]. He was an ardent student of Socrates and brought his teachings alive in the Academy. Aristotle was educated in the Academy for 20 years, devoting himself to the study of mathematics, philosophy, the natural sciences, and law and government. These ancient Greek scholars laid the foundation for Western philosophy [223, 224]. They were also greatly influenced by techniques in meditation [222, 223]. And in many ways, they created the foundation for modern science through the fundamentals of logic.

Further back in time, the ancient Egyptians who built the Pyramids of Giza, were well-known for their advanced techniques in meditation. Their system of education was very focused on meditation, mysticism, rebirth, and reincarnation. Their knowledge of architecture, physics, astronomy, material engineering, and clean energy was unsurpassed. Contemporary science is unable to match their accomplishments in structural engineering, even to this day. There is also clear indication that their system of education was far superior to the education system in our modern society [225].

Educating oneself by way of inner calling and intuition like the ancient Indians and Chinese

A system of education similar to that of the Egyptians was followed in ancient India, wherein meditation and the path of understanding oneself came before any other discipline. Did you know that the ancient Indians introduced the concept of zero? They also pioneered advancements in surgery and medicine way before any other civilization in history. Their understanding of particle physics was quite advanced, as there are accounts of atomic bombs having destroyed ancient Indian cities 4,000 years ago [226].

A testimony of their understanding in particle physics has been endorsed by CERN, the European Center for Research in Particle Physics. The Nataraja statue installed in Geneva, Switzerland, was given to CERN by the Government of India and represents the cosmic dance of Shiva. There is an inscription below the Nataraja statue by Fritjof Capra, the author of *The Tao of Physics: An Exploration of the Parallels Between Modern Physics and Eastern Mysticism*. Mysticism is based on the concept of using meditation as a technique in transforming of human potential [227]. Capra says, 'Physicists do not need mysticism, and mystics do not need physics, but humanity needs both.' His book has been acclaimed as a classic and is in its 35th edition. His take in the book is that modern physics is changing our perception of the world from mechanistic to holistic and ecological [228].

Ancient China has made several contributions to mankind in terms of its timeless innovations. Did you know that the ancient Chinese invented the first clock in the history of mankind? They are also credited to have introduced techniques for making paper, gunpowder, printing, and the compass. Ancient Chinese literature, architecture, music, martial arts, cuisine, arts, and religion have been deeply influenced by Buddhism, Taoism, and Confucianism. These are deeply rooted in metaphysical concepts such as knowing yourself by questioning your very being, in first principles. Clearly, the ancient Chinese education system emphasised the path to self-realization as a basic part of their culture and tradition [229].

What can be changed in our contemporary education system?

Our contemporary system of education is very outward facing. What I mean to say is that it makes us look at objects and things outside ourselves to get started on learning. If I were to go to school today, I would expect, knowing how things currently work, to be enrolled in a course with credit requirements; this would cause me to focus all of my time on finishing a project or solving a problem that would grant me enough credits for a certificate.

If I were to modify this sequence a little bit and focus on my individual state of mind, and my style of learning, then I would find the most optimal way to complete the course. For example, if I am trying to understand the positioning of a patient on a CT scanner machine, and if my school does not give me an opportunity to look at this machine in person, then I would find a way to see the machine at my own expense. This is exactly what the experts in any field or the game changers in history have done, time and again. They knew how their mind and learning mechanisms worked, and followed their instincts and intuition to enhance their learning. For Leonardo, in spite of being a polymath, he had trouble learning new languages. Whatever knowledge he missed due to the gaps in reading or learning from a new language, he made up for, by using his keen observation and interpretation. He had an innate ability to question the nature of things and an imagination that was not affected by the hurdles posed by his environment. What I mean to say is that Leonardo knew very well how to use his strengths and weaknesses in learning and creating something new [230].

Game changers in history spent a lot of time by themselves, in quiet, exploring things around them; and, as a result, understanding their own learning style. It is such a paradox that the greatest game changers in history did not go through conventional schooling. Game changers spent quiet time alone playing with ideas; they were self-realised. Einstein spent many hours in his bathtub, playing with bubbles and mulling concepts in his head.

Existing in a meditative state during daily activities is the core of vipassana [8,231] or mindfulness as a lifestyle. It is an impartial observation of events in life. It was also quite interesting to me when I discovered that most speakers, writers, top-tier management professionals, and artists who were a part of my journey in writing this book, knew how to transform themselves into similar meditative states during their daily activities. Suhas Gopinath, who became the youngest CEO that India had seen, at the age of fourteen, put me in a meditative state by completely focusing on our conversation, when he talked about how he made his first million. He had not only mastered the art of focusing on a conversation completely, but also the art of calming the person he is conversing with. What a great gift to have, in this day and age when we are all rushed and pressed for time.

In my Personal Experience

In my personal experience, most of my best speeches were delivered when I was in a meditative state, i.e., I felt completely thought-free before speaking. It is a subtle state of mind where I am aware of, but not distracted by, my surroundings. This was followed by a state where I felt intuitive about what my audience would like to hear, coupled with a strong inner calling to speak. Usually before I speak, the changes in my mind and body correspond to a state almost of high-energy, where I almost lose track of time.

My speech for the promotional video of the book, which I shot at Hakone Gardens, was an impromptu delivery. I had been thinking about the topics in this speech for many years, so I was well versed in the content. But for a whole fifteen minutes, the message just flowed through me, without any inhibitions. The speech was very well received by viewers. It was a slow delivery for me, as I was trying to speak intuitively. I am usually soft-spoken, and I speak fast. But when I am speaking with intuition, I am a slow and clear speaker.

Many people have come up to me at various speaking forums and complimented me about those speeches that I delivered when I was in a meditative state. The takeaway for me is that, while I am in intuitive and meditative states during a speech, my words and bodily movements have a certain grace reflecting a harmonious flow of ideas and are well received by the public. For me, this is the greatest testimony to how intuition and meditative states can be effective and useful in daily life.

> If I were to dissect the concept of living in meditative states, at the core of such a lifestyle is the ability to treat every single passing moment as an individual entity. This means focusing on the task at hand single-mindedly, and being intentional, purposeful, intuitive and slow in your movements and actions in dealing with the present. Such a mindset has given great power to luminaries and game changers in history.

Moment Therapy

The more you give yourself to every passing moment, the more powerful and effective you become in your life as a whole. For example, when you are dining with your family, be completely tuned into the events associated with dining, like eating, tasting the food, listening to conversations at dinner, or focusing on the courses in the meal. This way, every time you dine becomes a refreshing experience. When your actions are driven by a specific purpose, your movements become more refined and graceful. When you are focused on dining, your table manners become more refined. If you focus on chewing the food properly, your tastes sharpen and you start becoming a better cook. Eating itself becomes a relaxing activity, or it becomes eating in meditation. This is the greatest effect of meditating regularly or existing in meditative states during daily activities. All the interviews and interactions that led me to write this book, more than endorse this fact. I call this lifestyle, of living in the moment or being tuned into the moment, vertical living or living in the here and now.

Life is a sum of moments, lived one at a time. Why not focus on each moment with our full attention, focus, and love?

- *End Chapter* -

Chapter 3: So, what are high performers like?

In this chapter, I would like to highlight the fact that if you need to meet stellar goals or realise moonshot thinking, you need to be a high performer, who is driven by your inner calling to a strong purpose. I paint an idealistic picture of what a high performer carries with him/herself in daily life and help you register that vision by way of examples of game changers in history and contemporary world.

It is important to focus on specific aspects of your life in becoming a high performer. You need to be very clear about your inner calling or purpose in life, and be able to translate that calling into a vision. To realise that vision, you need to be able to leverage high performing teams and develop efficient communication skills to share your goals.

In the section below, I would like to express the ideas in *Chapter 3: So, What Are High Performers Like?* using charts. One of them uses a linear or step-by-step representation of the entrepreneurial approach to self-realization; the other chart uses a non-linear or cyclic approach. A detailed explanation of these charts can be found by checking the following section Self-realization using an entrepreneurial approach. The terminology foundin the cyclic and linear charts below, have been explained in the*Chapter Self-realization: Using an Entrepreneurial Strategy to Maximise Your Inner Potential*

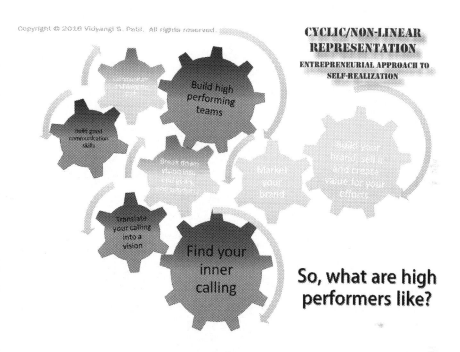

CYCLIC/NON-LINEAR
REPRESENTATION
ENTREPRENEURIAL APPROACH TO
SELF-REALIZATION

Build high performing teams

Build good communication skills

Break down your goals and priorities

Market your brand

Build your brand, sell it and create value for your efforts

Translate your calling into a vision

Find your inner calling

So, what are high performers like?

LINEAR REPRESENTATION
ENTREPRENEURIAL APPROACH TO SELF-
REALIZATION

The end result is to become an overachiever or an entrepreneur

Build a high performing team and leverage their skills effectively

Develop and build good communication skills to share your goals

Break down your priorities, goals and priorities

Translate your calling into a vision

Find your inner calling

Be a high-performer with purpose

-Chapter begins-

'The art of war consists, with a numerically inferior
army, in always having larger forces than the enemy
at the point which is to be attacked or defended . . . it
is an intuitive way of acting which properly constitutes
the genius of war.'
— William Duggan, *Napoleon's Glance:*
The Secret of Strategy

In this chapter, I talk about a few distinguishable traits of high performers in history and the contemporary world. It is important to understand the lifestyles and driving forces that cause high performers to deliver stellar results. My inspiration for writing this chapter is to help *readers move from aiming to be a high performer in their daily activities toward becoming a high performer as a game changer who can alter the course of things,* i.e., who can raise the human capacity and thinking of his/her fellow beings to a higher plane of achievement. For instance, think about making desalinated water available to the drought-stricken, and those people affected by natural calamities. How can you harness crowd sourcing or social media to achieve this?

My vision of a high performer is idealistic. It encompasses the summation of many traits across game-changers in history. *It is an idealistic vision, so you can visualise it in your mind all the time and live by it.* This can be done very much as part of your adherence to vertical living or working towards existing in awakened states as best as you can, so you can tap into maximised states of human potential.

There were many factors that helped high performers become game changers, i.e., people who significantly altered the course of technology, art, politics or any other domain that they touched in history. There can be several supporting factors as part of education, stimulating environment, lifestyle or upbringing may have been contributing factors in creating game changers; other factors like the time and circumstances they lived in, may also have influenced their importance in history. For instance, if Albert Einstein were to have lived in this day and age, his career path may have been different from what it was in the early 1900s. On another note, his theories may have found quicker acceptance in this age of digital publication and social media; he may have collaborated with Nikola Tesla to support the theory of ether. Who knows! The point I am trying to make is that high performers could become game changers due to influences from many parameters that may not be under human purview or human control. However, in this chapter, I will talk about factors that are under the preview of human control.

> *If you are a high performer, ideally, you*
> *will be great at motivating others.*
> *You are so driven by your purpose and goals*
> *that you will be brimming with energy; being*
> *a leader will be a way of life for you.*

Let us start our study by looking at a few examples from history. Albert Einstein, who shook the world with his ideas in physics, was a high performer; Leonardo Da Vinci, who embraced all knowledge as he moved from engineering, to physiology to painting to philosophy and kept reinventing himself, was a high performer. They were also game changers in their domains of expertise, but they were high performers as well.

Now let me introduce a game changer of this day and age—John R. Adler, the inventor of CyberKnife, a frameless robotic radiosurgery system used in treatment of cancer. He is a neurosurgeon and an emeritus professor of neurosurgery who conceptualised and realised the frameless robotic radiosurgery system. He acknowledges that his ability to focus persistently on his inner calling, and his open-mindedness in nurturing ideas both good and bad, are factors that contributed to his success. During his interview for this book, he reiterated that he was able to see past the detracting forces like peer jealousies, and stay focused on that one purpose to which he dedicated his life. He is definitely a game changer in the fields of image-guided radiation therapy. The take away from Dr Adler's interview is that, being a high performer requires you to be super-focused on that one purpose and learn to manage yourself when negative influences are acting on you.

Vidyangi

> *All game changers in history are high performers, but*
> *all high performers need not be game changers.*

In the book *How Google Works*, there is a concept called **smart creative,** which I think is a great way to represent a few consistent traits in high performers in the tech industry. Smart creative people are very passionate about what they do. They continuously risk experimenting, they are thorough in their work, they are driven by a strong sense of purpose, and they dare to dream the unimaginable and the unthinkable. A smart creative is also someone who is confident, assertive, and compassionate of the surroundings he/she is a part of. Many working mothers I know are high performers, as they are great at setting reasonable goals and meeting them.

Let me give you an example of a working mother who is also a game changer for women in India. I was listening to a talk on philanthropy by Sudha Murthy, who is the chairperson of the Infosys Foundation and a member of public health care initiatives of the Gates Foundation in India. She is the wife of N.R. Narayana Murthy, the founder of Infosys, which is one of the biggest IT companies in India. If there is one lady who has understood the power of being a high performer and is growing into a game changer for women in India, it is definitely her. Back in the day and age where women were not considered for jobs in factories, she became the first female engineer hired by India's largest auto manufacturer, TATA Engineering and Locomotive Company (TELCO) [300]. She always took up one cause at a time and affected her ecosystem at various levels, very deeply.

When she was an engineer, she changed the rules of the game for women in a male-dominated workplace. As the wife of Murthy, she motivated and supported him to build one of the biggest IT companies in India.

As a mother, she made social service a way of life for her kids. And now, she spends most of her time in improving the infrastructure in many Indian villages [301]. She thinks and talks like an entrepreneur; she pursues her passion for philanthropy while always being mindful of how she invests her time and money to help people. She is also very deeply involved in healing people struck by natural calamities in India. Now, that's the sort of person that I endorse as a high performer and a game changer, in our contemporary world.

I believe that most people, who play multiple roles in their families and at their workplaces, have learned the winning formula to becoming a high performer. The point I am trying to make here is that <u>a high performer is someone who is smart in tapping into resources around them, is creative, and is driven by a strong purpose, energised, and happy in their own skin.</u>

If you are a high performer, you will be great at motivating others. You will be so driven by your purpose and goals that you will be brimming with energy. You will always communicate from the positive energy in yourself. You will become good at communicating and leading. Being a leader and a good communicator are two visible traits of a high performer.

If you cannot lead or communicate well, there is no way you will be able to wear multiple hats and accomplish challenging goals. <u>All great personal achievements are team efforts as well.</u> If you need to do well in your business, you need a team of people to help spread your message, create a brand for you, and help you sell your product. It is all teamwork, at the end of the day.

Let's look at a few more examples from my daily life. My mom is a high performer too. She was not only a busy medical practitioner, but also a sponsor of education, food and shelter for many adults and kids that I know. She is an entrepreneur's wife (a tough role to play, I must say!) and the mother of two daughters whom she continues to inspire. She taught me the art of writing and speaking, and also gave me a primer in music and singing. You can spot a self-realised high performer either in history (e.g., Einstein or Da Vinci) or next door (e.g., people like my mom) because of the way they live and create and are completely driven by a purpose. Here are some pointers on how *you* can launch yourself on the path of high performance.

Start by Loving Yourself

Let me state that this is top priority: <u>be kind and compassionate to yourself first! This is because only in this state can you transmit love and compassion,</u> realise the purpose of your life, and be of service to the world around you. An unhappy and unloved person is always seeking solace and can give nothing. What is the point of living a life of affluence if you cannot love yourself and others? Start loving yourself.

It is in accepting and loving yourself that you begin the process of self-realization, and it is indeed the most important tip for vertical living.

When you are in love with yourself, you will take good care of your mind, body, and soul, i.e., physical health, mental health, and spiritual health. You will eat healthy, learn to stay as productive and as positive as you can, and lead a life that is gratitude-centric. In this process, you will not only impact yourself positively, but also the surrounding environment.

FIGURE OUT THE PURPOSE OF YOUR LIFE

If you succeed in finding the purpose of your life, you will succeed in becoming a high performer. I say this very confidently, because I feel a shift in my energies whenever I write or whenever I speak in public. Let us consider the case of a focused and purpose-driven high performer: Elon Musk thinks that eating should not consume ANY time, because he would rather spend that time on realizing his visions for clean energy and space travel. Elon Musk was fascinated with space travel at the age of fourteen. He had started focusing on his inner calling very early in his life. He has been able to sustain a chain of entrepreneurial ventures because he set the course of his future very early in his life. If you know that ONE purpose in your life, you will also start tapping into your maximum potential immediately. But how do you know the purpose of your life?

I wish it were as easy as taking a Jung and Briggs-Meyers Personality type test, or a personalised brain training program on Lumosity.com, or estimating your strengths in leadership with StrengthsFinder2.0. You could visit a vipassana meditation retreat or the Ayahuasca Retreat in Peru. It could start with any of the above. But, my dear reader, finding an answer to this question is going to take more work. It is a journey, and you will know when the answer pops into your heart through insight or intuition. You can start by observing all your daily activities very deeply. Note those activities that bring you maximum joy and success.

You may discover several purposes in your life as you evolve with time, but there is certainly one major purpose that will draw your potential toward maximum success and bring out the best in you, or invoke the greatest passion in your life. For instance, when I was talking to a friend who is a serial Silicon Valley entrepreneur, he told me that he knew as a child what he wanted to do with his life. He said that he had a passion for leveraging resources, be it technology or a corporate team or wealth. He explored literature of varied kind very early in his life, explored the fundamentals in finance and in graduate school; very early, he became an expert programmer. Today, he is a serial entrepreneur and investor.

As I spoke to a greater number of entrepreneurs and study game changers in history and contemporary world, I realised that most of them knew very early in their lives what they were born to do. Such clarity of purpose is a consistent trait among high performers.

> *Most high performers know very early in*
> *their lives what they are born to do.*
> *The more number of entrepreneurs and game changers I*
> *spoke to, the more I realised that this was a consistent trait.*

If your life has clouded you with a lot of negative influences about things you cannot achieve or things you are not built to achieve, or things you cannot change, *IT IS YOUR JOB TO DE-PROGRAM YOURSELF! I call this process self-realization.* This is definitely a lifestyle tip for vertical living.

Engage in different forms of creativity and challenge yourself regularly by learning something new and different.
This is a lifestyle tip for vertical living.

I have experienced the realization of the purpose of my life at several different moments. All the actions that I undertake, like writing, speaking in public forums, and connecting with people for their self-development, unleash tremendous potential and love in me.

Here is an excerpt from my blog that I think will help you as you seek self-realization:

BLOG POST: MEANING IN LIFE

My heart says: Through my writing today, I would like to help people who are lost in the process of finding meaning and purpose in their lives, by directing them towards creativity as a means of finding that answer.

The child plays in coloured water. He/she feels joy and splashes the colour on the wall to make a pattern. The pattern has a meaning, and it *means* the child is happy.

A scientist creates a product that disproves the critics and the logic of the savvy businessman. Maybe the product gets discarded. This incident can have many meanings, but for the scientist, it *means* he has expressed his inner potential. For him it *means* creativity.

I listen to music that passes through my heart and exits me as a tear drops in my eye. People say I am emotional and imaginative. To me, this teardrop *means* that the musician has succeeded in his art and has made me forget myself.

A very altruistic yet unpolished person who gets his language wrong and his approach wrong looks very imperfect to the cultured world as he tries to help someone. But he does it anyway. This means, he is bigger than the critics who are judging him by his appearance, and critics who cannot read his good deeds. This *means* he has transcended the critics by acting in good will.

Meaning happens when there is some sort of action or change, or when you risk something; something has transformed or changed in your life. To find meaning and purpose in our lives, we have to start acting and creating! Find the meaning of your life by creating something today!

Create something when you are feeling lost or are unable to realise meaning and purpose in your life. This is a lifestyle tip for vertical living.

Embrace Creativity

If you feel it is helping you to relax and unwind, continue to create. I know a lot of busy working mothers and homemakers who meet for random paint and wine sessions; it is called a 'paint night'. I know a friend who meets with her peers for cartooning sessions. She has reached almost professional levels in her endeavor, but it all started off as a hobby to nurture her creative instincts. Michael Chojnaki, a popular executive coach and also the President of Aikiway Professional Development, says that he encourages people to create using their hands. He says that creating something with your hands not only improves your connection with your surroundings, but also enhances intuition and creativity.

Creating something will change the states of your mind and body and the framework of your world for a while, so you can gain perspective and new insights into your current situation.

Create something when you are feeling lost or fail to realise meaning and purpose in your life.
This is a lifestyle tip for vertical living.

What you create may or may not be useful; however, it will align and activate the energy centers in your body and will give you a new perspective on your existing situation. I mean to say that it will change the states of your mind and body, and alter the framework of your world for a bit; this way you can gain perspective and new insights into your current situation. FYI: Energy centers are energy counterparts of the glands and organs existing in the body. They are used as points of diagnostics in Reiki and other healing techniques.

Find quiet time regularly

Chojnaki also recommends that in order to learn about the purpose of your life, you need to find some quiet time every day. This will allow you to connect with the purpose of your life. Such a connection with yourself can be accomplished by meditation. Most people ask the question, what can one accomplish by sitting quietly in meditation? Perhaps, one of my blog posts can serve you the answer.

BLOG POST: SIT QUIETLY, DOING NOTHING

Art and Illustration: Megha Vishwanath

My heart says I should write about the clarity and purity of purpose that emerges from a simple, quiet submission to the current moment: **'Sit quietly, doing nothing, spring comes, and the grass grows by itself.'** *(inspired by Zen)*

Sit quietly, doing nothing, spring comes and grass grows . . .

Sit quietly, doing nothing, eyes meet and love flows . . .

Sit quietly, doing nothing, we breathe in and life happens . . .

Sit quietly, doing nothing, creativity strikes and hard work follows . . .

Sit quietly, doing nothing, the heart opens and the mind explodes . . .

Sit quietly, doing nothing, the clouds lift and the rays of the sun flow . . .

Sit quietly, doing nothing, life is felt so very deeply . . .

Sit quietly, doing nothing, tears flow and our being is cleansed . . .

In a world racing against time and ambition, the chance to sit quietly, doing nothing, is a treasure to be cherished.

In the end, what matters is how deeply you have experienced life, rather than how much of it you have!

Chojnaki also talks about purposeful movement; it means driving your thinking, your bodily movements, and your actions with purpose, intuition, and a sense of empathy to your surroundings.

This is the most basic way to realise the purpose of your life. Once you start engaging in regular quiet time, you will start utilizing this quietness to initiate purposeful movements and actions in daily life.

Lifestyle tip for vertical living: Practice purposeful movements driven by intuition and empathy, e.g., purposeful speech in an executive meeting, purposeful suggestions for a family get-together, and purposeful deeds to cheer up a friend who is going through a difficult time.

Practice purposeful movements driven by intuition and empathy, e.g., purposeful speech in an executive meeting, purposeful suggestions for a family get-together, and purposeful deeds to cheer up a friend who is going through a difficult time.

This is a lifestyle tip for vertical living.

Michael Chojnaki also suggests that intuition is an inherent trait of every individual. We just need to recognise the decisions and actions that have been driven by intuition and appreciate it in ourselves. This way, he says, we can improve intuition in ourselves. In the book *Working with Emotional Intelligence,* Daniel Goleman points out the importance of following an inner rudder or inner guide for purposeful actions. This inner rudder will come alive when your intuition is working strongly in your heart against all the odds posed by your logic, surroundings, or data. Goleman goes on to add to this idea, stating that the decisions may not sound right at first, but decisions guided by gut feeling maximise the energy and attention available for pursuing them.

Richard Abdoo, a former CEO of Wisconsin Energy, mentions that he took long walks, worked in his home workshop, and rode his Harley away from the hustle and bustle of life to be in touch with his true self. Giving yourself regular quiet time makes space for your intuition to come alive and stir you to purposeful movements, which in turn align you with the purpose of your life. As Edward McCraken, a former Chief Executive Officer of Silicon Graphics puts it, 'The most important trait of a good leader is knowing who you are. In our industry, very often, we don't have time to think. You have to do all your homework, but then you have to go with your intuition without letting your mind get in the way.'

Most decisions based on intuition are powerful decisions, as they are better able to direct the intellect involved in decision-making. As Saar Bitner, VP of Marketing at SiSense, highlights the Fortune Knowledge Group study: 'Only Human: The Emotional Logic of Business Decisions,' which reports that that '62 per cent of executives feel it is often necessary to rely on gut feelings and soft factors when making big decisions on partnerships and proposals.' To invoke intuition and better perception of situations, give yourself quiet time regularly to connect with the purpose of your life. This is a lifestyle tip for vertical living.

To invoke intuition, and gain a better perception of situations, give yourself quiet time regularly to connect with the purpose of your life. **This is a lifestyle tip for vertical living.**

Why performers lead a Purpose-driven Life

Gary Keller and Jay Papasan talk about the power of purpose in their new bestseller *The One Thing*. They say, 'The more productive people are, the more purpose and priority are pushing and driving them.' This implies that if you would like to be productive at home, work, and other areas in life, let the decisions in your life be guided by purpose and priority. Life is meant to be lived happily, and in a fulfilling way; realizing the purpose of your life is one of the most optimal ways to accomplish this. I would like to share one of my blog posts, which I wrote when this idea was resonating with me.

BLOG POST: RESONANT FREQUENCY

Image courtesy: Nikki Zaiewski www.dreamstime.com

My heart says: I should write so that I can capture the feelings arising in a person who is realizing their inner calling or acting in alignment with the purpose of their life. I call this process resonance.

Every object on earth has its own natural frequency, at which all particles in the object resonate with the largest amplitude. This particular frequency in the object is called as resonant frequency. For instance, have you ever played with a tuning fork? A tuning fork has two metallic prongs. When you hit either of the prongs against a hard surface, it resonates with most of the vibrational energy at the fundamental frequency, and little at the overtones. This one particular frequency, at which the tuning fork makes the loudest sound, is called the *resonant* frequency of the tuning fork. It is the natural frequency of the tuning fork at which it has the loudest amplitude.

Human beings also experience resonance of various forms. Some of mankind's greatest creations, which seem to have beaten human logic or imagination, were fueled by a creative resonance in the creator. If we observe some of the mind-boggling creations of mankind, be it Rabindranath Tagore's Nobel Prize winning composition of Geetanjali, or Leonardo da Vinci's concepts of flying machines, we see that the creativity of these masters exploded into newer horizons when they resonated with their innate sense of creativity. The resonance they felt with their true inner natures was independent of the support or encouragement they received for their works.

We can experience resonance in so many other forms; we can experience resonance in smells, taste, touch, thoughts, and lovemaking, too. Every human being has a setting in which he/she is excited to, or realises the ability to experience resonance, i.e., the realization of maximum human potential. In other words, each one of us has an individual way of exploring inner resonant frequencies. Some people explore their resonance by connecting with more people outside them; some others find their potential in quiet silence and solitude.

The purpose of our life, knowingly or unknowingly, is to find our inner resonant frequencies. Because, in realizing our inner resonant frequencies, we have the greatest joy. We experience the maximum realization and *release* of our inner human potential . . .

The purpose of our life, knowingly or unknowingly,
is to find our inner-resonant frequencies.

If you wish to be a high performer, it is imperative for you to know why purpose and priority will matter in your life. If you lack clarity in your thinking on what your priorities and goals are, and what matters most to you in your life, your inner human potential will not be optimised. You will tend to feel a disconnect with yourself as the things you may be doing to occupy your time and energy may not be aligned with your true calling or purpose in life. In the next section, I would like to iterate the importance of purpose and priority in life.

On Purpose and Priority in Life

Deepak Chopra says, 'A life of meaning and purpose is one focused less on satisfying oneself, and more on others. It is often a life rich in compassion and altruism.' I agree with Deepak Chopra, but would like to add a primer to this statement, which is also my first tip for vertical living. Start by loving yourself and taking good care of yourself. If you are not fit in mind, body, and spirit, you will not able to spread joy and be compassionate to a fellow being, or altruistic in your endeavors. Aligning the biological, emotional and psychological states of a human being to a specific purpose, impacts the health and efficiency of a person positively. Such a state is a precursor to achieving the state of a high performer.

If you would like to be productive in a given time frame,
let the decisions in that particular time frame be guided
by an inner sense of purpose and priority.
This is a lifestyle tip for vertical living.

Purposeful living, i.e., a life driven by a specific goal or purpose, in compassion and a search for the betterment of your fellow beings, is a great starting point for every high performer in maximizing his/her potential; this is your pathway to a happy, healthy, and fulfilled life. Deepak Chopra quotes in one of his articles on compassion: 'cellular inflammation, which is hypothesised to be one of the root causes of cancer (supported by research at UCLA) [302], is low in people who believe they are leading a purposeful life.' *Lifestyle tip for vertical living: if you would like to be productive in a given frame of time let the decisions in that particular time frame be guided by your inner sense of purpose and priority.*

Create the Right Work Culture

In the book *How Google Works*, Eric Schmidt, executive chairman of Alphabet and ex-CEO of Google and Jonathan Rosenberg, Senior Vice President of Products at Google, talk about hiring the right people and creating the right work culture to foster talent as the most important steps in building a great company and great products. They talk about hiring *smart creatives* who are unafraid to express their opinions and take risks, even if it might end in failure. The idea of a *smart creative* is the closest parallel to the idea of a high performer. According to the book, the single most important trait of the employees hired by Google is that they are strongly driven by a purpose and hence are *high **performers***. In the book, they talk about smart creatives daring to challenge the data from market research and analysis and creating products that feed the user's imagination.

> In the book 'How Google Works', Eric Schmidt and Jonathan Rosenberg talk about hiring the right people and creating the right work culture to foster talent as the most important steps in building a great company and great products.

If Google has been able to realise such a work culture, then it has been successful at creating many self-realised people who are happy and fulfilled. Such people are <u>less likely to get into negative emotional states or traps of negative thinking.</u> Their time, creativity, imagination, and emotions are probably invested in meeting challenges that can raise the awareness and capabilities of humanity. Once you have realised the purpose of your life, happiness and fulfillment become perpetual side effects. Such a person can only create happiness, wealth, and find progress in all aspects of life.

68

Let us take the example of an employee in an unhealthy workplace, or a subject matter expert who is always driven by specific opinions and lacks the empathy to listen to people; such people are not only putting themselves through negative states physiologically, but also impacting the people around them negatively.

Self-realised people do not have time to engage in negative emotions like jealousy or pick on people with genuine, creative voices, or shoot down ideas without really examining them. They are always for building and creating something useful.

Negative states of mind and negative emotions set off a chain reaction in your body and affect you psychosomatically. Feelings like hatred and jealousy sap your human potential. If you would like to stay healthy and be a high performer, learn to appreciate people who are more successful than you are and treat them like role models.

> *Self-realised people do not have time to engage in negative emotions and actions, as they are too busy building and creating something useful.*

Most people engage in jealousy and criticism when they find a colleague or a friend who is more successful than they are. *Try not to be one of them!* **It's a loser's attitude.**

India's youngest millionaire-entrepreneur Suhas Gopinath, who currently works for the Prime Minister's office, runs his own company and advises two other companies, says he never hesitates to hire people who are smarter than he is.

> *Appreciating someone wholeheartedly, on a job well done, is the most consistent trait in leaders of high performing teams.*

A similar approach was used by Head of Engineering and ex-Chief People's Officer of Flipkart, India, Mekin Maheshwari. His voice rung with strength and clarity when he told me that the most important reason for the stellar growth at Flipkart was the work culture that fostered appreciation of good talent, good work, and creativity in his employees. He often refers to his employees as his family or team. He said he always believed in hiring, training, and delegating work to people who are more skilled than he is. He recalled distinctly, that he gave a lot of freedom to his team in executing tasks per their abilities. He mentioned an example about an intern he had hired, who created a specific feature in a product without asking permission to do so. The intern had been so motivated about his work that he felt he owed it to the company to build that feature in that product. It was indeed a proud moment for both Mekin and his team, and a feather in the cap for the intern.

Once you get into the habit of appreciation, you will notice that you are learning a lot of new things from your friend who is successful [303]. You are improving yourself as you start acknowledging the progress made by your friend. Appreciating someone wholeheartedly on a job well done is the most consistent trait in leaders of high performing teams.

Here is a blog post that I wrote that can better express how to transform jealousy into appreciation.

BLOG POST: APPLAUSE

My heart says: It is obvious that people lose out on valuable things in life because of personal jealousies. I want to write so that we can learn to appreciate each other wholeheartedly.

'The OSCARS have grandeur, showmanship, finesse and more importantly, the large-hearted quality to applaud others. WE DON'T HAVE IT.' – Anupam Kher (Veteran Bollywood Actor)

Applauding someone wholeheartedly means expanding our potential. People who cannot applaud others are scared of losing their power. They think that if they support another's growth, they will lose their power.

As humans, we are social beings. We grow by sharing, connecting, and caring. A person, who understands that power decays in accumulation, and power grows when shared, will learn to applaud!

Image courtesy: Wavebreakmedia Ltd. www.dreamstime.com

The world of a person who does not know how to applaud openly and acknowledge someone when they succeed, is so small!

People who cannot pay a genuine compliment are so limited in their ability to experience the world! Attention and power, which are always directed to yourself, are of no use. I have experienced this countless number of times: people looking away intentionally to avoid saying words of appreciation, or degrading someone who is successful. How I pity these people!

Maheshwari of Flipkart, fondly refers to his first manager as his mentor and mentions that even to this day, he looks up to his former manager for guidance. People who mentored me, inspired me, and encouraged me to write for the Toastmasters newsletter, have attained the best jobs and achieved stellar heights in their personal and professional lives. They were consistent high performers who were extremely emotionally adept at motivating and driving teams toward higher goals. When I was a junior speaker and struggling with being a Toastmaster, they did not hesitate to let me know when my speeches were better than theirs. My blessings are with them. I wish wholeheartedly for their continued success.

> Every human being is a unique expression of life. When we start interacting and acknowledging life through others, we become more intelligent ourselves. When we acknowledge, appreciate, and embrace a larger number of individuals, we develop their intelligences and expressions in ourselves as well. In summary, we become a collective total in our resourcefulness, of all those people we appreciate and applaud. *Applauding someone is a great way not only to empower the other person, but to also develop those abilities in ourselves!*

In the book, *How Google Works*, people who harbor negative emotions like jealousy and hedonism are called **knaves** or elements to be avoided. They exhibit behaviors that need to be fixed early. The book also refers to people with tenure, who discourage newer thinking and ideas, as **hippos,** i.e., people who are powerful and can crush you. Hippos are to be avoided completely as they most likely come in the way of the growth of a company and cause high rates of attrition or migration of talent into a competitor's ecosystem.

Self-realised people are usually aware of their surroundings and do not have time to snub new ideas. They believe in being open-minded to both good and bad ideas.

Dr John R. Adler, the inventor of CyberKnife, talks about one significant change he would like to see in the education system, i.e., it should become open enough to encourage all types of ideas before deciding which ideas to keep and which ones to discard. He detests the thought that ideas should be denied a place if they don't fall into a particular framework or school of thinking.

When Dr Adler talked about being open to an idea as-is, he reiterated **vertical living** *or the state of acceptance of ideas in the here-and-now.* This attitude is of prime importance in building a progressive and open society. Most high performers and game changers in history have consistently displayed this particular trait of appreciation and acceptance of newer ideas.

Be a STRATEGIC AND PURPOSEFUL planner

There is a quote by Rhonda Byrne, the creator and executive producer of the film *The Secret*: 'Create your day in advance by thinking how you want it to go, and you will create your life intentionally.' I vouch for this quote with my personal experience in interacting with friends, family, colleagues, and other Toastmasters. I studied high performing, successful, and productive people who are busy in customer-facing roles, in jobs that involve a lot of travel and require making frequent presentations to a large audience. I have keenly observed for many years now, the habits of professionals who face situations involving high-pressure decision-making, and leaders who envision roadmaps for products and portfolios in large multinational firms. This is what I found from my study: I hardly came across anyone without a planned calendar, filled with activities several days in advance. I hardly met anyone who was not strategic and succinct in his or her conversations. Even during casual conversations, they were strategic in their physical movements; they moved with purpose. They were also alert and open-minded to ideas because they were always open to learning and absorbing ideas to improve productivity.

For these high performers, being strategic in most aspects of life is a sophisticated way of expressing creativity. Being strategic makes the whole process of expressing creative ideas much easier for such people because of their focused and incremental efforts, and the optimal utilization of time. For instance, they know exactly how to pitch an idea to a client or a customer when there is a time crunch, because they have already planned and thought about a scenario where there may be a time crunch before that big presentation. Being strategic, alert, and open-minded is one of the best ways to maximise human potential for creative endeavors.

High performers usually start their day very early, or plan their prime working hours to coincide with times when there is less disturbance in their office or home. They habitually make time to collect and compose their ideas and creative insights, and most importantly, plan their calendar based on that primary purpose in life or work [304]. They also exhibit traits described as part of *vertical living*, for example, the abilities to listen, to focus on one task at a time, and to stay unfettered amidst a barrage of commitments and stressful situations.

In summary, if you would like to be productive and profitable with your time and also feel fulfilled and happy in your life, it is of prime importance to know what is your purpose in life, and prioritise activities in your life around that purpose. Let me summarise this as a tip. Vertical living lifestyle tip: plan your calendar based on a purpose, and be assertive in saying 'No' to appointments that do not meet that purpose.

Plan your calendar based on a purpose and be assertive in saying 'No' to appointments that do not meet that purpose. This is a lifestyle tip for Vertical living.

In being a high performer, and feel fulfilled in your undertakings, it is imperative that your life is driven by compassion for others. If you are to lead a stellar team of people, learn to appreciate their strengths and be compassionate with their needs. Being a high performer means being comfortable with your strengths and weaknesses, and not falling trap to feelings of jealousy and peer pressure as well. It means accepting ideas both good and bad, and being open to learning. Such traits are consistently displayed by high performers, all throughout history. Being a high performer starts with being a leader in your own right. What is the next big change you need to make in yourself, to be that leader?

- End Chapter –

Chapter 4: Free to Realise your Dream

Life begins at the end of your comfort zone.
—Neale Donald Walsch

Most people fail to dream big because they do not give their minds the freedom to conceive grand ideas, but instead allow the fear of limitations to take over. This chapter specifically focuses on freeing the mind. The first step in dreaming big is to rid your mind of unnecessary thoughts and make room for creativity to be born. Let us start with the simple idea of being able to think freely without fears and constraints.

Think about the last time you truly wished you were free. Think hard! Were you in a situation where you wanted to be by yourself and do something you loved? Did you wish to play music or paint? Did you desire to be outdoors in nature and feel the air in your lungs? More often than not, the mundane tasks of being a responsible adult interfered and you could not follow your passion. What if there was a way to manage your schedule so you could get to do all the things you desire and love?

Think deeply and you will become **aware** of the
fact that all the limitations are in your head

Remember! You are a part of the human race, empowered with the ability to lead, to harness the power of technology, communicate, plan and delegate tasks, and to consciously develop a positive perspective to situations in life. When you free your mind of fears, you are in deep connection with your inner calling. This will help you develop clarity in your thinking and prioritise your choices in life. In following your heart or inner calling, your whole being will inevitably be compelled to rise to the occasion. Whether you are solving a problem you face, or tackling a challenge you have embraced, you will realise your true potential and understand your limitations. You will analyze problems from many angles, including the perspectives of others, and begin to find creative solutions. You will team up with people who complement your skill set and compensate for your limitations, and gain a fresh perspective on the ideas that matter to you most. As you practice and develop the ability to think freely, you will build the momentum you need to go after your dream. Let us now see a few examples of how high performers and game changers in history used the power of freethinking.

'Be the change that you wish to see in the world.'
-- Mahatma Gandhi

Mahatma Gandhi, who was a passionate advocate of nonviolence and self-sufficiency, led by example. He would often go on life-threatening hunger strikes or march great distances in campaigning for the causes he believed in. He proved that people could *fight* for something by being *nonviolent*. Such was the freedom in his thinking!

Gandhi was one of those rare people in history who had the courage to think beyond inhibitions imposed by the mind. He questioned the political, social, and religious status quo of colonial India. Achieving independence through socio-economic reform became the mission of his life. He was a man of

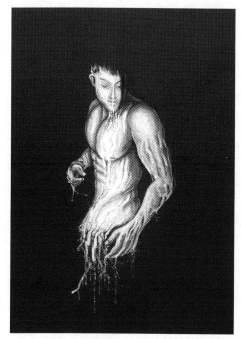

Image courtesy: Nivedita Gouda

simple yet eloquent action. He wore garments of *Khadi* that he spun from cotton himself, and followed a simple vegetarian diet that he advocated as part of a self-reliant and healthy lifestyle. He transformed his life in accordance with his philosophy of *satyagraha*—the attainment of truth or goals by peaceful resistance—and inspired a nation to form a powerful movement. He followed the path of nonviolence and led India to freedom from centuries of British colonization. A shining example of freedom and grand thinking!

It is important to obey the laws of the society that we belong to, but is there a way to bring about social change and freedom by becoming the change we wish to see in the world? Like Gandhi, many other luminaries in history have done it, even in the midst of dire circumstances like imprisonment. Here is a blog entry where I discuss the literary work produced by such leaders while they were imprisoned.

BLOG NAME: FREE AND IMPRISONED

My heart says: I know the joy of breaking free from mental inhibitions. I should write so I can share the ecstasy of this freedom.

Did you know that some of the greatest literary classics were authored in prison? *Don Quixote* was written by Miguel de Cervantes when he was serving a sentence. *Pilgrim's Progress* was penned by John Bunyan when he was imprisoned. *The Story of My Experiments with Truth* by Mahatma Gandhi, and *The Discovery of India* by Jawaharlal Nehru were written when the authors were incarcerated for political crimes. While the depth of their suffering provided the raw emotion, their solitude provided an outlet for them to express vivid ideas. Their dreams allowed them to look toward a grand horizon beyond the confines of the four walls of their prison cells.

Gandhi was free in his mind to follow his heart, even though the India he lived in was not a free country.

What is a prison? It is an enclosure that inhibits an individual's freedom. It is sometimes made of bricks and mortar, and sometimes by a few limiting ideas. Bricks and mortar can confine the body, but they cannot imprison the human will, imagination, or creativity. However, the prison of the mind—the prison of limiting ideas—is a stronger cage and can imprison a person even in a free world!

Alcatraz was one of the most notorious prisons in history and several spine-chilling tales have been told about the life of its prisoners. Robert Franklin Stroud, known as the 'Birdman of Alcatraz', was one of the most violent convicts who served time there. As he transformed gradually and broke free of his *mental prisons* inside a physical prison, he began to develop an interest in raising birds. Over time, with persistent efforts, he immersed himself in extensive research about the birds and became the most revered ornithologist who authored a book titled '*Diseases of Canaries*'.

Great freedom fighters like Mahatma Gandhi and Jawaharlal Nehru who spent many years in prison were quite unperturbed by the hardships they had to face. They saw their time in prison as the cost of attaining freedom for their country. They were revolutionaries at the forefront of India's freedom struggle and they were extremely driven by their inner calling. They endured years of harsh treatment in a government prison at the hands of the colonial forces. While they were physically bound by the walls of a prison, they were free from the prison of their ego and mind. They found the purpose of their lives by becoming freedom fighters, and used their free minds to author timeless epics in prison. These books are of eternal value to our society.

We tend to live in mental prisons where superiority and inferiority complexes can lead us to question ourselves and compare ourselves to others. We live with many limiting ideas that prevent us from connecting with our surroundings, and being a part of the bigger universe—the summation of infinite possibilities—or what I call as the *whole*. It is the universal whole to which we belong.

These mental frameworks and elements of restriction arise from our sense of *Ego*.

The ego is a sense of identity that we develop in our mind and body, based on our experiences, and the acceptance and rejection that we receive from the society around us.

The *ego is an armor of great necessity to all of us*. It is the source of our self-esteem and self-importance. It is our definition of *I* or *me* that resides in our memory. It helps us retain lessons from our upbringing and conditioning in society, so that we can find a predictable zone of comfort in which we can operate. In a sense, the ego is the ground we stand on to face the world. For instance, if you know that you are afraid of heights, you will probably not enjoy bungee jumping on your vacation. This fear is a facet of your ego, to which you will adhere faithfully.

However, the ego that resides strongly in one's memory as a sense of *self*, needs to evolve with changing circumstances. In the absence of such evolution, the individual, along with the ego, becomes less adaptive to his or her surroundings.

Why is the feeling of being free of your past experiences so powerful?

Let us consider the example of bungee jumping again. You can consciously work on overcoming your fear of heights, so that you can possibly attempt bungee jumping one day. This can be done by reprogramming your ego from 'I am afraid of heights' to 'I have figured out a way to master my fear.'

What are the consequences of adhering to your ego rigidly? Many of my close acquaintances and the parents of some of my peers, who were heads of large organizations during their tenure, enjoyed the respect and power they wielded at the workplace. They identified themselves deeply with the ego of a boss or a CEO, and were unable to step out of their role when they came home. They continued to be dominating or bossy after coming home to their families. Do you see a problem there? The head of a large corporation cannot carry the same attitude home and expect harmony. In fact, he or she may not be performing the role of a parent or spouse adequately in carrying memories of work home. When one goes home, it is best to clear the mind of being a boss at work, or clear the ego that feeds off the rank and power in society. It is best for them to blend in lovingly with family and friends. As you can see, it is important to be free of specific parts or aspects of ego, at specific times in your life.

> Awareness is the beginning of becoming free of the
> ego, because then you realise that your thoughts–
> and the negative emotions they produce–are
> dysfunctional and unnecessary.
> - Eckhart Tolle in *A New Earth*

As Eckhart Toelle writes in his book, *A New Earth*, 'Awareness is the beginning of becoming free of the ego, because then you realise that your thoughts, and the negative emotions they produce, are dysfunctional and unnecessary.' One of the ways to achieve this state of mind of is by meditation. Let us look at the formal definition of meditation: 'Meditation is a practice in which an individual trains the mind or induces a mode of consciousness, either to realise some benefit or for the mind to simply acknowledge its content without becoming identified with that content [400] or as an end in itself [401].' To acknowledge the content of your mind without being identified with it, is to acknowledge your ego without getting identified with your ego. This is because your thoughts are processed based on your previous experiences, which reside in your memories of past events, and your ego tends to keep you attached to an illusion of living in the past.

Coming back to the question, why is being free of your past experiences so powerful? We all need to rely on our memory to learn and grow as careful, responsible individuals. But when our memory starts interfering with our understanding of the current situation, we certainly have developed a mental block. We feel confused and helpless, when we are not able to see things as they are. Let us take a look at the fear of public speaking—a common fear that people harbor—of embarrassing themselves in front of others, especially, when they need to address a large audience. When you are worried that you don't have anything intelligent to say, or that people are going to make fun of you when you say something, or the way you look when you are addressing a crowd, etc., you are not accepting the reality of the situation. The fact that you are in front of an audience, who are just like yourself, and that they are waiting to hear from you, is not something to be afraid of.

The ego is an artifact of your memories, which can imprison you and take away your courage to speak freely. One must stay free of the negative chatter of the ego, and focus completely on the speech and its delivery rather than its detractors. This kind of ego (or a negative chatter in the mind) can weaken your ability to be creative and freedom to respond in the present moment. *Free yourself mentally, of this part of ego. It is a part of your identity that you need to dissociate from, to feel free—free to learn and grow, and outdo yourself!* This is another lifestyle tip for vertical living.

Meditate to get rid of that inner chatter
before you apply yourself to a task.
Lifestyle tip in vertical living

Meditate and get rid of that inner chatter while you apply yourself to a task. I will get into more detail on how to do this well in the chapter *Tuning Into The*

Present. For now, I would like to share my personal experiences on how to deal with the fear of public speaking.

I currently mentor people in public speaking, as part of my Toastmasters curriculum. My first order of business is to help my clients identify the incessant chatter of ego or memory, and have them work towards silencing it. I ask them to reasonably size up their new speech project, and evaluate their progress towards a chatter-free mind. Once they feel up to the task, I train them to belittle their fears.

One of the candidates I mentored had an irrational fear of making eye contact with people when he spoke, since making eye contact was considered rude in his culture. I asked him to wear sunglasses and practice making eye contact as a first step, which produced some good results. Wearing sunglasses calmed his mind and freed up his potential to explore strategies in effective speaking. I then asked him to remove his shades and look in the eyes of the people in the audience, but keep his focus on the message. I made him realise by experience that making eye contact with his listeners and audience made them comfortable, and then they were able to focus on the message. We later joked about how he was afraid of something that came so naturally to him—looking people in the eye and making that first connection. His speech turned out to be quite effective and as time passed, he got much better at public speaking.

Mastering any skill requires training. **Belittling that part of your ego, which resides in you as fear, also requires training and practice. Train yourself to belittle your fears by overcoming them over and over again.**

Identify your fear and describe it in detail on paper. Next, accept the fact that you will need to work hard and practice overcoming that fear, because hard work and practice are the magic mantras! Sweat it out! Sweat it out until you go past old limitations that are obstacles on the path to excellence. Conquer your fears, but go after them *one at a time*. Belittle those fears that belittled you, by mastering the skill that takes you to the point of **_no fear!_**

Belittle those fears that belittled you, by mastering the skill that helps you conquer those fears, and takes you to the point of no fear! This is a lifestyle tip for vertical living.

Practice techniques such as delivering one speech in front of a different audience every day, no matter how big or small the audience. Try it out with family and friends who can support your personal journey. Dress for the role of a speaker; it raises your confidence when you look polished. Record your speech each time you practice. Note down where you stammer or make mistakes, and rework the content so you achieve fluency. Don't be afraid to seek help if you are not able to do it yourself! I will talk more about speaking skills in the chapter titled 'Icebreaker'.

Achieving perfection through small steps, targeting one fear at a time, indeed leads to the zenith of self-realization. It is *this* moment of realization, I promise, that every high performer or overachiever seeks and longs to experience.

The founder of Aikido, the iconic martial artist Morihei Ueshiba, worked on improving his techniques well into his eighties. According to his biography, *Invincible Warrior*, by John Stevens, a Professor of Buddhist Studies and Aikido instructor at Tohoku Fukushi University, Japan, Ueshiba was popularly known as invincible warrior in real life. He also mentions in the book that Ueshiba had such mastery of Aikido that he could not be attacked, even in his sleep. Ueshiba had dedicated his life to the discipline of Aikido, and is said to have achieved superhuman abilities to perceive sights and sounds several hundred metres away from him. He was physically so well-conditioned that he could practice his art until the day he died. It is this kind of dedicated honing of skills in a domain of choice, that aspiring game changers should devote their time to. The trouble is, in an ordinary life, there is so much time to idle away, so much energy at one's disposal to be destructive and nurture unwanted emotions like self-deprecation, jealousy, and low self-esteem. *If so many negative emotions are playing on your mind, is there any other way to feel but imprisoned?*

I would give up my ego altogether if doing so meant feeling free and living a fulfilled life. I would free all the imprisoned parts of my human potential and use them to construct my inner being: an overachiever, a leader, and a person in love with life and her fellow beings!

Becoming a game changer or a high performer in life means being able to master your fears constantly. In fact, it is a way of life.

How do you achieve self-realization by freeing yourself from your ego? Chanakya, a brilliant political strategist and economist of ancient India, who architected the birth of one of the most powerful empires in its history states: 'Before you embark on a task, always ask yourself three questions:

Why am I doing it?

What might the results be?

Will I be successful?'

Find satisfactory answers to these questions, and then give yourself the green signal to go after those goals. Intuition and purposeful living, are the powerful under currents that can guide you to express your talent to the maximum. But only objective goal setting, and strategic efforts will help you in realizing your true potential.

Lifestyle tip to vertical living:
Leading the life of a high performer is not only living purposefully guided by intuition, but also working hard and starting off by finding the best answers to the questions above three questions, i.e.,

---

'Why am I doing it?
What might the results be?
Will I be successful at it?'

'It' can be any task or challenge you choose to take up, such as training in a new language or skill, having that first difficult conversation to sort out a relationship issue, or starting your own business. The 'it' in the above set of questions, is the part that is closely influenced by your inner rudder or intuition and your purpose in life: a purpose that makes your eyes brighten up when you think of it.

There can only be one conclusion to this chapter, i.e., there is no point in living a life filled with fear. There is no great achievement in posing limitations to our true inner abilities, because of our pre-programmed sense of identity, or the influence of a few failures.

Do not be afraid to imagine and dream big, because all game changers in history started on their journey of self-realization without inhibiting their dreams and imagination. They set reasonable goals and persisted with their dreams. Enjoy this freedom to dream, and realise yourself in realizing your dreams. This is the greatest path to self-realization. Joseph Fernandez, one of my mentors and a veteran Toastmaster, has a favorite quote: 'You are your own limitation.' In other words, there are no limitations to the limits one can set for oneself.

Here are a few more quotes that highlight the joy of awakened living or vertical living.

'Arise, awake, and stop not till the goal is reached.' This is one of the most popular quotes from Swami Vivekananda, one of the key figures in spreading the Indian philosophy of Vedas and Vedanta in the Western world [404].

A similar quote can be found in the Katha Upanishad, chapter 1.3.14, where Yama suggests to Nachiketa [403]:

उत्तिष्ठत जाग्रत प्राप्य वरान्निबोधत,

क्षुरासन्न धारा निशिता दुरत्यद्दुर्गम पथ: तत् कवयो वदन्ति ।

The above excerpt in Sanskrit means:
Arise! Awake! Approach the great and learn.
Like the sharp edge of a razor is that path,
so the wise say—hard to tread and difficult to cross.

- *End Chapter* –

Chapter 5: The Icebreaker

In this chapter, I show you a few ways to break ice with your fears. I specifically refer to fears in experimenting with unknown or unfamiliar territories in your life. I feel the fear of expressing oneself by way of public speaking is the most commonly faced impediment to career advancement. I share a few techniques in overcoming fear of public speaking as well. If you are strongly driven by a purpose and inner calling in your life, you will be easily able to face fears which come in the way of you realizing your goals. In following your inner calling, you will feel a high degree of motivation and self-realization. That is why I recommend following the path of inner calling, or vertical living, as a lifestyle.

In the section below, I would like to express the ideas in the chapter *Icebreaker* using two charts. One of them uses a linear or step-by-step representation of the entrepreneurial approach to self-realization. The other chart uses a non-linear or cyclic approach. A detailed explanation of these charts can be found by checking out this section in the book: Self-realization using an entrepreneurial approach. The terminology found in the cyclic and linear charts below, have been explained in the section referred to above.

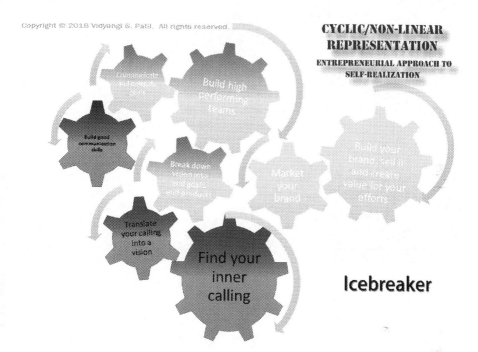

CYCLIC/NON-LINEAR REPRESENTATION

ENTREPRENEURIAL APPROACH TO SELF-REALIZATION

Icebreaker

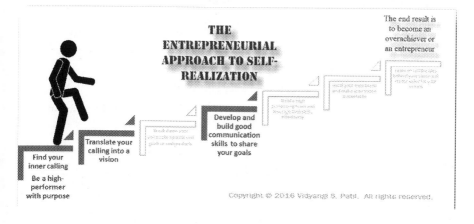

THE ENTREPRENEURIAL APPROACH TO SELF-REALIZATION

-Chapter begins-

Image courtesy: Somypt Sutprattanatawin www.dreamstime.com

In the last chapter, I talked about freeing the mind of unnecessary fears and limitations so you can dream big. Once you learn how to free your mind, the next step in realizing your vision is acting without fear. To be able to act without fear requires you to manage the states of your mind and body efficiently. You need to be able to bring yourself out of states of fear and negative thoughts in order to create the personal power to act without fear. Overcoming any sort of fear requires a lot of hard work and regular training in mastering that particular fear. You need to understand how your fear works. Fear is a mental conditioning. It can be dealt with systematically by understanding how your brain and body are responding psychosomatically to the idea of fear.

In his book on the plasticity of the brain, *The Brain that Changes Itself*, Norman Doidge a Canadian-born psychiatrist and psychoanalyst mentions that people can undergo neuro-plastic transformation and overcome diseases like Obsessive Compulsive Disorder (OCD), mental retardation, or conditions that induce a perpetual sense of falling even. For me, it was both proof of my real-life experiments at work and a pleasant revelation. I have always believed in the neural plasticity of the brain and I have used it to overcome my fear of public speaking, and my back pain. Doidge talks about reinforcing or training specific mental or neural pathways that are associated with a particular behavior or mental condition and using them to cure specific diseases. He proves that the brain is capable of undergoing changes in its architecture throughout a person's lifetime.

There are specific mental conditions that are associated with the firing of specific pathways of neurons in the brain; these pathways were ascertained by PET and MRI scanning techniques. For instance, there is a part of the brain called the cingulate gyrus, which is present in the deepest part of the cortex; it is known to trigger the physical sensations of dread to the gut and the heart and is associated with the 'mistake' feeling. It goes away as soon as you have done something to correct the feeling of having made a mistake.

Just like the feeling of dread, the feeling of fear is also a sequence of neurons firing in the brain. You need to break this sequence and instead train your brain to reinforce pathways of confidence and personal power. I call this process of breaking your fear *icebreaker*. By this, I mean shattering that inertia to act, because of fear. 'Icebreaker' in common usage refers to a game or activity that relieves tension between people, helps people open up to each other, and helps initiate a conversation. In this case, 'icebreaker' means training your brain to overcome your fears; this way, you can not only reverse the patterns of fear and failure that occur in your brain, but also control manifestations of fear, i.e., psychosomatic reactions like sweaty palms, trouble speaking articulate sentences, pain in the stomach, shivering, or a quivering voice.

Icebreaker: the pathway to eliminate points of weakness in your ego

---

When I developed the content of this chapter as part of a speech one year ago, I was new to Toastmasters. I was a huge success at every event where I delivered the speech and got invitations to speak at many clubs. Back then, I did not realise why people liked it so much, but now I do. What this speech essentially did was, get people to come out of their shells and do something different. I share this speech with you with a lot of joy. I believe the techniques shared here can be customised to not only achieve mastery over fear of public speaking, but also help erase deeper fears you may harbor when moving into unfamiliar territory in your life.

These techniques are relevant to the theme of the book, i.e., adopting the here and now or vertical living as a lifestyle. If you are training yourself to *get rid of one fear at a time*, such as the fear of public speaking, then you are essentially dissolving that negative part of your identity/ego. (I elaborate on the concept of ego in Chapter 4, 'Free to Realise Your Dream'.) You are emptying your mind of that inner mental chatter that holds you back from embracing new opportunities such as public speaking, moving on from your job as a developer and embracing your calling in taking up the responsibility of a manager, exploring the option of starting a new business, sorting out a relationship issue by taking the initiative, being persuasive in making a sales call, asking someone out on a date, etc.

Dissolving your ego, one part at a time, is one of the greatest ways to lead a purposeful life.
Lifestyle tip to vertical living

Swami Chinmayananda says, '"Renounce your ego" is the Lord's only request. And I will make you God is the promise.' Renouncing ego may be a drastic step for anyone to start with, as ego gives us a sense of identity (refer to Chapter 4 'Free to Realise Your Dream' on how to interpret the ego). Once we renounce that identity, we will have no ground to stand on while assessing the world. But, if you can renounce your ego, the whole world, free of any judgment or political or social frameworks driving it, will become your stage to stand on. You will start identifying with and connecting with everything around you. If you are in Russia, you will feel Russian, if you are in China, you will completely identify with the Chinese. This is a position of great power to look at things from, if you can achieve it, my dear reader!

I believe the techniques shared here can be customised to not only achieve mastery over fear of speaking in public, but also erase deeper fears you may harbor when moving into unfamiliar territory in your life.

Before I introduce the techniques, I want to prepare your mind to receive them. I would like to introduce an excerpt from my blog. It talks about the power of a non-ego state, which gives a person tremendous resilience to take criticism, face failures and come out strong.

BLOG POST: I DON'T MIND

Image courtesy: Kobrin Nikita www.dreamstime.com

My heart says: I should write about the freedom of thinking which a non-ego state puts us in. Non-ego here refers to a state of acceptance regarding the definition of 'Who am I?' This definition is subject to change all the time. I can live life with much more creativity and freedom if I detach from my perceived definition or sense of ego.

I don't mind if you praise me,
Because I am nobody and nothing in this existence so vast.

I don't mind if you put me down,
Because I am infinitely powerful as I connect with every living and nonliving being in this universe.

I don't mind if you criticise me as right or wrong,

Because what I think is right or you think is right, does not matter. What matters is reality.

I don't mind if you love me or hate me

Because both love and hate are different forms of the same energy.

I don't mind what you think of me

Because what you think of me, what I think of myself, and what others think of me, are totally different from what I am. I keep changing with life, and life changes all the time.

In defining myself with a definition, I will only be limiting myself.

Image courtesy: Erwin D'Souza

If I were to imagine myself to be as vast as an ocean, a few droplets taken out of my body or a few specks of dust added to my being, would not affect me. In acting to dissolve our egos, let us merge and grow into our surroundings to be as vast as the ocean in our power and presence. This way, a few variations in our neighbor's attitude to us or a few ups and downs in our path to fulfillment will no longer affect us as much.

TECHNIQUE 1 IN OVERCOMING YOUR FEARS
MAKE IT A HABIT TO FACE YOUR FEARS

One way to slowly renounce the negative parts of ego is by facing your fears regularly, and overcoming them one at a time. Indu Navar is a role model for upcoming women entrepreneurs. She has been a single parent, a start-up executive, investor, and a founder and CEO of successful companies in Silicon Valley. In her interview at Navika, an international Indian cultural event held in Pasadena, California, she talked about facing her fears. Once fearful of heights, she decided to face her fears by taking pilot lessons, and even engaged in skydiving with her co-workers. In an interview for School of Herring with Marten Mickos, she talked about overcoming her fear of communication and presentation using the 'fake-it-'til-you-make-it' attitude. She used to memorise her opening lines and deliver them without much thinking before she started a conversation with accomplished clients.

Get over your fears by strict discipline, and persist in
your efforts until you master your fears.

There is a lesson here for all of us, that if we can work on facing our fears regularly or make facing our fears a habit, then we can open ourselves up to bigger opportunities. Let us start on our path to self-realization by breaking the ice with one fear at a time. In the next section, I will specifically talk about one of the most common fears faced by people in a new environment, i.e., the fear of breaking ice with surroundings. The process I am referring to in common parlance is called the *icebreaker*.

THE ICEBREAKER – a popular speech at Toastmasters

Icebreaker is a term used to refer to techniques that help people open up or warm up to a social setting; it could be a new workplace or a new team or a new family, or a social event like a distant friend's party. Imagine that you are in a situation and setting you have never been in before, and are obligated to open up and take on a role in order to meet a higher social objective, for instance, lead a fundraiser for earthquake victims or recruit volunteers for cleaning up your neighborhood. Let me explain this further with more specific examples.

Many jobs and social roles may require you to do an icebreaker with your surroundings; for example, imagine you are a business partner in a company or married to a person of high social standing in any industry, political arena or in academia. You are most likely to be in social situations *where being graceful and self-confident in your speech and presentation are minimum expectations.* Imagine that you do not know the people in this new setting very well, although you are required to fit in smoothly. *You are not only expected to dress for the occasion, but also to be intelligent in your responses.* This is a situation that calls for an icebreaker. I have been put through many such situations time and again, as life has taken me through unusual highs and lows where I needed to connect and collaborate with people to make a living. In the rest of the chapter I list a few tips, which works for my mentees and me at speaking clubs effectively, in accomplishing a successful icebreaker. If you find my tips superfluous, feel free to go to the next chapter; maybe you already know what I am talking about. But for the reader whose heart beats rapidly at just the notion of opening up to a bunch of strangers, I offer the following techniques.

TECHNIQUE 2 IN OVERCOMING YOUR FEARS
EMPTY YOUR MIND BEFORE YOU STRIKE AT YOUR FEAR

Image courtesy: Neil Lockhart www.dreamstime.com

In life, changes can happen in one second.

Your decisions can occur in one second. Your gut feeling can strike you in one second. Your intuition can flash to you in one second. There is a term called 'the moment of realization'. It indicates that the realization of the truth, or reality of the situation, can hit you in one moment where the tipping point of change, is again, one second. Your decision to face your fear and start a conversation can happen in one second. The icebreaker that enables you to open up to your surroundings or to any specific fear can happen in your mind in one second.

The question is, how to make that one second flip in your favor? In what state should your mind be to make that icebreaker happen?

The answer is, your mind should be *empty*. Bruce Lee was a legendary martial artist; this is the crown jewel of his teachings: 'Empty your mind.' But why do we need to empty our minds?

An empty mind is fully available to perform and to break ice with a fear or with a new situation. The mind should be empty to allow a meaningful conversation or action to flow. Just like an empty pipe is free of dirt, the mind should be free of unnecessary mental chatter before that 12-15 seconds of initial conversation, when we break ice with our surroundings and make that first impression.

Image courtesy: Erwin D'Souza

My heart says that the feeling of emptiness in space, in thoughts, and in time helps us connect with life more deeply. How energizing this feeling of emptiness is!

In life, changes can happen in one second.
Your decision to face your fear and start a conversation can happen in one second.
In that one second, your mind should be EMPTY.

What are the different ways to empty your mind?

Image courtesy: Oocoskun www.dreamstime.com

Laugh wholeheartedly! When you laugh wholeheartedly, you are not thinking, your mind is empty. Just before I walk into a difficult meeting or a large audience to speak in front of, I listen to the sound of farts on my phone. I have been gifted with a book of farts, and I love flipping through it when I am nervous. It makes me laugh wholeheartedly. Even if am not able to laugh openly, I am so amused by those sounds, my mind goes empty and makes my whole appearance relaxed and pleasing.

Smile genuinely by looking into someone's eyes and connecting fully before starting your first conversation. This pause will not only put both your minds into a state of emptiness, but will also help create a moment of relaxation before breaking ice. Is your heart filled with love, compassion, a genuine interest in connecting with that other person? To align powerfully with that intent, your mind and heart should be fully present in the process of connecting; you should be in a **vertical state** of mind.

Breathe deeply! I recommend the practice of Kapalabhathi, under the guidance of a competent yoga instructor. It is an aggressive breathing technique that not only clears out your breathing tract, but also makes you squeeze all the muscles involved in breathing until you reach a state where you cannot think. When you resume normal breathing, you reach a state where you feel completely thought-free and empty. After that, you will feel a surge of energy gushing into your system—certainly a great feeling. Within the next few moments, you can definitely do an icebreaker with one of your fears, or practice a speech, or maybe even deliver one.

Try out fight-or-flight sports! There are sports like bungee-jumping, deep sea diving, bull-chasing, kung fu, combat sports, etc., that help make your mind empty because they put you in a state of **fight-or-flight** or survival mode. These are sports of great risk and danger where staying alert and focused in the current moment is the minimum requisite. However, it is imperative that such sports require a lot of preparation, practice, professional guidance from certified professionals, alongside physical conditioning and mental focus acquired by regular practice. This kind of focus requires you to keep your mind in a state of emptiness or *staying* vertically *invested in the moment.*

Image courtesy: K. walkow www.dreamstime.com

Love someone or something passionately! When you are in love with someone, you are not thinking. Drowned in the world of digital data and communication, we are so disconnected from the world of touch and feel and attention to a fellow human being, that loving someone or something passionately is increasingly becoming rare. I love writing and I love some people in my life unconditionally. It gives me plenty of opportunity to be in a **vertical state**, i.e., a blissful state of empty mind, and helps me experience the maximum expression of my creative potential.

Let us get back to the next step in icebreaker, i.e., beginning that conversation, after you have overcome your fear and are ready to make your speech or icebreaking. When you meet someone for the first time it takes 12-15 seconds to make that first impression. To make those 12-15 seconds flow smoothly you need to be prepared. These are a few questions you need to answer for the icebreaker to proceed smoothly. When to prepare, what to talk, how to talk, and what does it take for your speech to flow effortlessly in those 12-15 seconds?

TECHNIQUE 3 IN OVERCOMING YOUR FEARS
VENTURE OUT INTO THE UNKNOWN FREQUENTLY

Let us start with the questions about when to prepare and what to talk about. Ideally, you should prepare for those 12-15 seconds of your icebreaker constantly. Your whole life is an opportunity to prepare. You live the act, you walk the talk, and you become your speech! At least that's what I do. I practice my speeches when I am waiting my turn in the grocery store line, or waiting for the red light to turn green at a traffic signal. If you listen to tips about great public speaking by Patricia Fripp, my role model in public speaking, you will realise that she preaches the same idea.

In order to make interesting conversations, you need to expose yourself to new experiences; you need to try out something new as often as possible by changing the activity patterns in your life. These changes should make you more productive in general. For instance, you could make a pattern change of keeping away from a familiar group of friends who indulge in drinking frequently, and engage with acquaintances who are training for a marathon.

This is a technique in reinforcing newer pathways in your brain. It eliminates the fear of getting into the unknown and causes you to develop alertness, awareness in exploring newer options, and allows you to feel comfortable in your own skin. Such a practice not only helps in connecting with your surroundings using the five senses, but also the sixth sense or intuition. It is more natural for you to feel heightened in your sense of intuition. I say this because most human beings tend to have a gut feeling about a person or a situation, when they walk into one, especially for the first time. When you do something for the first time, there is no history of being in that situation or knowing that person before. When you are in a new situation, your mind is chattering less, and observing more. Doing something new is like taking a risk, as you are venturing into the unknown. Intuition kicks in when your mind has stopped chattering and you are feeling and sensing your surroundings, as opposed to thinking and rationalizing about them. Very similar to the way a seasoned martial artist defends himself against an attack, because he has not only sharpened his five senses as part of his training in martial arts, but also learned to tap into his sixth sense, which keeps him super alert and able to defend himself from untimely attacks.

Now let us look at a few more ways of venturing into the unknown. If you are used to hanging out with a certain group of friends who always talk about stocks and money, try hanging out with friends who talk about hiking and traveling. This way, you become knowledgeable enough not only to break ice with people interested in finance, but also with people interested in fitness and health.

Start reading non-verbal cues and emotional responses to your conversation. This is a great way to develop a sense of empathy. In doing the above exercise, you will also develop clarity in understanding the dynamics of integrating into a new environment. By putting yourself through new experiences time and again, you are essentially training the neural pathways in your brain to adapt to newer environments easily.

You have to keep up this effort of learning and trying out something new. This is the whole purpose of living fully—to learn, experiment, and grow knowledgeable, and evolve as a human being rich and fulfilled in experiences. This approach to self-discovery and adventure will also give you a number of interesting stories to talk about.

TECHNIQUE 4 IN OVERCOMING YOUR FEARS PRACTICE YOUR ACT

What does it take to talk spontaneously with a person or group of people you've never met? To be able to talk about a topic spontaneously, you must be able to connect with the person you are talking to. It is important to treat him or her with respect, and acknowledge their point of view. Feel passionate about the topic you are conversing about, so you start from a place of confidence. In order to develop such a comfort in conversation, practice talking with strangers as often as possible. Picking a stranger to make a conversation with is not easy. You need to sense by way of a gut feeling or observation if the other person is open to communication. By practicing such conversations regularly, you develop muscle memory in your body language, physiology, and psychology to overcome fear of speaking in front of an audience.

When I refer to physiology in the above paragraph, I refer to the panic that you may experience the very first time during an icebreaker—you may sweat, or feel your heart race. Eventually, these symptoms will go away and you will start feeling normal while speaking in public or speaking with someone for the first time. Remember: belittling that part of your ego that is fear also requires training and practice! Train yourself to belittle your fears by overcoming your fears again and again. This is a lifestyle tip in vertical living.

Here is a practical tip to all first-time speakers. Video-record your speech; listen to and watch yourself speak about your favorite topic. This way you will know how you come across to others when you open a conversation. Critique yourself on your content, clarity of speech, level of confidence, and ability to engage the other person. These are important metrics in gauging the effectiveness of any speech or conversation. Think of your speech as a tool in connecting with another fellow being.

Practice this technique of observing your own speech as you choose topics of various levels of comfort, and be disciplined about it. Make it a habit to assess your abilities in terms of speed of talking, use of appropriate pitch, tone, and degree of humor. Try to make the conversation interesting by talking about something new.

Be a good listener to find out how people respond to what you say. This can happen only when your mind is completely empty and receptive to the present moment, i.e., in a **vertical** state. It is a mental discipline of being completely attentive to the person you are talking to.

Lifestyle tip in vertical living:
Get over your fears by strict discipline, and persist in
your efforts until you master your fears.

TECHNIQUE 5 IN OVERCOMING YOUR FEARS
FOCUS ON THE MESSAGE

Karthik Kalpat, a distinguished speaker at Toastmasters, had this tip to share. 'One of the things I learned is that the nervousness in speaking goes away when you concentrate on the message rather than on how the audience is responding to you.' Karthik is another outstanding example of **vertical living**, speaking by retaining a vertical state, and staying focused on delivering the message to his audience.

As Kalpat puts it, 'My reluctance to talk to a stranger has vanished. I have learned to strike up many an interesting conversation, and I am comfortable. In return, I get smiles, compliments, and friends. This has improved the quality of my interactions and made a positive impact on my life!'

Kalpat also mentioned that working hard to become a good speaker at Toastmasters energised him to do well at his day job too. Kalpat, who focuses on the task at hand during public speaking by staying **vertical** or completely focused on speaking and delivering his message to the audience, uses the same approach to be a successful team leader. He always keeps his focus on his vision or game plan for the team and stays away from his detractors. This is the very core of vertical living as a lifestyle—to be able to stay tuned in to the vision, as you live in the moment, and tuned out of the negative forces which are getting in the

---

Being a leader of a team and being able to influence a large
number of people, starts
with being a leader of your own human potential.

---

way of realizing your purpose or calling. Lifestyle tip to vertical living: approach your fears in communication, specifically the fear of breaking ice, as a leader. Being the leader of a team and being able to influence many people, starts with being in touch and being a leader in developing your own human potential, i.e., knowing yourself and your strengths and weaknesses. This way you will lead by setting an example, and being a leader will come naturally to you.

I would like to conclude this chapter on *icebreaker* with an example. Think about a martial artist who is blindfolded and shatters multiple layers of ice with his fist, in one single punch. The martial artist's fist is conditioned. But remember! He works on conditioning his fist every day and that is why he is able to pull off such a difficult trick with ease. The fist is an analogy for your personal power and presence. You need to work on your personal power every single day of your life, and keep exposing yourself to new situations and learning experiences all the time, as part of your conditioning. Again, you need to be disciplined and work on it regularly.

Once that is done, empty your mind in that one psychological moment or harness that state of **vertical living** and get into the flow. Once you are able to achieve a state of flow [114], you can start executing a task that you truly fear. Again, staying super focused on your goals and considering yourself as a leader in managing a given situation, also helps you overcome fear, and get into a state of flow. Your fear could be in public speaking, handling a tough negotiation, making that sales call, or asking a girl out on a date.

Approach your fears in communication, or otherwise, as a leader.
This is a lifestyle tip in vertical living.

Physiologically, this state of flow translates into expanding human capacity and human potential by harnessing newer pathways in your brain, to experience a state of fearlessness and maximised performance. With your physical and mental potential conditioned for optimal performance, you will be able to explore newer challenges in your life with ease. You will be able to beat your fear down and be ready to make that first golden impression!

- End Chapter -

Chapter 6: Tuning into the Present

-Chapter begins-

In this chapter, I talk about three different techniques for staying focused on the present:

1. Focusing on one task at a time and achieving a meditative state while applying yourself to the task.
2. Using pauses effectively in your daily activities.
3. Ignoring negative and energy-draining thoughts.

I also talk about the relationship between finding your inner calling and maximizing human potential by staying focused on the present.

There are many books in the market that talk about how to live your life in the here and now. Living in the here and now is increasingly being seen across the globe as the secret to maximizing happiness, health, and human potential. It requires a lifestyle that asks you to be fully present in the current moment. It may be hard to practice focusing on the present all the time. However, in my personal experience and from my study of the biographies of great scientists, artists, and entrepreneurs, if you can focus on your inner calling, it will not take you long to learn how to be present in the moment. **Focusing on your inner calling will give you immaculate clarity in life.** Once you develop clarity of purpose, you will be able to delegate, communicate, and lead the way to realizing your vision. In the following paragraphs, I will show you why.

If you are connected to the purpose of your life, you will love what you do and will be able to fully immerse yourself in realizing your inner calling. Every moment of your life will contribute to this inner calling and allow you to be connected to your true nature. In such a state, you will be able to focus on the present moment efficiently. It will be a pleasure to wade through the waters of life because you are heading toward your purpose. Life will make more sense to you. When you are truly being yourself, the hardest tasks become easy to tackle, because you are brimming with determination and personal power.

In doing what you love, you are resonating with your maximum potential. You will estimate your strengths and weaknesses accurately, become realistic in building your team, and hire the right talent to complement your inner potential. You will also be able to clear the mental blocks that inhibited your inner potential from expressing itself. If you are not good at managing finances, you will team up with the right talent to do that. You will be able to eliminate all the clutter that keeps you from focusing on the present moment. To be able to have a razor-sharp focus on the current moment, you need to be driven by a higher purpose. If your purpose is strong, you will be drawn more toward it in every moment, and your personal potential, i.e., your ability to act, make conscious decisions and create something, will align with it completely. **You will be able to accept and focus on the present moment, and brace to meet the challenges it brings, or simply enjoy being in the moment.**

While analyzing the profiles of overachievers for this book, it struck me as an insight that most people who are successful in influencing others by way of their presence or speech, do so by being completely present in the moment. I now know this for a fact because, when I asked each person that I interviewed for this book about what they were thinking before they answered my questions, or during our conversation, they said that they loved talking about personal development and were completely focused on our conversation.

When I interviewed Suhas Gopinath, CEO Globals Inc., hailed as the *Bill Gates* of India by BBC, and also the youngest ever Indian millionaire, he talked about his innate ability to focus on a task. He had to switch back and forth between our interview call, and a call with his investors from the United Kingdom. I recall that it was late at night in India, and it had been a long day for him. I asked him if he found it taxing to switch between the two phone calls. He replied that he was completely focused on one call at a time, adding that he was not under pressure to move on to the other call while he was finishing the interview, or vice versa. By doing what he loves, he has developed an innate ability to focus on the task at hand and be present in the here and now.

Most public speakers are bound by time because they have to respect a certain program schedule. They usually go through several drafts of their speech to structure their message so it fits within the given time. When I gave my first Icebreaker speech at Toastmasters, it took me a lot of practice to convey five concepts in seven minutes. I also had to ensure that my voice sounded natural and engaging. At that early point in my journey in public speaking, it required strategic planning for me to time the content, pitch, emotion, and key points in my speech within the allotted minutes. I enacted my initial speeches in my mind until I could recall them almost from memory. I then focused on pacing my words, emphasizing certain phrases, and giving time to the audience to respond to my humor or questions.

After countless practice sessions in presenting ideas to varied audiences, I observed that I had developed an ability to deliver a speech without being stressed by the factor of time. I learned that if I am genuinely motivated by a message, and clear in my mind about the concept that drives the message, I require less preparation before speaking. Most of my recent speeches have been impromptu, and I have enjoyed the feeling of not being bound by time, in my speech. I can speak from intuition, only when I am aware of, but not stressed by, the time factor. When I am free of the stress of time, I feel completely present in the moment and can accommodate the surrounding audience in my *flow* [600] of speech. This ability to be present in the here and now, while delivering a speech, is a powerful experience. I call it powerful because such a presence has time and again—for me and other successful speakers that I interviewed for this book—helped establish a connection and a creative flow [114] between the speaker and the audience.

The point I am trying to convey is that there are many ways to reduce the stress of time and enhance the perception of timelessness and depth in any experience. In this particular case, I am referring to public speaking. Practicing any skill until you reach a level of mastery unleashes your ability to surpass the sense of time. It is a great way to overcome your fear in any specific area in your life. Mastering a skill, by practice, strategy and delivery, allows you to feel a sense of joy or of timelessness. For example, when you work with an expert in dancing or martial art, you can clearly see that he can perform with a great degree of grace because he is in a timeless state or a flow [600, 601]. His mastery of his art allows him to not be stressed by time. In fact, mastering any skill, sport, or performing art, enhances our ability to be present in the current moment. This state is referred to as *flow* in psychology. [114]

If you think about how Bruce Lee was able to stun the world with his abilities to push the realms of fighting, it was only because of his ability to surpass a sense of time and fear.

> Mastering any skill, sport, or form of art unleashes your ability to surpass the sense of time. It allows you to feel a sense of joy, fearlessness, or of timelessness in using that skill, sport or art.

In my interview with Jayalaxmi Patil, a successful television artist, writer, theater professional, and activist from south India, she mentioned that she felt no inhibition or fear in playing roles that mocked the political system in India. She has portrayed characters associated with rape and victims of corruption, and has also voiced personal opinions about the political system in India. Her courage, determination, sense of higher purpose, and love of her art is hugely apparent in her personality on and off stage.

It was easy to sense her vibrant personality, so I asked where she derived so much inspiration and courage, as an artist, to initiate social changes. Her answer was quick: 'I know and listen to my inner calling.' She attributes her success in life to her love for art, and in this feeling, is able to dissolve any sense of fear. Her mastery in theater has endowed her with a sense of timelessness (i.e., she forgets time and other parameters when she performs) when she is conveying a message with a higher purpose, or initiating social change by way of her performances. She clearly knew how not to let fear get in the way of her social activism, which is quite a daunting task for a woman in a male-dominated society like India.

When I attended a performance by Mallika Sarabhai—a renowned Indian classical dancer—at the Asian Art Museum in San Francisco, I saw her gracefully address a very sensitive and controversial social subject of how a woman is severely judged as immoral and punished over the man, when it comes to topics related to infidelity. Mallika enacted a scene where Ahalya, a sage's wife, committed infidelity with Lord Indra and she is cursed for the same—but Lord Indra is set scot-free. This is a story from an ancient Indian epic Ramayana. Mallika, by way of her act, mocked the social system that favored the superior class over true justice. I asked her if she felt any fear or inhibition in expressing such a bold message that mocked the status quo of men in society. She responded that she knew how to carry off the message without antagonizing the society in expressing her cynicism. She also added that she felt so immersed in the art of dance that she had surpassed the factor of fear. Thus she had successfully managed to transmit the feeling of timelessness to her audience. By timelessness, here I mean, Mallika was able to make the audience forget about a parameter called time.

I turned to historical accounts to learn about this concept of the here and now, and found my answers in the principles guiding Buddhism, Tao, and Zen. I then started questioning the Newtonian interpretation of time that uses a clock to measure time, and standardises it across the globe.

> As I experienced the sense of time being distorted, when I was in love with what I was doing or who I was with, I felt that time is not just a physical quantity that can be measured; it is a very mysterious concept, indeed!

When I learned about Einstein's theory of relativity as applied to time, my whole perception of life seemed to change. I experimented with my life by dealing with time in both a fixed and a relative sense. My upbringing in India emphasised the wisdom that time is relative to the experience and the individual in question. But when I moved to the US, I got used to the linear concept of a deadline-driven, sequential, and task-oriented sense of time. I studied the differences between the two approaches, which helped me better understand the changes and turns of events in my life. I then saw the importance of the factor called time in my life. To be able to tune into the present moment, it is essential to understand what the concept of time means to you.

It's high time you know what time means to you!

What is time, really? It is just a reference used for social convenience. It is also a useful metric that keeps us aligned with the rhythm of nature, i.e., helps us pace ourselves to harness sunlight and keep track of the past, present, and future. For many of us, some of the best experiences in our lives cannot be measured in terms of time, but only by the joy we experienced. However, in my interactions with top-tier management from the corporate world and academia, which I was a part of, I have also met people who feel alive from the thrill of working within or beating deadlines.

> The concept of Agile Project management or lean thinking in business emerges from a circular treatment of time.

I realised when working with people from Asian, European, and American cultures that *time* is of utmost importance to them in strategizing business decisions and carrying out projects across countries. This experience helped me get better estimates of deadlines for projects, and also to improve my overall productivity at work. But the question is, why do people perceive time differently across the globe? Should the varied treatment and perception of time be viewed as more of a cultural difference?

> What kind of treatment of time is most suited to you?
> Do you believe in adhering to time precisely, like

the Swiss do, or do you believe that there is a bigger
poetic entity driving the world, and so time is not really
the most important parameter? This is probably the
most important question you will ever ask yourself.

Richard Lewis is a British polyglot, a cross-cultural communication consultant, and author; he claims to speak eleven languages. Lewis has been able to explain the varied perceptions of the concept of time by different cultures in the world.

His theory can be summarised as follows [601]: In the western world, time means money. Time is divided sequentially into the past, present, and future; the idea is to focus on a single task within a given time frame.

To the Japanese, time is relative, because they believe in doing the right thing at the right time rather than keeping up with a specific task as planned in a schedule [601]. The concept of Agile project management, or lean thinking in business, emerges from this idea of time.

If you know how various references to time affect you,
you will be able to choose a framework that will allow
you to achieve peak performance.

Americans and Northern Europeans have a natural tendency to quickly approach the heart of an issue. Asians use a more indirect, layered, formal, ritualistic approach to problems, owing to a circular perception of time; they revisit ideas to see if new issues surface.

In the Arab and Latin countries, time is subjective. It can be manipulated, molded or stretched to suit an event or a personality, despite what the clock says [601].

So, what kind of treatment of time is most suited to you? Do you believe in adhering to time precisely, like the Swiss do, or do you believe that there is a bigger poetic entity that is driving the world, and so time is not the most valued parameter in your life? This is probably the most important question you will ever ask yourself.

If you know how time affects you, you will be able to choose a framework that will allow you to achieve peak performance. Depending on the clarity of your perception of time, you will have successfully eliminated one of the most important stress factors in your life; you may even have introduced the most important motivating factor in revitalizing your inner potential. In short, you will have taken a major step toward maximizing your human potential.

Personally, I need to use a western treatment of time when I am acquiring a skill. Once I acquire that skill, I like to use an eastern approach or a circular interpretation of time, where there is a sense of trust that events will align naturally toward producing optimal results.

So far, we have discussed the concept of time and how it can be used effectively. In the rest of this chapter, I suggest three different techniques to stay tuned in to the present. Each technique is **illustrated by way of a blog post,** which captures its essence. In the first post, I talk about staying tuned in to the present by trusting your complete potential to the task at hand, with a sense of calm and awareness. Technique 1 for tuning into the present can be summarised as: Focus on one task at a time, and strive to achieve a meditative state while applying yourself to the task.

BLOG POST: 1/N

Image courtesy: Rolffimages www.dreamstime.com

My heart says: I should write a book to help people see how the power of focusing on one task at a time maximises their potential to eventually handle many tasks.

1/n is a concept that works for me in beating stress and staying focused; I will define it below. It is an analogy that I drew from people whom I consider efficient in managing stress. Since the success and stress meters are closely linked, I have always looked for people who are successful in their profession and also know how to enjoy the better aspects of life. Forty years from now, I would like to recount the moments I lived fully and happily, the chances I took with courage, and the plans I executed to perfection. Are all these possible in a world where being successful means taking on more stress and competing hard? I still have to find a suitable answer to this question. I will try, however, to address the issue of reducing stress.

I am a new mom. Balancing work, family, and social life along with adapting to the needs of a baby is quite overwhelming at times. I am enjoying this new phase in so many ways, but I am also very aware that sometimes I feel like giving up on my own comfort and simple joys. Being able to sustain success and meet the demands of personal timelines come at a price. If I am to schedule going to my favorite play or a movie outing with my girlfriends, it is going to take a lot more planning than it used to. I can't make a date as spontaneously as I used to. If I were to believe in the concept of timeless existence and enjoying every moment in life, how can I cope with an entire society that is driven by time? It is a tough call to have to give up our natural states of being in order to sustain the demands of a structured framework. Let me elaborate on this concept by using an analogy.

I watched the movie *Gravity* yesterday and loved it. I am not sure if the situations can actually occur in real life, however. For me, the essence of the movie involved the unexpected twists and turns astronauts face in space. It boggled my mind as to how astronauts fight gravity while staying alert every single moment.

Staying alert means staying in a space of emptiness. If we believe our mind is thinking of 'n' different thoughts at any given time, our alertness is reduced to '1/n' in the current moment (assuming that we give $1/n^{th}$ attention to each of the 'n' thoughts). So we have $1/n^{th}$ of our capacity to deal with the present moment. As the number of thoughts that cross our mind increases, we have less potential to focus on the current moment. This means we are less alert in the current moment (with decreasing value of 1/n).

How should a person who has to juggle several aspects of life at once within a fixed time frame behave? The answer is to get rid of 'n' thoughts in the current moment and make oneself completely free and alert. In the movie *Gravity*, the protagonist has to breathe from a limited supply of oxygen to stay alive. But she is under stress and struggling to breathe; many negative thoughts are crossing her mind. She is succumbing to fear and so is taking too much oxygen. The command she receives from her superiors is to stay focused and relaxed, and breathe very slowly. In order to make it through such a perilous situation, where her very survival was dependent on the amount of oxygen she was breathing in, there was no other option but to focus.

To maximise your potential, make n=1, i.e., stay in the present moment, focused on one single task or thought. Make the number of thoughts running through your mind equal to one. Then make n=0 for 'zero' thoughts, and 1/n becomes infinite, implying that you have infinite potential in the current moment. *This happens in a meditative state and sometimes in a state of creative flow [114] when you start acting out of intuition, experience thought-free state, and have optimised the utilization of your brain and body.*

A perfectly meditative state can be achieved either through systematic meditation techniques, or simply by pursuing activities like painting, singing, writing, playing a musical instrument, etc., in a state of immense love for what you are doing. The concept of 1/n can be analyzed and used in many ways. I hope that we can all reduce the 'n' factor in 1/n so that we will be very **alive** in the present moment, alert, happy, healthy and fulfilled, and not distracted by unnecessary thoughts. Focusing your human potential on the current moment, and enjoying it thoroughly can contribute to a life well lived.

Staying alert means staying in the space of emptiness. It is a state of no-mind or thought-free-ness.

This is a lifestyle tip for vertical living.

The decision about whether the task at hand is more or less important than an irrelevant thought, should be guided by your awareness and intuition. Complete awareness and grasp of the current situation happens in a state of empty, thought-free, or calm mind. *Intuition comes alive when you are thought-free.* There are three easy ways to focus on the current task in complete awareness, clearing the path for your intuition to come to the forefront:

1.   ***Use breathing techniques to calm your mind***: Focusing on your breath will help you minimise external distractions. Breathing deeply itself improves oxygen supply to your cells and improves blood circulation in the body. Breathing-based meditation is known to decrease posttraumatic stress disorder (PTSD) symptoms in U.S. Military Veterans [603]. In my interview with Amandine Roche, a humanitarian rights expert, U. N. Peace Keeper in Afghanistan, Women and Youth empowerment expert at United Nations Development Programme—who had suffered PTSD— she stated that deep breathing, yoga and meditation helped her come out of PTSD. After being taught and blessed with Buddhist meditation techniques by the Dalai Lama, this brave lady went back to Afghanistan and started classes for the locals, inspiring them to look to Yoga and meditation for dealing with PTSD. This is the core of many meditation techniques like vipassana and sudarshan kriya yoga, etc. Meditation heightens awareness and intuition and helps you in getting into an awakened state or a state of ***vertical living.*** When you completely focus on the task at hand, your mind becomes still and rid of unnecessary thoughts; then you will start acting out of intuition.

2.   ***Train yourself to calm your mind by learning to focus:*** Convince your mind to focus on the task at hand, no matter where a new distracting thought wants to lead you.

3.   ***Try to use your body and mind fully when applying yourself to a task***: Improve your posture to focus on the task at hand, then spend some time preparing for your task in different ways, i.e., cleaning your desk, getting organised for your meeting ahead of time, figuring out smarter ways to plan your vacation, or learning a few jokes to make your company more enjoyable to your friends on a train ride.

I have quoted a few tips that work for me—and many people that I interviewed for the book—effectively. The ultimate trick for you to focusing on your task is to choose a methodology that attracts all your potential into one powerful stream of focus.

As adults, how different are we from children who learn their first letters and words through touch, feel, or music in pre-school? We are motivated by our strengths to apply ourselves to a task, or to learn something new. A child, whose strength is in being hands-on, learns and focuses better by choosing to be hands-on while learning a new skill. A child who is a thinker tends to spend more time speculating mentally about a task before accomplishing it. So it is important for you to know what technique motivates you to still your mind.

I would also like to add that, when you are genuinely motivated and guided by a strong sense of purpose, you can retain your focus. You can accomplish many challenging tasks without being distracted by external factors, fears, obstacles, or irrelevant thoughts.

My goal in this chapter is not only to help you focus on the current moment, but also to help you feel happy about it. What does it take to be genuinely happy as a high performer? I will share a blog post that was quite well received by my readers; it talks about pausing effectively to maximise human potential. Technique 2 for tuning in to the present: Use pauses effectively to stay focused.

BLOG POST: EMPTY EYES

Image courtesy: Shirley Henderson www.picturekidz.com

I have said this many times in my previous writings, and I would like to say it again. Given a choice, I would say it every day, in infinite ways.

My newborn is changing every day. I feel I am being reborn every time I see her outdo herself. I look forward to getting home from work and staring into the eyes of my newborn. It is very therapeutic and unimaginably soothing to me. Sometimes, I wonder if I am comforting my daughter, or if she is giving me solace by loving me unconditionally. The greatest pleasure I know is in looking into her seemingly expressionless, crystal-clear, fresh eyes, which carry no memory, no bias, no desire, and no anguish. There is a strange pause to all my thoughts, my entire being, in fact. I feel merged with everything around me, and very powerful. This is probably what people call a meditative state.

I am living my life all over again with my daughter, by experiencing her innocence. I want to be absorbed into her eyes, which can accept everything around her without judgment. Now I see why it is so powerful to look into her eyes. She can happily accept the situation, and yet is filled with the energy to move forward. Now it is clear to me why children are so playful, optimistic, creative, and happy all the time.

We live in an analytical and competitive world so completely driven by memory, i.e., people carry an impression about us by the way we talk, walk, interact with our surroundings, and present ourselves. For a few moments, can we afford to see life with clear, thought-free, receptive and empty eyes? Empty eyes are meditative—reflective of a clear, calm, and yet powerful mind.

When we make our eyes receptive, i.e., free of judgment, we encourage a slight pause within ourselves. I have discovered that the most powerful interactions happen when this pause is timed effectively. Learning to pause at the right time is important, purposeful, and rewarding. Michael Chojnacki, President of Aikiway Professional Development, recommends taking suitable pauses before speaking to a group of people, or a one-on-one conversation. Incorporate slight pauses before you start any activity in your daily routine to initiate purposeful movements and actions. Pausing means you are in a vertical state of mind and hence your actions that follow will be mostly triggered by intuition. If you watch an expert martial artist in a fight, his mind is most likely empty as he ignores the constraints of time, intuitively selecting and executing the best techniques of defense or attack.

In my experience, training in Kung Fu or Bombay Jam, I have felt that once I have mastered a kick or a move, I am fighting or dancing without thinking, and more by intuition. I can vouch for the fact that intuition played a major role when I composed and delivered my winning speeches. When I am giving my punch line, I am totally and blissfully consumed by the moment of delivery; in my mind and body, I am one with that moment. Basically, my mind is thought free.

Technique 3 for tuning into the present: Turn negative and energy-draining thoughts around into positive energizing actions. This is yet another way to stay focused on the current moment, or be in a state of empty mind. The following is an excerpt from one of my blog posts that shows the reader how the power of directing negative and energy-draining thoughts in a positive direction, would allow for better focus on the present moment. In such a positive mindset or framework, finding solutions to problems and clearing roadblocks to progress, become much easier!

BLOG POST NAME: THE POSITIVE ARROW

Image courtesy: Kamil Macniak www.dreamstime.com

My heart says: I should write about small split-second decisions that we can make consciously, which, in the long run can work in our favor.

Topsy-turvy it was; not a usual weekday at all by any means! Everything went wrong from the get-go. I had lost my entry badge to work, I was late for an appointment by 10 minutes, and I couldn't get my car to start. Somehow, I tapped into my creative genius and managed to get everything going and walked into the meeting.

This was not the usual 'me.' I was so glad the person who was supposed to meet me was calm and collected and nullified this wrong start I had. This response from my colleague was a 'Positive Arrow' targeted at me. Things hadn't gone smoothly between us earlier that week. But my colleague had let it go, and turned the situation positive by being nice to me. I started to feel calm even though I was late for the meeting by almost 20 minutes.

I had a very hectic schedule through the day. For some reason, the way my colleague had hit me with a 'Positive Arrow', I was able to leave the wrong start behind. I was coping, even though it was not an easy day; *let's just say it was one of those days!*

Later at noon, I walked into Subway for lunch and placed an order for my usual sandwich. It was the busiest time of the day at Subway. I was totally famished and had not even an ounce of energy or patience left in me. I like my sandwich a certain way, and the person who took my order got it all wrong. I could have yelled at her, as the store manager whom I knew very well, stood right there, but I remembered the way my colleague had treated me that morning. I deliberately chose to use a 'Positive Arrow' and shared a joke with the Subway attendant instead. I let it go and politely asked her to redo my sandwich. She told me with a smile, 'I am so glad you are being patient with me. This is such an all-wrong day; this is one of *those* days for me!'

I call this choice, of letting go of the issue about the wrong sandwich and turning it into compassionate, positive and reinforcing words as 'Positive Arrow.' People who shoot positive arrows create a positive field and the positivity gets enhanced in the process of interpersonal interactions. The attendant at Subway was indirectly benefited by the way my colleague had treated me. Try to shoot as many Positive Arrows as you can, because you never know you may somehow, end up being the target of your own arrow!

- *End Chapter* –

Chapter 7: The Heart of the Matter

In this chapter, I would like to emphasise the importance of being connected to the people around you at the heart level, by way of intuition. Whether it is your family or workplace, great achievements happen when you are able to drive people towards a vision, as you help them unleash and feel fulfilled in their creative juices and help express their innate potential. I always believe that even an individual feat is the result of a teamwork. Even the winner of an individual sport needs helps from a good coach, a good nutritionist, and a team of friends or family or well-wishers to work with. However, when you realise your calling and need to work with a team of people, you also need to develop adequate communication skills to share your goals and supervise the end results. The trick is to allow people the freedom of expression as you manage them towards goals and milestones in realizing your vision.

In the section below, I would like to express the ideas in the chapter 'The of the matter' using two charts. One of them uses a linear or step-by-step representation of the entrepreneurial approach to self-realization; the other chart uses a non-linear or cyclic approach. A detailed explanation of these charts can be found in the following section in the book: Self-realization using an entrepreneurial approach. The terminology found in the cyclic and linear charts below, have been explained in the section mentioned above .

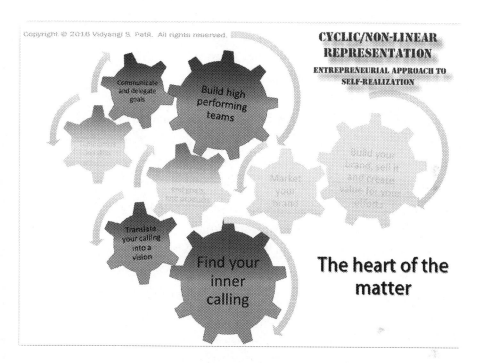

CYCLIC/NON-LINEAR REPRESENTATION
ENTREPRENEURIAL APPROACH TO SELF-REALIZATION

The heart of the matter

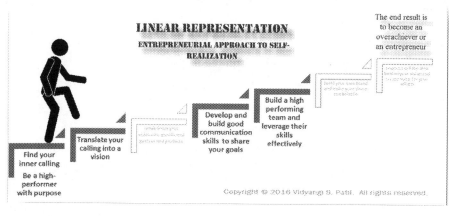

LINEAR REPRESENTATION
ENTREPRENEURIAL APPROACH TO SELF-REALIZATION

-Chapter begins–

'For more than 40 years, I have felt that one of my most important jobs is to attract and motivate great people who genuinely feel their job is more important than just money.'
Richard Branson
Mega entrepreneur

Renowned cardiac surgeon, **Dr Devi Shetty**, hailed by the Wall Street Journal as the 'Henry Ford of heart surgery,' is a game changer in the field of affordable health care. In my conversation with him, he mentioned that if he finds something he loves and is passionate about, he goes after it with all his heart and soul. He dreamed of being a cardiac surgeon very early in his life, when he did not even know that he was required to become a doctor before he could become a cardiac surgeon. Blessed by Mother Teresa, he believes in heartfelt interactions with each of more than one hundred patients he examines every day, so he can connect with them as a human being rather than simply as a doctor.

Mekin Maheshwari, former Head of engineering and Chief People Officer at Flipkart, an e-commerce company, talks about the importance of connecting with employees as human beings, rather than resources, which was the most important game-changing move for Flipkart. Flipkart made unprecedented progress in e-commerce because he and his team believed in focusing their lives on building the company. Such focus, he says, comes from hiring the right talent and establishing a culture of trust and a high degree of ownership. The company has turned out to be a game changer in the domain of e-commerce, reshaping the psyche of the Indian masses into embracing online shopping. Mekin fondly recalls that when he decided to move on to a new venture in the education space, some of his best mentees at Flipkart reciprocated with very high expectations of him and the change he could effect in this new space. This ability to raise the bar for a peer or team member stems from a culture of trust and mutual respect; such a feeling of trust can only reside in the heart.

Great companies are envisioned in the <u>hearts</u> of people, and built using the faculties of their <u>minds</u> (or vice versa if need be). This indeed is the heart of the matter in this chapter.

I interviewed Suhas Gopinath, the youngest Indian technology entrepreneur when he launched his first enterprise, Globals Inc., as a 14-year-old. He was later referred to as the *Bill Gates* of India in a BBC documentary. He talked about his calling to be an entrepreneur, and his true driving force—his passion for computers and the Internet. Though he finds it hard to focus on reading for too long, he devours inspirational books by game changers and leaders in technology. He does not like to be pushed into things his heart is not connected with, and he cannot stop himself from excelling in things with which he finds a true connection. The people in his life had so much faith in him that when Gopinath dropped out of college to be an entrepreneur, one of the first things he received was a request from a former teacher asking Gopinath to hire him in his new company. Gopinath fondly jokes about it. He recalls that early in the day that he decided to drop out of college, the Head of the department would not give him permission to attend his term exams, because he was short on attendance. Gopinath was busy building his new company and had missed out on classes. However, when Gopinath quit, immediately, another faculty member asked him for a position in Gopinath's new company. The point I am trying to convey by Gopinath's example here is that when you follow your heart, and start fulfilling your dreams, you are bound to meet people who disapprove this move. But there will also be people who understand and acknowledge your path in following your heart, for example, the faculty member here who understood that Gopinath had set a new bar of excellence in being self-taught and self-realised. He had been a game changer in the Internet industry in India, back in the 90's, and had done it without requiring to complete a college degree.

Have you ever wondered what states of mind allow people to dream big? What makes people pursue their dreams relentlessly and set goals that are beyond their limitations? What makes people fearless in the face of risks and challenges? This chapter focuses on the answers to these questions and more. Money has great potential to drive success; however, to sustain success, your motivation has to be more than just monetary returns. In this chapter, I talk about how to harness the power of *love* and *the beginner's mind*, which have rendered people fearless and made them persistent enough to change the course of history. I have used my blogs and personal experiences to substantiate the concepts of love, beginner's mind, and ego. I believe that if you put your body and mind into a state of love when you are pursuing specific tasks, your human potential is maximised to accomplish them. I call this the '*Heart of the matter*,' because the heart is indeed the seat of love, compassion, gratitude, and intuition [704]. It provides the ultimate driving force that helps us find the meaning and purpose in our lives.

If you love your work and find love in the relationships that matter to you, you will almost automatically reach your goals. Being in love invokes a higher degree of perception and intelligence in all of us. I refer to such intelligence, which is driven by love and compassion, as simply *higher intelligence*. The greatest marvels in engineering and art came from people who loved their profession and cared about others who would benefit from their work. I bring to light in this chapter, an association between love and higher intelligence as applied to managing teams and the process of innovation.

Have you ever loved someone or something very deeply? You will know the answer to this question even before you can think, because *the answer is in your heart*, and it lives with you as part of your intuition. You will also know by intuition that, perhaps a particular hobby brings out the best in you; so you will love pursuing that hobby. When you talk of the things or people you love, there is no delay in your thought. The head is almost shut off and the heart takes over; your mind is empty in that very moment when you think of love. Being in love is a great way to stay in a state of empty mind. Being in love puts you in **a state of vertical living.** It is a state where you feel blissful, your eyes light up and your whole body and being are filled with energy. It is indeed a state of non-ego. I am not a big fan of being guided completely by love when I make important decisions in life, but there is great power in loving something or someone deeply.

Physiologically, being in a state of love can be explained by the effect of dopamine, a neurotransmitter that is released in the brains of people who are in a state of love, according to Dr Helen Fisher, a biological anthropologist and a senior research fellow at The Kinsey Institute [701]. Dopamine increases energy, reduces the need for sleep or food, and helps develop better focus on tasks. It also enhances the feeling of exquisite delight in tasks related to the things you love [702]; being in love puts your body in a state of *desire and reward*. It stimulates the reptilian part of the brain that controls feelings such as want, motivation, craving, and focus [701].

A post from the archives of my blog talks about the power of love:

BLOG POST NAME: BEING IN LOVE

Art and Illustration: Nivedita Gouda

I would like to write in such a way that I can uncover the most consistent nature of love and its true power

Love for cricket! Love for football, love for dancing, love for good food. Love for something means you connect with that thing deeply, for reasons you can't explain.

Love is a connection that exists, come what may. Think about your favorite sport, pro football for instance. Are you a fan of the Cowboys? You love the Cowboys even when they don't play well. You jeer when they play badly, but you love them nevertheless! I am Indian and I know how crazy my folks back home can be about cricket. We love the Indian cricket team even when they are not quite in their best form. Such an unconditional love for national sport, has time and again, spurred a sense of patriotism in us.

There can be no bad mothers, they say. A mother's connection with a child is unconditional. A mother's connection with her child is called love.

The world has seen true lovers—Romeo and Juliet, Anthony and Cleopatra, Odysseus and Penelope, Paris and Helen—who were deeply in love, and fought against the whole world just to be together. True lovers look past the life they have lived so far, or even the future for that matter, in their struggle to be together. Love is indeed a strong and deep connection. Feelings, thoughts, and actions align and submit to this connection. Many of my friends and relatives have given up smoking or drinking, or turned vegetarian because they wanted to please their prospective life partner. Such is the power of love!

Some of the best speakers at Toastmasters love the topic of their speech. They love it so much that when they are delivering a speech, their whole body and being are in a state of high energy and exhilaration that is simply infectious. I have learned several useful speaking and writing techniques from speakers who resonate in this state of love for their message. They are like beacons of inspiration, classic examples of how being in love with a certain aspect of your life makes you powerful and effective in that facet of your life.

While we can experience love in specific aspects of our lives, is it possible to feel such love for life as a whole? Can we fall in love with life unconditionally? Just like two lovers who accept each other no matter what; just like we embrace the performance of our national sports teams, no matter what. I think we can.

Let us connect with life through a deeper emotion called love, without preconditions or judgment. It is certainly a great way to maximise our inner human potential.

Michael Chojnacki, President of Aikiway Professional Development, talks about a concept called *beginner's mind,* which is commonly used in Aikido. The term refers to the skill by which one can look at a situation with fresh eyes, dropping all judgment. You must have experienced such a state when you were in love. I have felt nonjudgmental about the people and things I love. For instance, I love writing; I believe in my message, and I continue doing what I love in spite of the critical feedback that I receive quite often.

Chojnacki explains that even though Aikido practitioners have practiced their techniques tens of thousands of times, they still strive to retain a beginner's mind before using a technique. He adds that retaining a beginner's mind is the goal of every master in Aikido! He goes on to say that the opponent to achieving one's goal always lies within. In our daily life, the opponent could be a simple thought, which clutters the mind by way of associating unnecessary fear or judgment with certain activities. I will talk more about factors that drain human potential in the section on ego in this chapter.

The beginner's mind is an essential prerequisite for connecting with your surroundings. If you cannot clear your mind of unnecessary thoughts before you meet someone, address a large group of people or perform a routine activity that you are uncomfortable with, you may not be able to fully tap into your potential. Your memory of an unpleasant experience or bias from the past will prevent you from performing freely.

When you feel free in your heart and mind, you can perform actions freely, be it connecting fearlessly with an audience; managing a team at work or fitting into a new environment, like a new city or a new group of friends. In other words, you need to retain a beginner's mind to embrace situations where you would like to harness your abilities freely, and be yourself completely, without inhibitions. This way, you can connect with your audience, your team or your surrounding environment, with nothing to hold you back.

Power of harnessing love as an Emotion

- Being in love with something helps you attain a beginner's mind.
- Retaining a beginner's mind is the goal of every master in Aikido.
- Retaining a beginner's mindset helps you to excel at tasks, even if you have failed at them previously.
- A beginner's mind can be attained by clearing your mind of negative experiences and dropping all judgment and preconceptions before walking into a situation.

When I interviewed successful Toastmasters and entrepreneurs for this book, it became obvious to me that it was second nature to them to effortlessly connect with the people around them. When you connect with the surrounding ecosystem, you will be able to read the requirements of your audience and play your role efficiently. For example, if you are the leader of a team, you will have worked with the team for a long time, and very likely will have shared many victories as well as setbacks as part of your work. Put those ups and downs from the past behind you when you take on a new challenge or task. If you approach your team with a beginner's mindset, if you are more empathetic to your team, you can maintain a long and healthy working relationship with them.

Intuition is the most powerful way to connect with your surroundings. Intuition is heightened in a state of love.

Retaining a beginner's mind enhances your intuition and the ability to connect with the need of the hour. In his book, *Strategic Intuition: The Creative Spark in Human Achievement*, William Duggan talks about beginner's mind and strategic intuition, which were at the heart of great achievements throughout the history of humanity: the computer revolution, path-breaking works in the physical and biological sciences, the civil rights movement, modern art, etc. Duggan is a senior lecturer at Columbia Business School [703], where he teaches strategic intuition in graduate and executive courses. With intuition, you will be able to read the requirements before anyone else. It is almost always the secret of game changers in history. If you ever have a conversation with mega entrepreneurs like Richard Branson, Bill Gates, or Elon Musk, you will almost always feel that they spend a lot of their time reading the requirements of the future.

Connecting with your surroundings is of prime importance in any form of communication. There are specific techniques for connecting with your surroundings. Having a beginner's mindset is the first step.

Kirubakaran Periyannan (aka PK), a Distinguished Toastmaster and contender at the May 2015 Toastmasters International Speech Contest, has this to say about the importance of connecting with one's surroundings via communication: 'I guess Toastmasters provides the ability to connect with different people. I feel that's where the magic of Toastmasters lies. When you start connecting with the people around you, you become a happier person.'

Michael Chojnacki quotes a specific example of the power of connecting. He describes how his wife talks about hiking intuitively as she feels connected to her surroundings. This helps her not only to enjoy her hiking experience but also to move intuitively across the terrain on the hike. When I interviewed Chojnacki, he was able to completely connect with me, and my state of mind. When we talked about the practical applications of intuition, one of the things he mentioned was that people who use intuition and the beginner's mind are able to solve problems in the corporate world faster than others.

Chojnacki gave the example of one of his mentees at IBM, who was able to fish out solutions more quickly after learning how to develop and guide his intuition. Most successful people feel connected with, accountable to, and eventually intuitive about the environment around them.

During my interaction with a kind and altruistic lady, who did not wish to be named, I observed that she feels connected with and accountable to the insects in her home. She never kills them; instead she ensures that they are safely shooed out of the house. She donates money to a needy person every single day, without being judgmental. She is highly intuitive in her decisions and fearless in carrying through with them because she feels integrated with her surroundings. If you observe people who practice martial arts or sports involving a lot of danger, e.g., climbing precipitous mountains, bungee jumping or obstacle racing, you will see that they are very aware of their surroundings; so much so that they plan their movements and strategies by blending in with their surroundings. They are using not just the five primary senses, but also a sixth sense—intuition.

Intuition comes alive when we feel completely integrated and blended in with our surroundings. According to Lynn Robinson, the bestselling author of *Divine Intuition: Your Inner Guide to Purpose, Peace, and Prosperity*, intuition has been found to be active in states of heightened awareness, gratitude, and compassion [700].

At this point, I would like to introduce a small blog post that I wrote about how people might connect better with their surroundings with a beginner's mind. Feeling connected with your surroundings is an essential precursor to vertical living.

BLOG POST: ON CONNECTING

Art and Illustration: Nivedita Gouda

My heart says: After all these years of wondering why people act and talk superficially, I would like to help them realise the value of connecting genuinely from the heart!

The friend who hurt me, the person who took away my peace of mind; the love who cut the cord with me, and people who belittle me—have I really connected with them at all? If I remove the burden of all that they did to me, and connect with them, how powerful I feel! *How free I feel! How happy I am!* They are all made of the same basic elements as I, but so differently evolved; such is the wonder of nature!

We are in the most connected world of all. We have a device to connect us in every corner of our home and every corner of our world. But how often do we really connect with the life force in everything around us?

We walk past the office space and say a superficial 'Hi' to a colleague. There is no connection in our 'Hi' with the person we say it to. We don't even look the person in the eye. Life has become a protocol without feelings.

Connecting with someone or something means seeing past the 'past' of that person or object, forgetting for one moment, our thoughts about the person or object in question, and being one with that person or object.

Try connecting with life today and see how powerful you feel! Connecting with life is fun; there is joy in blending in with people and the environment around us.

In accepting life as it is, with a beginner's mind, there is a deep connection with life. Such a connection allows us to experience life in meditative euphoria. We are all so used to living life in the compartments inside our heads, that anything that falls outside the compartments gives rise to a sense of insecurity in us. The truth is, life cannot be classified into compartments. The true nature of life is chaotic; it is capable of evolving in innumerable ways. *A true connection to life is felt in the complete submission and acceptance of its chaotic nature.*

Most of the people I chose to interview in the course of writing this book are good at retaining a beginner's mindset even while performing simple tasks. The tasks could be as simple as listening to someone talk, or appreciating the flavors in a dish. Such a state of nonjudgment and zero preconceptions is the nascent state in which creative solutions show up as insights. I learned this as part of my interactions with engineering managers and executive management in a corporate setup. I have seen them use a beginner's mind for rebuilding a failed team, approaching a dissatisfied customer, winning over a lost client, and recuperating from the failure of a product. Teachers in preschools use this approach when dealing with one- and two-year-olds, because every child is different, and they need to start with a fresh mindset every time. They specifically use this approach when getting the children to learn something new or accomplish a list of tasks.

Using a beginner's mindset for your task will keep you glued to your task or goal. It will give you the persistence to embrace a new approach to that particular task even if you have failed at it before.

I have used this approach when coordinating social events for family or friends who usually do not get along well with each other, due to mutual disagreement in points of view. When they arrive at these events, and engage in group activities like praying, chanting and singing together, helping set up food, music and the stage for the event, they find an opportunity to reconnect and put the past behind them. I also make sure that I set off this process of clearing the past, by making the present moment energizing and motivating in using an energised pitch to get them to talk to each other and complimenting them for their contributions to the event. A beginner's mindset is indeed a great approach to maintaining successful long-term relationships.

People who do not retain a beginner's mind end up reacting to a situation instead of responding to it. Overachievers are calmer and more responsive, i.e., less reactive. They maintain a beginner's mind—a mindset inherent to vertical living as a way of life. Due to this approach, they brim with energy and feel fully aligned with their surroundings. It helps them become overachievers as it unleashes tremendous human potential in them to rebuild and reinvent themselves from failures. Let me illustrate with an example.

Amitabh Bachchan, a veteran Bollywood super star and an actor of international repute, enjoyed a near impeccable career for almost two decades. However, he hit a rough patch in the 90s, and Pritish Nandy, one of the most influential journalists in India at that time, called his career 'Finished,' in the front-page headline of the Illustrated Weekly. Bachchan, writes in his personal blog, 'I tried to bear it as bravely as I could and silently swore to myself the possibility of proving him wrong. I placed the magazine on my desk and allowed it to stare at me ominously every day. It remained in that position for years . . .'

Bachchan had failed in his stints at politics and business, which badly affected his career and financial prospects. At that critical juncture, he decided to restart his career using a different medium—the television. Bachchan went on to host 'Kaun Banega Crorepati' (based on the UK TV game show 'Who Wants to Be a Millionaire?'). This show captivated television audiences, topped the charts, reinstated Bachchan's stardom, and paved the way for his successful comeback into Bollywood. Later in an interesting turn of events, Bachchan applied a beginner's mind strategy and went back and collaborated with Nandy productions for the movie *Kaante*. This is a classic example of how a beginner's mind can be used to rebuild a career, and help re-collaborate with people who didn't believe in you, i.e., Nandy here, and this strategy of retaining a beginner's mindset, seemed to have worked very well for a renowned celebrity.

Using a beginner's mindset for your task will keep you glued to your task or goal. It will give you the persistence to embrace a new approach to a task at which you have failed before. John R. Adler, inventor of CyberKnife, talks about persistence as his most promising trait as a game changer in the field of image-guided radiation therapy. His life has been extraordinary, considering the degree of transformation he has had to make in a domain that spans neurosurgery, radiosurgery, engineering, people management and even concepts in Agile Project management, alongside his tenure as Dorothy and Thye King Chan Professor of Neurosurgery at Stanford University School of Medicine. During my conversation with him, there was one message that rang clear in his voice: he uses the approach of a beginner's mind in persisting with his tasks and seeing them through to completion. *Persistence, in a way, is the ability to retain a beginner's mind while attempting to go back and start afresh on a task at which you have failed, but with a fresh perspective and energy.* This is the same mindset that is retained by Aikido masters.

> Dr Adler stresses the importance of retaining a beginner's mind when listening to new and creative ideas. In fact, he is a great proponent of retaining this mindset when listening to both good and bad ideas. His latest venture, Cureus.com, is backed by his motivation to allow for innovative ideas to flow freely in the medical industry.

Distinguished Toastmaster PK displays a beginner's mindset in accepting objective criticism to improve the quality of his speech. In preparation for his participation in the Toastmasters International Speech Contest, he delivered his speech at countless locations, each time as if it were the first time. I have seen him accept criticism during evaluation; he comes across as calm, strong, fresh, and open to incorporating the feedback constructively. He exemplifies someone who can retain a fresh mind, while delivering the same speech repeatedly, improving it iteratively. He would revise his speech immediately based on the feedback and deliver it again, right away, with the changes incorporated. His relentless energy and beginner's mindset have served him well, and ushered him all the way to the top tier of the contest.

A beginner's mind is a trait inherent to a long-lasting love for something or someone. If you can love someone or something deeply, and connect with that person or thing, having let go of the past, you have mastered the art of retaining a beginner's mind. In a sense, being in love with someone is the best way to maximise your human potential because it teaches you to be patient, compassionate, perseverant, and persistent in dealing with relationships. Your life is an outcome of how well you have managed your relationships; and retaining a beginner's mind is vital to managing them well.

One of the first things Nelson Mandela did as the president of South Africa was to love, embrace, and empower the very people who had imprisoned and plotted to kill him. He parted with the bitterness of his past experiences by forgiving his enemies; he did so for the love of his nation, South Africa. Such ability to forget wisely can also be interpreted as parting with a memory that defines a part of your identity or ego. If he loved his ego more than his country, he would never have patched up with his enemies and facilitated the rebuilding of South Africa. Living in a non-ego state empowered him throughout his tenure. It also served him well during his struggle for the freedom of his fellow citizens from apartheid and various other atrocities.

This state of love for fellowmen displayed by Mandela, exemplifies a beginner's mind. The saga of his struggles and eventual victory shows how a beginner's mind or the state of non-ego can enable someone to become a game changer; in this example, in the history of an entire nation.

Art and Illustration: Megha Vishwanath

I would like to take a moment to reiterate what I mean by the term 'Ego,' which I use in this book. When I use this term in my articles, online blog posts, and speeches, I receive mostly defensive responses from people who wonder how someone can give up their ego. After all, the ego is the safe place where we store our experiences and lessons learnt in life. In fact, it tells us who we are and gives us an identity. It would only be foolish to renounce our own identity, wouldn't it?

The ego is an artifact of the memory residing in us, and it summarises the things we like and the things we do not like; it includes memories of people we do and do not get along with; it defines the specific set of ideas that we agree or disagree with; it also records our love or dislike for specific kinds of people and behavior, so that we can keep loving people who give us joy in return, and be indifferent to people with whom we do not get along.

The ego guides us by way of the mind, in energizing areas of life where we get maximum returns, and conserving our emotions, thoughts, and resources in areas where we do not get returns. It is a framework that we carry in our head, which helps us preserve our personal power, sometimes even at the cost of disdain for our surrounding habitat or ecosystem. For example, you may, on occasion, decide to not help someone who has been rude to you in the past. You may not attend a talk by a professor whom you admire professionally, but dislike for his personal habits. Essentially, you are missing out on the knowledge he could impart, due to the prejudice you carry in your heart, which is a part of the ego.

An ego that wills you to focus only on yourself can, in its advanced forms, isolate you mentally in games of power and wealth and render you rigid in your ideas. Adolf Hitler is an example of how one person, blinded by his ego, directed the massacre of millions of innocent human beings. However, a positively directed ego, like that of Mahatma Gandhi—a proponent of nonviolence—could inspire an entire nation toward the path of freedom, self-sufficiency, and compassion. *The power of ego is expressed in both constructive and destructive ways, based on how we choose to express ourselves to the world outside.*

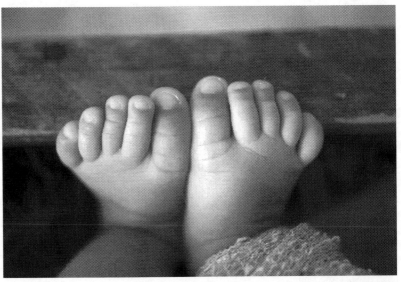

Image courtesy: Shirley Henderson www.picturekidz.com

In our journey from birth to death, all our experiences add to our self-image that we conveniently call our ego. Each day from the day of birth, we grow a little older and our experiences change as well. Unfortunately, some of the memories in our vault called ego do not change with time at all. For example, if we are constantly fed with news that a certain country is a dangerous place, and that people who live there are violent, we may judge the people from that country as violent throughout our lives. If we do not dissolve this component of our ego, we will likely be prejudiced against anyone from that country, anytime in our lives. And while the world around us may change and lovingly embrace people from that country, we will remain rigid and old, if we are stuck in our egos or ideas of the past.

The ego is a component of our psychological makeup. However, it also has the ability to influence or our ability to think logically, when it casts a negative filter on our perception of specific situations. Terrorists who wouldn't hesitate to kill innocent people in order to serve their mental conditioning, are examples of people whose ego is getting expressed negatively. What is the use of a fine analytical and logical mind that is crippled by the narrow avenues of the ego? *Giving up your ego completely is not wise, because many positive accomplishments are guided by the ambitions and targets embraced by your ego.* For instance, if you have it in your ego that you are a fine athlete, you will, in all likelihood, work hard to stay fit and meet the requirements of that part of the ego. *Lifestyle tip in vertical living: Use your ego wisely; free yourself of that part of your ego which brings you down or introduces negativity instead of helping you express your full potential.*

There is a simple way of looking at people and objects without being cluttered in the mind, or being influenced by the limitations of the ego. One of my blog posts may perhaps describe this technique better:

BLOG NAME: WONDERING

Art and Illustration: Megha Vishwanath

My heart says: I should write about how wondering can free us from inhibitions of the mind and help rejuvenate and reinvent ourselves.

I recall a time from my first year in the US. I had had a gloomy day at school, with lots of setbacks in my schoolwork. On my way home, I had a bitter fight with my best friend that left me feeling like I never wanted to talk to her again. When I got home, I barely took off my shoes before I crashed on my bed. Almost everything I had expected to work had fallen apart that day.

I am not sure how long I lay on my bed sobbing. I missed my home in India terribly, and not even the cup of tea my dear roommate made for me pacified me. I felt hopeless and sad. Life seemed to be as gloomy as the evening sky that was visible from my bedroom window. The bedroom in our third-floor apartment had huge windows overlooking an intersection. I lay on my bed, just staring into the nothingness of the sky. At one point I felt numb, and sank into a deep sleep.

Suddenly, something woke me up: I'm not sure what it was. I opened my eyes slowly. Everything seemed so bright, like I was in the middle of a dream or a fairy tale. I woke up and peeked outside my window. My heart skipped a beat. Everything was blissfully white. In fact, it was snowing—it was the first time I had witnessed snow fall! I could not stop staring in wonder for a long time. I forgot everything that had happened that day. For one moment, I did not regret that I was far away from my home country, because I had just witnessed the finest moment of my life. I had earned it! I felt alert and alive again, as if I could jive and dance and create something new and fresh. I felt I had the energy to rewrite my destiny.

Even to this day, when it snows unexpectedly, I feel like I have been offered a slice of heaven so generously by nature. *The power of wonder is so great that it can erase sadness, bitterness, and pain.* What makes us wonder anyway? To wonder is to surrender the burden of our memory, whether good or bad, for a few seconds and make our minds still, our hearts lighter, and become like children again.

A state of wonder can provide immense power to build and create, solve problems, envision new ideas, and even shape the course of history, as in the case of Einstein and Archimedes.

Albert Einstein changed the face of classical physics forever by questioning its fundamentals. He admitted to solving great problems in physics and math when he was daydreaming, and playing with bubbles in his bathtub. He is known to have said, 'Play is the highest form of research.'

Archimedes was one of the greatest mathematicians of all time and is credited as one of the pioneering visionaries of calculus. He solved the problem of assessing the purity of gold used in a crown while he was in the bathtub, where he discovered how to use the volume of water displaced by an irregular solid to measure the solid's density. In a state of wonder and ecstasy, he supposedly leapt out of the bathtub naked and ran through the streets of Syracuse, exclaiming, 'Eureka!'

To wonder means to light up your eyes, to expect without expecting, to accept life as it is, not knowing the future. It means living and existing intensely in this very moment. **To wonder is to feel alive.**

To wonder amidst a busy and hectic day, to wonder amidst an atmosphere of stress and harshness, is to nurture a flower in the heart. Wonder fosters the power to be reborn.

It is important to wonder about things, both infinitesimal and vast. At the deepest core of the wondering mind is a heart filled with love, which has the ability to give birth to life itself! Take the time to wonder and love life in its totality.

A person who has not kept the power of wonder alive has missed out on living life deeply, because his life has been lived in the head, and not in the heart. Living without wonder is like touching without sensing, listening without understanding the speaker's intent, and breathing without appreciating life. To be able to wonder about life means feeling life in its depth and power! It means **living vertically by living in the here-and-now,** with a deep sense of compassion and hyperawareness about life.

Human ability to be curious, to explore, to wonder and draw this experience to come up with path breaking ideas, is only the beginning of innovation. I am now going to introduce the concept of *higher intelligence*. It is a prime requisite in sustaining great innovations and creative endeavors, which have helped humans transcend the limits of their innate human potential, time and again.

The heart is the seat of intuition. Intuition is
the highest form of intelligence.
The more sophisticated you become in your approach
to life, the higher is your level of intuition.

In transcending the limits of conventional thinking, they are also trying to stay rooted in your human nature. I have introduced this term *higher intelligence* for the first time in this book. I choose to use the word higher intelligence here, because the intelligence I am trying to describe here is the root of many great accomplishments across history, and is one that has raised the plane of human thinking.

BLOG POST NAME: THE HEART OF THE MATTER, HIGHER INTELLIGENCE

My heart says: I should write about the greatest form of intelligence, which evolves with the wisdom to accept and care for life.

Have you felt the difference between using a desktop (a personal computer or PC) with which you interact by proactively providing all input, and a smart phone that alerts you via apps about your calorie intake, or the preparations needed for your upcoming event? Have you felt the difference between writing a letter and posting it, and sending an e-mail over the Internet? The phone app and e-mail are media of *higher intelligence*. These media make lengthy, laborious actions really simple for us. But in reality, the app and the e-mail service are media with a more complex inner composition than that of a PC or postal service. Their *sophistication* arises from the fact that these devices are able to anticipate your needs before you know, and absorb the mundane, laborious tasks into the subtleties of their higher intelligence. Here, I refer to higher intelligence in machines.

Is it possible to sense higher intelligence in human beings as well? *When someone is able to read your thoughts without talking to you, is empathetic about your situation and shows compassion, that person is displaying higher intelligence.* A person using higher intelligence does not need to talk to you to get input from you, but senses you and responds to you. This feeling of compassion is at the heart of intuition.

If you love someone, you are bound to be intuitive about him or her. I am a mother and I know by intuition and a deep connection, when my daughter needs me. The ability of a mother to be compassionate, care for and be connected to her child makes her endowed with a very high level of intelligence in understanding the needs of her child; sometimes even before the child can verbalise its needs.

Compassion and intuition have always driven creativity to stellar heights. Have you ever wondered what was running through the minds of Leonardo da Vinci, Arthur C. Clarke, or H. G. Wells when they created designs and concepts of the future? They were driven by a strong sense of purpose and intuition, the ability to envision a future with great clarity when it did not exist; such intuitive insights, such clarity and creativity, arose from a deep connection, a sense of compassion, the ability to care and show empathy for humanity, and what the collective human potential can do. Such a deep sense of connection and compassion is indeed a sign of *higher intelligence*. Being able to care about something makes us intelligent, strategic, and sophisticated in dealing that aspect of life. That is why these inventors and writers of sci-fi were extremely sophisticated and intuitive in their writing and visions about the future of humanity and its potential. Great innovators and thinkers were not only curious about their surroundings, but also felt connected to them and cared about the way they were improving their inventions and discoveries to contribute to the surroundings that they were a part of. Such ability to care is indeed the sign of a certain degree of sophistication *or higher intelligence*. I will elaborate more below.

Sophistication as a sign of 'higher intelligence': A sophisticated being is capable of adjusting and adapting effectively to situations in a harmonious way, because she has developed the intelligence to do so. For example,, if you have interacted in-person with a competent business executive who handles delicate and sensitive company matters with high stakes, you may be able to appreciate the effort she has put into developing her appearance, body language, and tone and content of communication, because she cares about the value she brings to the situation she is in. Such individuals are used to delivering results in a high-pressure situation by being alert, aware, and empathetic to the people they work with, and compassionate towards their surroundings. This makes them purposeful, slightly slow in their responses, and hence graceful in their overall disposition. They are also highly aware of their mental, emotional, and physical energy levels— parameters they constantly modulate to meet the demands of timelines and competition in the market. A friend of mine who worked in a customer-facing role for a long time, never missed her workout sessions because they kept her calm and productive. In fact, she trained herself so thoroughly in the nuances of yoga that she could very well pursue an alternate profession as a yoga instructor.

I have seen professionals who work in sales and marketing, being very informal and open-hearted when they interact with a team in house, because they have a certain comfort level with their colleagues. The same people are formal, strategic and very composed when dealing with a difficult customer. I know this for a fact based on my interactions with coworkers in customer support, product management, marketing, applied physics, and engineering during my time as an engineer in supporting medical imaging equipment, and in building and supporting equipment in a mission-critical environment. It was a great learning experience for me on how to balance my emotions, professional expertise, and a sense of empathy in a high stress work environment, where the end product entailed mission-critical accuracy for the patient who is being treated for terminal illnesses. Such an ability to balance technical expertise and display of emotional intelligence and care is a facet of higher *intelligence*. My dad and mom are doctors and I have seen them pull off miracles in saving a patient's life. They have almost always experienced a high degree of intuition and quick insights, which occurred to them in a state of a deep connection and compassion that they felt about the patients they were trying to save.

Many a time, sophistication comes with a conscious training to meet the challenges of the tasks at hand. An unpolished or unsophisticated individual (a person with an 'I don't care' attitude) cannot create a pleasant environment for people of different temperaments and intelligence, because he or she does not use higher intelligence to care about them or the surrounding ecosystem. Sophistication stems from the core of a person, from thinking, 'I do care about myself and the framework that I am a part of!'

<u>Sophistication is more than skin deep.</u> A person who appears sophisticated on the outside, but does not carry the same degree of care, feelings, and connection at a deeper level, falls out of harmony with his or her surroundings very easily. In such cases, sophistication is short lived—very focused on specific targets and an entirely self-centered approach to interacting with the surroundings. A businessman who appears very polished to his clients and friends but comes home and ill-treats his family, cannot enjoy the worth of his earnings. He cannot feel pure joy—or a good night's sleep every night—but can only enjoy short-lived joy associated with results and money. Superficial sophistication does not aid wholesome personality growth or lead to genuine happiness.

What is the basis of complete and well-rounded sophistication, or 'higher intelligence'? The desire for sophistication is rooted in the ability to care for life within and around you; the ability to care for not only the details that are visible and apparent, but also those that are subtle, hidden, or not easily comprehensible. ***Sophistication or 'higher intelligence' is rooted in the business of caring.*** The attitude of caring comes to a heart filled with patience and the ability to nurture, empathise, and love.

Sophistication or higher intelligence lies in the ability to care, to feel *compassion.* An engineer who builds sophisticated products cares about or is compassionate towards his customers. He cares about, among other things, the ease of use of his product and the ability of his products to enhance the productivity of the customers.

> Sophistication in caring about the simple aspects of life makes you successful in strategic endeavors. Sophistication is at the heart of intuition, which indeed is a sign of higher intelligence.

Robert Noyce, who founded companies that changed the face of Silicon Valley forever, was the first to introduce a culture of open communication between different tiers of management. He started the cubicle system, and for the first time, people in upper and lower tiers of management could freely walk into each other's cubicles, mingle, and share ideas. He eventually turned out to be a game changer in the semiconductor industry. Very early in his career, he had realised and harnessed the power of an open culture that fosters creative thinking and communication. He believed in encouraging his employees to take on risks and translate path-breaking ideas into real products.

Mekin Maheshwari, former Head of Engineering and Chief People Officer at Flipkart, endorses the power of an open culture, where people are treated as people, not mere resources, and allowed to take ownership and deliver. In his interview for this book, he expressed great admiration for the culture at Google. He said that the single most important reason for Flipkart's ability to achieve stellar growth and create a great line of products in India within a short period of time was hiring the right talent, and creating the right work culture—a culture that believed in the freedom of expression and mutual trust between employees. He describes a creative work environment as a place that fosters the freedom to think and wander in space and time, and not necessarily enhanced by artificial external factors, which could be a creative work space or fancy gadgets and gizmos to fuel creative ideas.

Create great products and foster higher intelligence

To encourage creative thinkers and foster higher intelligence in your employees, it is important to:

1. Place trust in their individuality.
2. Allow them to express their ideas openly.
3. Encourage their spirit of risk-taking and experimentation.
4. Be compassionate towards creative thinkers because innovative ideas have subtle beginnings. Being negative towards creative thinkers kills these ideas even before they can be visualised completely.

On a different note, Google invests a lot of money in its infrastructure; resources and tools are easily available to all employees so they can collaborate and be productive. The work environment does not isolate people based on their position in the company, and encourages them to communicate openly. The company is genuinely compassionate towards the employees, and is invested in their comfort. Google is able to innovate relentlessly because its management knows how to keep the creativity and intuition of their employees alive. The management treats employees as entrepreneurs, values what each of them brings to the table, and enables them to work towards a common goal with a strong sense of purpose.

Google's philosophy of management has been described in greater detail in the book *How Google Works*. If you are a seasoned management professional who is rebuilding the culture of your company, I highly recommend this book to you. The underlying message of **respecting the individuality of every employee** is powerful and can be effective in boosting your company's productivity. In a healthy and successful product company, the leader of a team is most likely to be as sophisticated in dealing with technical issues as in managing or being compassionate towards the team.

Caring entails more than spending money and providing material comfort to the employee. It involves tuning into the dynamics of the team, or adopting vertical living as an underlying rhythm in team dynamics. *A good leader usually cares about the skills of each member of the team and constantly senses the interpersonal dynamics and comfort levels within the team during every phase of a project or product lifecycle. Tuning into your team dynamics at such a deep level is a practical application of vertical living in a corporate setup.*

From Leonardo da Vinci to Arthur C. Clarke, Benjamin Franklin to Steve Jobs—creators who have touched the lives of people have cared about their creations, about a higher cause, and most of all about the people who use their products. A lot of care went into the making of Google maps and rendering it on an iPhone, giving the common man extraordinary tools of connectivity beyond just navigation. This goes to show that a sophisticated gadget or application is a gift from an engineer who genuinely cares about raising the plane of human capacity. As a result, these products speak for themselves.

From building successful teams to meeting tall targets effectively, the basic requirement for any kind of work culture is trust. Mutual trust is the driving force at the heart of every successful organization. At this point, I would like *to emphasise the importance of a culture of genuine trust in every aspect of our lives.* Trust is a pathway to happiness and joy. Trusting someone or something is a great way to reinvent yourself and regenerate your mind, body, and spirit. It strengthens your ability to meet daunting challenges in life. In the following blog post, I emphasise how trust can be used to regenerate inner human potential.

BLOG POST: FROM ONE WOMB TO ANOTHER

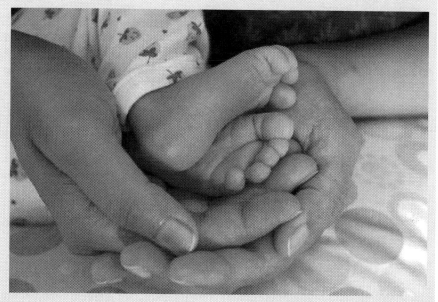

Image courtesy: Vidyangi S. Patil

It was a frantic night. Sixteen hours into labor and I was super exhausted. My mom was standing next to me and urging me to be strong. The doctor almost said if I did not hang in there, my baby would have trouble making it out into this world safely. Yes! All this happened just a few minutes before my daughter was born. I have never waited for anyone so eagerly in my life. This cute little stranger who kept talking to me for nine months from inside my *womb* had tested my patience. I had tasted the droplets of sweat and felt the pain; I was waiting to taste the teardrops of joy . . .

It was my first pregnancy and I remember feeling nervous about even small changes in my health and asking the doctor if my baby was doing fine. She used to reassure me that my baby was in the safest place in the world— my **womb**. She told me that nature had equipped my womb with several nurturing and defense mechanisms to protect my baby from different forms of danger. It was comforting to know that my baby was in the safest place that nature had so immaculately designed.

A few minutes before she was born, when I had almost given up, I recalled the concept of **womb,** which had given me much comfort during my pregnancy. I reassured myself that it was not just my baby who was **living inside a** *womb.* *I was living inside a womb too* – in the **womb of nature**. When I thought about how my body had physically and emotionally transformed through the nine months, I felt that nature had taken care of every need of mine. I was safely and delicately carried through all the changes of pregnancy in nature's own special ways.

During phases of insecurity, I had friends and even strangers, sharing love and strength in the form of words, gifts, calming talk, and kind gestures. My food cravings were all satisfied by people I had never imagined would come to my help. My emotional roller coasters were patiently tolerated by friends, family, and co-workers. I was taken care of by amazing doctors and nurses who held my hand and kept my spirits up. I thought I had become a baby again, being cared for so delicately. Today when I think about my life, I realise I have been safe in *nature's womb in a million ways.*

Giving birth is rebirth in itself; it is also a near-death experience. There is so much pain and discomfort before and during childbirth that your whole life flashes in front of your eyes. There is a lot of insecurity and yet joy, which is only earned through lots of patience and prayer. The whole universe conspires with your will to nurture your little one and pave his or her way into this beautiful world.

When I look back through all the phases of my life, I realise that nature had woven a safe haven for me in *its* **womb.** I have been cared for in every possible way, whenever I asked for help. In the last few minutes of labor, when I had no more strength left, I asked nature for strength, trusting that I would get it back. And **in nature's womb** I found the strength to give birth to **my daughter, Ananyaa—my precious!**

Image courtesy: Mausam Hazarika

Each of us is a unique expression of life, evolving in **Mother Nature's womb.** All we need to do is ___trust___ the *womb*. It is like trusting that when we breathe in, we are bound to breathe out. It is like trusting that the heart will beat, reflecting the continuity of life; trusting that the cycles of day and night, life and death, happiness and sorrow, and the ecstasy of variety in life will never cease to exist. It is that profound trust in the prowess and largesse of nature as a provider that I call upon all of us to cherish. I have felt it through my child's birth. It is simply magical!

Here's to the feeling of trust and security, and to the joy and peace of living in the *womb of nature!*

Being Creative as a Sign of Intelligence

If you haven't questioned an existing belief, you haven't really experienced the joy of creativity. Dr Tina Seelig is professor in the Department of Management Science and Engineering at Stanford University and teaches courses in creativity, innovation, and entrepreneurship. An article in her book, *What I wish I knew when I was 20*, makes a compelling case for the power of creativity in building profitable, purposeful businesses. She talks about how people can recreate frameworks of thinking to build great products where the seed investment may hardly be of consequence.

Her anecdote is reminiscent of the attitudes that nurtured path-breaking inventions and discoveries throughout history. She conducted an exercise where she gave fourteen teams each an envelope with five dollars as seed funding and two hours to do whatever they wanted with that funding. Her winning team brought back over six hundred dollars in returns. What did the team do differently? They did not rely on the seed funding; instead they used the value of time—the two hours that they were given—as the basis for their venture. They bought tickets to shows and blocked reservations at upscale restaurants, and then sold these to people who did not want to spend their time waiting in line. They quickly figured out that female students were better at selling the tickets since people were more comfortable when approached by women. They also traded vibrating pagers for cash, since people found them to be good value for money when they paid for the reservation.

This article by Dr Seelig illustrates the rewards of being open-minded about choosing the means to an end, and even redefining the end if required! It highlights the need for a higher intelligence and free mind to be compassionate toward creative endeavors.

I strongly believe that creativity thrives in an environment of compassion. Compassion is a sign of higher intelligence. Such intelligence enables you to put yourself in another person's shoes, and to foster creativity. If, as a society, we cannot support a creative endeavor physically, emotionally, and financially, we will impede the progress of not only the creator, but also of the entire society.

This is a truth that companies like Google, Apple, and countless startups all over the world have identified; they do everything necessary to keep their employees engaged in tasks leading to a higher intelligence. They do not punish them for being creative or thinking out of the box. Sundar Pichai, CEO of Google, had this advice for the teachers in India about shaping the future of Indian education. 'I think the Indian education should allow a system of creativity, project-based, experiential learning. We should teach students to take risks and not penalise them', Pichai told an audience of over 1,800 people.

Let us aim to live a life of 'higher intelligence,' a life of compassion towards creativity and creative thinkers, a life of 'I do care' about the environment that we are a part of. Most game changing ideas came from scientists and entrepreneurs who genuinely cared about a higher cause or believed in improving the environment to which they belonged. **This is a tip for vertical living as a lifestyle.** A life of 'higher intelligence', is a life filled with the wisdom to accept and care for life and its resources. It is a great way to evolve as human beings. It is indeed the heart of the matter in fostering creative thinkers and game changers.

- End Chapter –

Chapter 8: On Goal Setting and More

In the chapter on *Goal Setting*, I talk about the importance of breaking down your calling or vision into specific realizable goals. Next, it is important to communicate these goals and motivate your team to execute these goals successfully. These ideas can be applied to the entrepreneurial approach in realizing your human potential as depicted in the charts below.

In the charts below, I represent goal setting in terms of non-linear/cyclic and linear representations of an entreprenurial approach to realizing your innate potential. Refer to the chart in the Preface section for details on the terms used in the charts below.

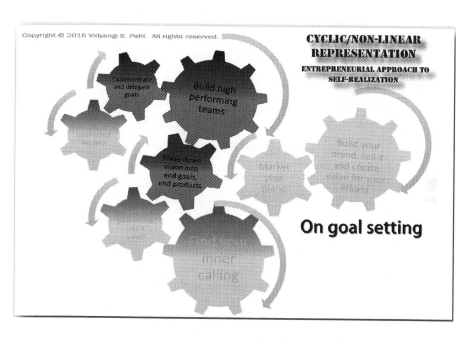

CYCLIC/NON-LINEAR REPRESENTATION

ENTREPRENEURIAL APPROACH TO SELF-REALIZATION

Communicate and delegate goals

Build high performing teams

Break down vision into end goals, end products

Market your brand

Build your brand, sell it and create value for your efforts

Find your inner calling

On goal setting

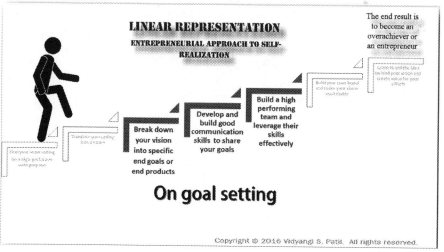

LINEAR REPRESENTATION

ENTREPRENEURIAL APPROACH TO SELF-REALIZATION

The end result is to become an overachiever or an entrepreneur

Break down your vision into specific end goals or end products

Develop and build good communication skills to share your goals

Build a high performing team and leverage their skills effectively

On goal setting

-Chapter begins–

Once you start sensing the purpose of your life, you will have unleashed in yourself tremendous talent and potential to create. But how will you go about realizing your creation or vision? Finding and resonating with the purpose of your life and hosting many creative ideas as part of your higher intelligence [refer to Chapter 7] is only 25 per cent of the job done. Choosing that one single idea out of the fountain of ideas and executing it is the remaining 75 per cent of the job. As all game changers and overachievers in history have done, the only way to go about this process is by goal setting and meeting those goals.

Does visualizing a creative idea and realizing it as an end product come naturally to you? Have you failed in realizing your grand vision in the past? The top 3 reasons *why people fail to realise their vision is:*

1. They do not know how to translate their visions into goals
2. They do not know how to extraordinarily decide what the immediate goal should be
3. They do not have a strategy to accommodate change if the current goal-setting schema does not work.

Let me rephrase these issues in the form of questions. Let me also tell you what a good leader will do when faced with these questions.

1. How will you translate your vision into goals? *Goal setting is a trait that comes with clarity of vision or thought.* You can set reasonable goals by customizing your goal to be SMART (**S**pecific, **M**easurable, **A**chievable, **R**ealistic, and **T**ime-quantifiable). Trying to lose two pounds in one week is a very specific, measurable, realistic, and achievable goal. Trying to lose twenty pounds in two days is not a reasonable goal even though it may sound specific and measurable, because it is taxing to the natural physiology of the human body. Good leaders not only set SMART goals, but also assess the strengths and weaknesses of their team members in meeting those goals. An integral trait of any good leader is being able to communicate specific realizable goals—in a SMART way—to their teams

based on their inherent potential to meet those goals, and support the team as required.

2. How will you decide what your immediate goal should be? To do this, you should identify the constraint or problem that is holding you back. You also *need to be able to motivate yourself and your team* to stick to a plan in meeting that immediate goal. A good leader can perceive the reality of a situation very clearly, and knows what needs to be done, and what the immediate goal should be. For instance, he/she may be able to identify the problem, lay it out for discussion with the team and come up with a plan encouraging open exchange of ideas with the team.

3. How will you accommodate changes? Do you have a backup plan? In case things don't go as per the current game plan, good leaders have backup plans to deal with unforeseen changes. These goals can be individual goals for personal development; or for a team, for collective goal setting as well. For example, what do good leaders do if a teammate quit halfway through a project? How do good leaders make sure the team meets deadlines in that case? *A good leader is strategic in leading a team, and knows how to leverage the agility* in the team when there is a resource crunch or a problem. *A good leader understands the strengths and interpersonal dynamics in the team very well,* and knows how to steer the team toward its end goal.

Here are examples of three people whom I interviewed for the book and who are experts in goal setting, and have met stellar goals. They have pushed their limits to extraordinary levels in their ability to envision and realise tall goals. In the following examples, I intend to iterate the concepts in effective communication of goals; sustained and incremental efforts in training to meet those goals; and developing an ability to envision goals, trust your team members, and delegate those goals to them after profiling their strengths.

Dr Devi Shetty is a household name in India. He is a veteran cardiac surgeon, philanthropist, and someone who is slowly and surely changing the landscape of affordable health care all over the world. Being awarded the highest Indian civilian honors—Padma Bhushan and Padma Shri—for medicine by the

Indian Government has affected not his ability to connect with the poorest of the poor, and Dr Shetty is almost proud of this freedom.

Dr Shetty is stellar in communicating his goals to his team. Bringing down the price of heart surgery has become a mantra for Dr Shetty. He has been successful in bringing the cost of heart surgery down from $3000 to $1400 as his first incremental goal. Reducing the price of heart surgery from $1400 to $800 is the next goal for Dr Shetty and his core team. In the past few years, achieving this target has become his immediate, measurable, and concise goal. His ability to ingrain these goals in every member of his team and motivate them to achieve these minor goals incrementally, has helped him disrupt the myth that high quality health care cannot be made affordable.

To question the myth that the quality of health care is directly proportional to the wealth of a nation is his *major* goal. In one of his interviews to the media, he mentioned that every staff member in his chain of 1000-bed hospitals focuses on the goal of improving the health of the heart, and providing world-class health care at a minimal cost. If you are able to convey clear, concise, and measurable goals to your team like Dr Shetty has, it will help the team focus their efforts in one direction, and ensure that goals are not only set, but also met effectively.

Dr Shetty has a whole team that understands his short term and long term goals. With so many talented high performers focusing on one goal with integrity and dedication, what can prevent such an unprecedented and affordable health care system from being created? What can possibly stop a team that is driven by a higher purpose of making the best health care facilities accessible to the common man? What can possibly stop them from being game changers in the health care system in the world?

Charlie Serrano is not only a competitive runner and a fitness expert at Plus One Health Management Inc., but also a part time contemporary urban artist who experiments with mixed forms of media. He talked to me about his experience in competitive running, in setting tall individual goals and meeting them. He believes in setting incremental goals especially when training to run for longer distances. When he feels half way through a 10-mile run that his body is getting tired, he breaks down the remaining miles as smaller goals. Once he knows that he is entering a zone of running where he needs to push his body beyond its normal limits, he breaks the remaining distance into one mile at a time, one small goal at a time.

Serrano talks about a point in the running experience called a *runners high*; it is a state where the human body feels ecstatic, and there is a jump in human potential in terms of stamina in running. Most runners feel that this sudden elevation and euphoria in the mind and body induces a sense of expansion in human potential. This feeling is significantly powerful in increasing the runner's capacity to run. Serrano shared that he uses the runner's high experience to motivate him in meeting goals. The euphoric experience of runner's high motivates him to push himself as best as his body and mind permit.

Serrano thinks that he can meet his goals in competitive running effectively because he attends his training sessions in fitness and running like clockwork. He tries to stay away from influences that prevent him from waking up early in the morning and showing up at the workout sessions. He believes in training regularly with sincerity, and attributes this habit as the greatest reason why he is able to meet his goals. Jeff Bezos, the founder and CEO of Amazon, Inc., mentioned in *60 Minutes* television report that he believes in meeting his goals incrementally. He said that at Amazon, they constantly take incremental steps to do everything better. Even if Amazon is not making disruptive changes, the company is continually seeking to improve its existing systems. They are using this approach in fulfillment centers incrementally and regularly. According to Bezos, continuous and small improvements lead to major improvements. In conclusion, breaking down a major goal into one small goal at a time, is an extremely powerful and sure shot approach to meeting goals.

Suhas Gopinath became the youngest entrepreneur that India had seen when he started an Internet company at the age of 14, all by himself. It was during a time where owning a computer at home was indeed a big deal in Bengaluru. He has come a long way from the day he started this company. He currently holds a position in the Indian Prime Minister's office and he coaches and inspires young entrepreneurs in India. In managing offices in more than 11 countries while working on a second start up, and being actively involved as an investor in multiple ventures, Gopinath has mastered the art of goal setting and delegating his goals to his team.

When I asked him about how he manages to work with so many teams in meeting his goals, he says that he trusts his employees and he delegates work to them quite confidently. He believes in giving freedom to his team in executing the plan using their individual thinking. However, he has always been acutely aware of the fact that it is very important to profile the strengths of each team member and assign work to him or her accordingly.

He says that the ability to take on a role and do what needs to be done, at any given point in the product lifecycle is his natural trait. It has helped him integrate into and out of teams easily. Gopinath believes that all his visions and goals are realised twice: once in his mind, and the second time in the outside world. He believes that goal setting can be visualised and then made to happen in real life.

Gopinath believes that it is critically important to delegate work, to stay focused on the bigger picture, and save his best for the need of the hour. Managing a team towards the immediate goal is a strength he thrives on. He talks about his favorite cricket game quote by Harsha Bhogle, a highly regarded Indian cricket commentator and journalist. Bhogle quoted that 'if the legendary Indian cricket player Sachin Tendulkar loses a match, he will not complain that the pitch was bad or that his fellow players played badly; instead he will take accountability for the failure.' Tendulkar is regarded as one of the greatest batsmen of all time, and this quote on him by Bhogle inspires Gopinath, time and again. He does not believe in complaining about his team when goals are not met; he'd rather take accountability and deal with the issue himself.

Dreaming big should not hinder you from setting reasonable goals

What do you think was the essential difference between Steve Jobs and Nikola Tesla as inventors and visionaries? They were both moonshot thinkers; they were also the most radical thinkers of their day and age. But Jobs was better at communicating his goals to his team and to his family. His success was hugely due to the objective, detailed, and strategic execution of his planning, which was carried out to completion by his high performing teams—teams comprised of people who were well aligned to his purpose and vision.

Jobs was really good at profiling strengths of people and conveying his requirements for the end product very clearly. He made people see that one big goal and that drove his teams to work relentlessly toward that goal. Tesla, on the other hand, shaped the concepts in electricity, wireless, and many future technologies, but was not able to set SMART (Specific, Measureable, Achievable, Realistic and Timely) goals for himself, his patrons, and his teams. He eventually lost out on realizing many of his visions because of costly mistakes and lack of patrons who could fund his research.

Many of Tesla's great inventions and theories are still on paper or lost in time. He had designed many self-guided machines that used laser, but his designs were never realised. Both his Wi-Fi tower design and guided machinery design were not realistic and achievable for the budget and time constraints he worked with. Jobs' efforts to raise the potential of humanity were more fruitful. He realised this vision by way of several Apple products like the iPhone, iPad, iOS, and by revolutionizing the way we listen to music or view animated movies. He was able to do so because he inculcated a culture of minimalism and focus at Apple. It is known that Apple management has always followed a method of focusing on one product at a time and doing it well. He has had his bouts of failures in setting and meeting SMART goals. However, he always recovered from them and created a framework where innovation and goal setting work hand in hand.

Based on the above examples, it is implied that in setting SMART goals and working diligently towards them, anything can be accomplished.

Joseph Fernandez is one of my favorite mentors in Toastmasters. He is a person of great will who started off by declaring ahead of time that his Toastmasters Club would be a model club, and achieved the goal by working toward it with a clear and aggressive game plan in mind. I will explain more as we proceed with the chapter. Fernandez said that Toastmasters was a great platform for him to experiment with goal setting, team building, communication, and presentation skills. He had wanted to join an organization that would help him refine his presentations at work to upper level management. This trait was critical for his job requirements and when he started off at Toastmasters, he was having trouble communicating his ideas effectively to upper management.

When he started off at Toastmasters, he was the director of a business unit and he was finding it hard to articulate his message and goals to his team. He mentioned that Toastmasters was the only forum where he felt free to experiment and fail. He learned new techniques in leadership and communication in terms of active team building, and setting and meeting specific goals. This experience changed his life and made him self-realised, and a high performer at work.

Setting and meeting goals is a timeless and mandatory strategy for self-realization and high performance. As the saying goes, 'There is no shortcut to success and no substitute for hard work.' This is a lifestyle tip in vertical living. Intuition, brilliant management, higher intelligence, and smart approaches will not do it for you unless you set goals. Realizing your purpose in life boils down to goal setting and meeting those goals as best as you can.

'There is no shortcut to success and no substitute for hard work.'
This is a lifestyle tip in vertical living.

Are you in the habit of setting goals in your personal and professional life?

1. How often have you set a goal of completing a certificate program or meeting an activity group regularly to foster your hobby?
2. Have you been training for a marathon and regularly increasing your running miles every week?
3. If you are a software professional, have you picked up a new software language in the past three years of your programming career? Maybe you have, or maybe you have not; you may have gotten comfortable with your current paycheck. If you haven't already been setting these goals, now is a good time to start! The ability to set great goals also requires a lot of trial and error.

So, how do people who set tall goals—and achieve them—get it right? One of my favorite mentors at Toastmasters is **Joseph Fernandez**, who within the very first year of his tenure with Toastmasters, completed CC (Competent Communicator), CL (Competent Leadership), Advanced Leader Bronze (ALB), and Advanced Communicator Bronze (ACB), to achieve the Triple Crown (4 awards). Not only did he serve as the Vice President of Education and Vice President of Membership for Foster City Toastmasters Club, he also achieved the President's Distinguished (9/10 DCP Points) for this club, and increased its membership from 20 to 50+. He has a huge list of record-breaking accomplishments at Toastmasters, which can run to many paragraphs.

What I am trying to convey in this example with a Toastmaster, is that once you start experimenting with goal setting in your personal life, in extracurricular activities, in personal development, in your social life, etc., and make it a habit, goal-setting will come naturally to you. Your brain will train itself to look at challenges and milestones in terms of long-term and short-term quantifiable goals.

It is also important to create an environment for yourself and your team where experimenting with goals, and being able to see your creative ideas to completion, is rewarded. This way you can shoot higher and meet taller goals and not be afraid of failing.

Consider a workplace that rewards people who take interest in experimenting; a work place that does not punish its employees for failing. As Google CEO Eric Schmidt says in his book *How Google Works*, such an environment will encourage people to achieve tall orders in a short period of time, and be exceptionally creative and fearless in trying out new approaches. Ned Hallowell, author and psychiatrist, mentions that to reach optimal performance or get into the state of *flow* [114] one must be willing to take risks. Setting tall and stellar goals translates to taking a risk in pushing yourself harder. He says, 'To reach flow, one must be willing to take risks. The lover must be willing to risk rejection to enter this state. The athlete must be willing to risk physical harm, even loss of life, to enter this state. The artist must be willing to be scorned and despised by critics and the public, and still push on. And the average person—you and me—must be willing to fail, look foolish, and fall flat on our faces, should we wish to enter this state.' Such thinking is the bases of moonshot thinkers and game changers in history.

How to go about executing those goals SMART-ly? When I asked Fernandez what his secret recipe for constantly meeting club milestones is, he came up with the following ingredients. A good mix of individual development plans focused on members' personal growth and SMART (**S**pecific, **M**easureable, **A**chievable, **R**ealistic and **T**imely) goals for each club officer, i.e., goals that can be measured, clearly articulated, and connected with. He said that 'every club member has a specific goal for which they come to Toastmasters, and it is my job as the Club President or VP of Education to extract that.' He shared with me his own time-bound, clearly bullet-pointed, time-lined road map for becoming a Distinguished Toastmaster.

Fernandez said that once you work closely with people, you can start motivating them towards the bigger club goal by breaking the bigger goal into smaller, tangible individual club member goals. By working with each team member every step of the way to achieve the individual club member goals, you can negotiate club responsibilities to them constantly, and meet the bigger goals of the team. He talks about the 'Yes-but' scenario, where the club member says, 'Yes, I would like to help out, but reason A is coming in the way of execution.' Fernandez says that he shows empathy and recognises the 'but' part of their story and then uses his negotiation skills to help people out of that roadblock.

Communicate your vision and goals to your family and friends.
This way they will be co-operative and if need be,
you can negotiate smaller goals with them.

Your individual success in meeting your goals requires teamwork, so make your friends, family, and social circle a part of that journey. Communicate your specific goals to your family and friends so that they are co-operative and you can negotiate a subset of your goals with them. For example, when I authored the book, I sought help from friends and family in editing and restructuring my book. Since I had very clear, time-bound deadlines to be met, I was able to delegate many tasks to my close family and my team members in the publishing pipeline. In turn, help your team, family and friends, achieve their personal goals so that the whole ecosystem of your life maximises its potential.

Fernandez holds each of his team members at Toastmasters in high regard and places high priority on their personal goals. He mentioned that once any club member achieves a goal, they can share the lessons with other club members and get applauded. This way the whole club learns a new experience, is energised, and motivated. This is a positive environment of co-operation and growth. It works in Toastmasters, it works for a family, it has worked at companies like Google, Flipkart, and it will work at any level in any organization or community.

As Fernandez puts it, set reasonable goals for yourself or for your team. I would call your family as your core team, if you live with them or interact a lot with them. This is a fact: Whatever you do at home/with family affects your work and social life, and your social life and work in turn affect your home/ family. They are all interconnected. So being a high performer or realizing your maximum potential all boils down to managing effective teams at work, home, and in your social circles.

Again, how you pick your core team and how you communicate your goals to the concerned people, is all up to you. It is driven by your inner calling and a sense of empathy and compassion to the people you work with. Empathy and compassion are the most consistent traits of people who practice vertical living as a lifestyle. Practicing empathy and compassion with your team is a must for communicating goals and setting deadlines effectively.

Every time you meet your goal, cheer yourself and your team on a job well done, and the same holds for your friends and family. Every time your family or your teams at work or social circles meet their goals, cheer them. The human brain responds to acts of positive reinforcement.

It is good to have long-term and short-term goals in mind for important aspects of life like health, family, friends, education or hobbies, etc. For example, set goals like: I will meet with my extended family who live far away at least once a year; I will participate in one full marathon every year; I will complete one module in Toastmasters speaking series in the next five months; I will spend three weeks of vacation time with my family and friends every year, etc.

Fernandez also mentioned that respecting the rules of the framework that you belong to, is critical to achieving any goal. Conducting meetings on time and giving a chance to every club member to speak at the meeting even if there were a large number of speakers, were some of the considerations/rules, which he constantly prioritised. These considerations, I believe, stem out from a deep sense of empathy and higher intelligence. These traits are required to build a high performance model club that is constantly recreating itself. Such rules encourage creativity in its members, and hence allow for record-breaking achievements!

Image Courtesy: Creative commons licensing

Fernandez proudly mentions that his club membership outgrew his expectations and increased from 20 members to 50+, because of his winning formulae in building a rock star Toastmaster Club. To meet this unexpected growth, he constantly optimised (developed templates for mundane tasks) and revised the club programs and goals to meet the needs of the growing club. Revising goals comes with a possibility that the new approach may fail, and one should be open to that. He said that if we don't evaluate ourselves, the path we take, and our progress constantly, we tend to fall back in achieving our goal. He said he quickly identified both successful and unsuccessful approaches to meeting club goals and parted with unsuccessful approaches. Sometimes, he even had to part with winning formulae because they did not help meet long-term club goals.

When I shared with Fernandez, that I am doing a day job, participating in Toastmasters meetings and writing a book, he told me right away that I should focus on the main goal in my life. When we went over the various approaches that I wanted to use for the book, he told me, 'Don't pick up those shiny objects while you are working on your main goal.' By shiny objects, he meant that I was getting distracted with too many ideas, products emerging from the book, and the fact that I intended to market and sell the beta version of the book as I was writing multiple drafts. He asked me to slow down, and maintain focus on one small goal at a time. He re-iterated to me that in order to meet my target deadline, I need to stay away from the peripheral ideas or perspectives that may delay the book's scheduled release date.

How I went about goal setting and meeting those goals:

Have you read about the concept of *lean thinking* used by Toyota that shook the fundamentals of production management as it delivered legendary results at the lowest costs? Toyota used a Japanese style of over-the-shoulder management, where a sensei (older learned person) constantly alerts his team to remain in heightened states of awareness and comprehend problems and constraints quickly. The *Theory of Constraints* [1001] helps you identify constraints that need to be resolved immediately for you to meet your goals.

I encourage the use of the concept of lean thinking used in mass production, for individual human potential development as well. This way you can *harness your inner calling and intuition*, in order to make key decisions when you are hitting bottlenecks in your pathway to realizing your immediate goal [1001]. In asking the questions listed below, you are constantly encouraged to challenge the assumptions made by the market or the framework of your profession, for your own flexibility. By flexibility, I mean we can mold the rules slightly to suit our individual project and team environments. If the Toyota rulebook mentions over-the-shoulder management every day, you can do it every two days if you are heading a large team. I was facing a constraint in managing my timelines and revising the content to get approval from the reviewers of the book.

The assumption from the reviewers that I challenged was: *there are specific templates required to write a book.* The revised assumption that I have adopted for the book: *If the message in the book brings value, the template of the book should not matter.* The questions that are listed below, per *Theory of constraints* [1001] used in *lean thinking*, helped me resolve bottlenecks in the publishing process:

WHAT NEEDS TO BE CHANGED? For example, I had to ask myself what needs to be changed in the initial drafts of my speeches and the book, for the reviewers to approve it as publishable.

WHAT SHOULD IT BE CHANGED TO? For example, I had to look into my popular speeches and writings, to identify the distinguishing traits that made those particular speeches and writings popular. I had to create a template for creating better articles and speeches.

WHAT ACTIONS WILL CAUSE THE CHANGE? For example, I had to rethink my current draft, and before I wrote my new draft, I went on multiple writing retreats. I started brainstorming ideas in the wee hours of the morning when it was absolutely quiet, so I could focus better and think differently. A change of environment helped improve the quality of my writing.

WILL THROUGHPUT BE INCREASED? For example, my writing rate became slower than before; however, the quality of my writing got better. I focused on capturing stories and bringing out my author's voice in the book.

WILL INVESTMENT BE REDUCED? For example, I had to leverage my existing resources, i.e., high performers in my team in order to accommodate the cost incurred due to the change in the release dates of the book.

The chapter so far talked about *Goal Setting*, now we go for the peripheral issues in making goal setting effective for game-changers, overachievers, and moonshot thinkers, who need to harness the power of high performing and motivated team members.

AND MORE . . .

LEADING AND RETAINING TEAMS BY POSITIVE REINFORCEMENT AND LEADING WITHOUT MICROMANAGING

Vicky Iu and Karthik Kalpat, who have been stellar achievers in several senior leadership roles at Toastmasters, have some amazing thoughts on goal setting and team management. Kalpat mentions that good leaders are not threatened by team members who are more talented than they are. In fact, once Kalpat identifies a talented team member, he delegates some of his responsibilities to this member and frees himself to take on other responsibilities.

Be comfortable around people smarter than you are. Leverage the experience of working with people who are better than you are. All good leaders do it. That is why they are good leaders!

This is the same approach suggested by Mekin Maheshwari, former CPO of Flipkart. As soon as Maheshwari excelled in his role as an engineering leader and building the right work culture in the company, he started training his junior in taking on the role of the engineering leader. Maheshwari ensures that he hires smart people and then gives them the freedom to create and contribute. The whole culture at Flipkart, he mentions, is based on trust and freedom to be creative, and hence his employees are high performers. Flipkart is one of the fastest growing e-commerce companies in India till date.

Maheshwari says that he is deeply inspired by the work culture at Google, and his approach is inspired by the strategies adopted by Eric Schmidt and the founders of Google. Sundar Pichai, the India-born CEO of Google, in his address to Shri Ram College of Commerce (SRCC) in Delhi University, had this to say to students: 'if they are comfortable with what they are doing, then they are not pushing themselves enough.' He won kudos from the audience when he said, 'It is good to work with people who make you feel insecure. They help you push yourself to do better. That's an inherent part of learning.'

When you are the leader of a team, make the whole experience of working towards a goal, as enjoyable as possible for your team. That's what sets the good leaders apart.

Vicky Iu talks about making the whole Toastmasters experience enjoyable so that people who join have a good experience, and bring in more people. This is a great way to recruit people in meeting your club goals alongside personal goals in leadership and communication. She also believes in observing and appreciating positive changes in people. She believes in managing projects versus managing people. Iu leads by example and believes that it motivates people to adhere to a set of rules when she, their leader, follows them too. She believes that neither adults nor kids would like to listen to someone instructing them; rather they like to be treated as equals and be spoken to in the right tone of voice. She says that modulating the tone of voice when attempting to get things done is very important in leading teams.

Michael Chojnaki, a Distinguished Toastmaster and an executive coach, supports this idea of modulating your intonation during a conversation; in his definition of effective communication, he mentions that we should be aware of the state in which people are receiving the message. The delivery and content of the message is as important as the state in which the recipient is, while receiving the message. In communicating any particular message, a major component of the effectiveness lies in managing the state of the recipient.

---

*A good leader takes genuine pride, interest, and
happiness in seeing other people grow.*

Iu also takes genuine pride, interest, and happiness in seeing other people grow. Appreciating and applauding a fellow team member in their growth is a trait that I observed in Iu, Kalpat, and Fernandez who have displayed stellar performances in senior leadership positions at Toastmasters.

Dr John Adler, the inventor of CyberKnife, past CEO, chairman and founder of Accuray, Inc., in his interview for this book, describes a great workplace as one that fosters openness. In such a work place, great ideas are never discouraged; if they cannot be realised immediately due to a lack of time or resources, they are incorporated later when resources can be made available. Adler describes an ideal employee as a person who is unafraid to speak his thoughts and is not restricted in expressing his/her creativity. In such an open culture, he/she would be inherently driven to be a high performer. In such a team, both good and bad ideas are appreciated and talked about openly.

A good leader allows his team members to express
their ideas openly; be it good ideas or bad.

In conclusion, I would like to say that to realise the purpose of our lives, each one of us has to think like a good leader does, in leading his teams. We need to be able to set reasonable goals and realise them. No dream will ever get realised if you do not keep moving towards it, one small goal at a time. When I asked Dr Adler how he managed to stay focused on smaller and larger goals to realise his grand vision of building a robotic radiosurgery system, he mentioned that, 'The mundane leads to the sacred. The mundane is important!' The mundane here refers to the smaller goals in clearing the pathway for the bigger goal or vision. For instance, Dr Adler mentions that if you are an inventor in the field of physics who wants to realise his invention in the medical device industry, you may have to get up to speed on fundamentals in business, FDA regulations, maintaining a quality management system, etc., even though it may not be your core competency. He talks about sticking to neurosurgery as his field of core competency. He allows for the experts in other domains in his team to meet their goals effectively by being open and transparent in goal setting and communication, in meeting those goals.

If we can take goal setting to the next level, I would like to make the following statement: <u>In finding our inner calling and realizing it, we should not only be adept in setting and managing our goals, but also in invoking that entrepreneur in us.</u> Most entrepreneurs have to be able to relate to all phases of the product life cycle, from inventing the product to launching it in the market, and selling it to the right audience. Likewise, it is important to know how to market and sell your creation, which is again a small step in self-realization, in order to sustain yourself as part of a profitable business model. I think setting goals and meeting them is the most critical part in self-realization. In being entrepreneurial in our approach to goal setting, we will see fruitful expression of our creative endeavors.

- End Chapter –

Chapter 9: Life Makes Sense Through a Creative Lens

-Chapter begins–

Image Courtesy: Gow927 www.dreamstime.com

Have you felt that some things in life do not make sense to you? For instance, think of a situation where you are diligently working towards something you want and then out of nowhere, some unforeseen circumstances derail all your hard work? The emotional and financial efforts seem to go to waste. What if your loved ones walk out on you when you really need them the most? Sounds unbearable, but we all go through these situations in life, and our struggles make us stronger and wiser.

I feel that when life does not make sense in a given framework, changing the framework through which you look at your life helps reinforce our personal power. I remember that when I began to look at life as art, it began to make more sense to me. I could deconstruct its layers or levels: on one level was the interplay between masculine and feminine energies as represented by the Hindu archetypes Shiva and Shakti, or the Chinese yang and yin; and on another level was an expression of unspoken, yet powerful, laws of the universe, i.e., laws of cause and effect, action and reaction, law of attraction and rhythm, and of Karmic cycles, that govern us. Such analogies calm the restless mind by allowing us to look at life through many different lenses, in a different light, so to speak. Such a shift in perspective helps us to **be resilient or bounce back on our feet from failures very creatively**. I included this chapter to help my readers feel that there is a sense of art to life; a dimension where intuition comes alive.

This chapter revolves around a few of my blog entries on the topic of *Life as Art*, and focuses on understanding the principles of energy flow and energy states in life. I believe that one can approach life through an artistic process. From inception of the concept to the completion of the project, an artist must make decisions on what the message of the concept is, and how it can be conveyed through medium, composition, colour, and design. Following an inner calling and realizing the higher purpose of your life, is similar to the path an artist takes. You look at all your choices and then choose the one that appeals the most to your true nature, just like an artist sorts out issues of medium, composition, colour and design, to realise his vision and perfect his craft.

The process of self-realization can be as enjoyable as art! Let us look at polar opposites as analogies for the colours of life, e.g., the art of being quiet versus the art of expressing ideas; the art of talking versus the art of listening; the dynamics of being passive versus the dynamics of being proactive in approaching life situations; the karmic cycle of giving followed by receiving; the structure of life versus the chaos of life; being creative versus being conventional in expressing your ideas; being a risk-taker versus being cautious, etc. All of these aspects make the process of living an art in itself. When you treat life like art, failures and disappointments appear to be a result of choices made in pursuing your calling. Failures start appearing as a combination of decisions in life, and there will be much less regret applied to failures. In treating life as art, life will appear more as a process of blending decisions with actions and outcomes of actions. Life will become a process of creating art, as you pursue your inner calling.

To better realise life as art means to be able to manage the contrast in life with a certain degree of finesse. Just like creating a painting requires you to manage the texture of your canvas, and requires you to choose various hues and colours to enable the art work to meet your vision, the choices and decisions you make in your life allows for your life to evolve as art in helping you follow your vision and inner calling. These choices indeed determine your path of choice to self-realization. For example, if you are an unconventional thinker, your life would be abstract art not adhering to many norms of status quo in art. However, if you are conservative and conventional in your approach to life, your life may be compared to legacy art.

In my blog, I offer a few ways of looking at life creatively. I describe my own experiences of tapping into my creative energy. Looking at life as a constantly evolving process has given me emotional strength to recreate myself effectively and bounce back from setbacks and failures. The greatest benefit of creativity is that, it has the potential to pull a person out of negative emotional states. Negative thinking is a tremendous drain on human potential. Creative ways of looking at life's problems not only helps re-energise us, but also provides us with an opportunity to explore life differently than the way we did in the past, and allows for more positive outcomes. Let us look at one of the ways of looking at life creatively. In the blog below, I discuss the masculine and feminine energies present in all of us that provide us with a perspective of life.

BLOG POST NAME: THE DANCE OF EXISTENCE

Art and Illustration: Nivedita Gouda

My heart says I should write about the dynamics of focused (male) and creative (female) energies and their beautiful interplay, which causes evolution of life itself!

What do I want from my life and what does life want from me? These are two very important questions we need to ask ourselves.

When we ask ourselves what we want out of life, it taps into our ambition, a need to satisfy desires, the need to acquire and embellish the *self*, a need to satiate the senses, to dream, to be innovative, and to strive. These are examples of an aggressive or *masculine* gesture towards life.

In asking, 'What does life want from me?' there is a submission, there is an expansion, a humility to perceive, the *self* vanishes in perceiving life. The self exists in the present, observing, absorbing, feeling, and simply living to serve others. There is timeless beauty in this attitude and expression. It is a flexible, nurturing or a *feminine* gesture towards life.

A few more analogies to masculine and feminine expressions in life: a rock is solid and can resist forces of nature like wind, water and heat quite well; however, it can be transformed by a strong powerful blow, or a slow, or a gradual movement of air and water over time, that causes it to change its shape. The rock and powerful blow in this case is considered masculine. A rock cannot withstand the subtle power of air and water for too long and eventually, it is turned into grains of sand by these feminine elements. This is a common notion of truth and existence.

The feminine (creative and flexible) energy yields, and the masculine (logical and demanding) demands. These energies are always in interplay in various forms in life, and life is a continual dance of existence. This interplay is replicated in everything we know: from subatomic particles to the great expanse of our universe. If this cosmic dance of existence ceases, then life also ceases to evolve. This dance of energies is meant to be a magical way of life, and you'll find that eventually, what you want from life and what life wants from you will become one and the same. In that context, the masculine and feminine energies that represent various logical and creative aspects of life, merge; and maturity allows us to accept and embrace life with grace.

Each one of us carries masculine and feminine energies in various proportions: some call it the yin-yang; some call it the Shiva-Shakti. Its inclusive quality makes room for people of all personality types. Spend a couple of minutes assessing your masculine and feminine energies in quiet solitude. When you master the expression of masculine and feminine energies, for instance, *commanding versus submitting, giving versus receiving, talking versus listening, being quiet versus expressing thoughts, being simple versus being glamorous, being judgmental versus being non-judgmental, holding on to power versus sharing it,* you will then slowly start exploring various dimensions of life, within you. In this process of mastering the masculine and feminine expressions within yourself, you can develop a sense of overall awareness, which is nothing but an enhanced emotional and intelligence quotient. You will become a better team player as you will start gelling effortlessly with any kind of team or work environment and eventually become a high performer. You will achieve *a state of vertical living* as you realise the purpose of your life.

The next blog is about ensuring continued progress in all areas in life through the perspective of energy. I use the word 'energy' because energy forms the basis of life. When the flow of energy stops, life ceases. Our physical and psychological well-being requires various forms of energy to be sustained, and to be in circulation. For example: circulation of breath, circulation of blood, circulation of ideas, etc., are all a representation of life, of progress and of well-being in an individual, and eventually, a society as a whole. In the current article, I go further into the interplay of giving and receiving energy, and the many forms that it can take. It is a rather abstract perspective on life, but it can also be a quite powerful one, if one is to look at as being fundamental to our harmony with life itself.

GIVING AND RECEIVING: THE FLOW OF LIFE

Art and Illustration: Spoorthy Murali

The concept of giving is one that is very dear to me and countless others, and thus it carries the weight of emotion. **Giving** is most commonly perceived as sharing something that is a part of our persona, or a part of our life, or a part of our energy.

Giving is embedded in **receiving.** Anything that is alive is part of the process of **giving and receiving.** No giving is complete without receiving, and vice versa. Let me explain how and why.

Anything that is a part of our life is a product of our environment around us, positive or negative, and it has received our attention and energy.

If we continuously share our wealth, without earning or replenishing it (a form of **receiving** wealth from the source), our wealth will diminish. If people who share knowledge, for example teachers, do not engage in a constant process of learning, they will stagnate, and their future ability to share knowledge will be reduced.

Have you noticed that people who share wealth, are always looking for new avenues of giving and sharing, because their wealth never decreases? I call them social magnates. They are always attracting people, hosting parties, making new connections, and are in the habit of staying in touch with their family and friends regularly. People who are actively involved in many aspects of life, e.g., sports, art, charity (energies circulating actively in **giving** and receiving), always seem to have room for more and they get better at welcoming newer challenges in life. This implies that to be in a position of **giving,** there has to be a constant circulation of energy in **receiving** as well. For example, when I was looking for jobs during recession, I focused on my job search almost all the waking hours of the day. It was not a very effective approach. When I switched gears and started mingling with networking groups, developed a fitness routine, took classes in technical writing, and met new people, my whole perspective on life changed. I started becoming more productive with every new experience that I faced as part of my effort to circulate my physical and mental energies, and stay happy and fulfilled.

During my job hunt, I looked up to such social magnates as my role models. I wondered: what do these people receive by giving away their time and energy to charity, art, sports, etc.? I figured by way of my interviews with them, that they **receive** energy by learning to explore newer dimensions of life, by interacting with different people, and taking on newer experiences. They become more perceptive and intelligent about the dynamics of life when they **give** their time and effort to challenging tasks. However, I was aware of the time when they did not feel their best. I wondered why and now I know the answer to what these busy social butterflies could do better to enhance their personal power. When I interviewed a few such candidates from the corporate world and from the music world for my book, I realised they were skipping their fitness routines often and eating unhealthy to overcome stress and lack of sleep. In our lengthy in-person discussions, we mutually agreed that they would be able to better receive from life, in return, for all the energy they are giving away in terms of their hard work and efforts, when they spend some quiet time or pursuing their favorite hobby and re-charging and re-connecting with themselves by realizing meditative states, by way of their favorite pastime, or by going to a retreat or spending a few moments in solitude and self-reflection, every so often.

Now another question is, do all people *give* in the same way? The answer is obviously a 'no' because of the variety in the nature of people.

People who are unwilling to *give* in kind may instead choose to give to others their time or the wisdom of their words. People who are frugal with words and their wealth may instead choose to pour their tremendous energy reserves into their work. We can **receive** from such people through their actions and benefit from their accomplishments in society. A busy and wealthy entrepreneur who may not have much time to give to others may instead choose to *give* by creating jobs for people and building products that benefit society.

This cycle of giving and receiving in terms of knowledge, skills, wealth, and love should be kept in circulation, to keep these aspects of your life alive. For example, when you stop expressing love to someone by way of actions or words, it will affect the health of the relationship, and soon the relationship will die. This concept of flow is important even in a corporate environment, and a clear example of the application of this concept is the use of *Agile methodology* for better project management. The *Agile methodology* believes in establishing a constant flow of communication and feedback across development, engineering, and product marketing teams, in an effort to fail fast and build products that are aligned to customer satisfaction and customer need. Agile methodology of project management was conceived to keep ideas flowing constantly and help in evolving the right product.

Let us look at two kinds of people, to better understand the concept of giving and receiving: people in power, who do not believe in sharing their wealth or love; and people in power who believe in sharing their prosperity and empowering others. In the novel A *Christmas Carol*, there is a character called Ebenezer Scrooge. He is a wealthy and cold-hearted miser who despises Christmas because he has to give gifts and donate money to the needy on Christmas Eve. How can someone like him be encouraged to give, and what can we receive from him or her? The answer is nothing, unless people like him are willing to change and accept the natural flow and cycle of giving and receiving. In the story, he is visited by three ghosts who enlighten him by taking him back to instances in his life when he had chosen money over the exchange of love with his friends and family. In the end, he repents all those instances where he walked away from his loved ones, and understands that life could be much more meaningful if he could share his treasures as he earned them. He is allowed to witness the generosity of people who do not have much wealth but have a heart filled with compassion and a hand that reaches out to the helpless and needy. However, this is an example from a novel.

Let us look at a few examples from real life. Bill Gates is the richest man in the world today. He has donated several billions of dollars in charity. So has Warren Buffett, another American business magnate, investor, philanthropist, and the third richest man in the world. He is known to have pledged to give away 99 per cent of his wealth in charity. Buffett and Gates are the world's most generous philanthropists and proponents of *giving*. They started *The Giving Pledge* in 2010, encouraging the world's wealthiest people to commit to donating at least half of their fortunes to philanthropy, during their lifetime or after they die [90]. Some of the richest people in the world understand the power of exchange and flow of energy. It is a concept that requires serious thought by every one of us.

Let us learn to keep our energies *alive* and flowing by *giving and receiving* in good will and love. Let us move toward the flow of life every single moment, by opening up our channels of *receiving and giving*.

In the next blog post, I would like to illustrate how you can expand the realms of your thinking by looking at life as art.

BLOG POST NAME: ART

Art and Illustration: Ashwini Bharadwaj

My heart says: I want to write to express the state an artist is in when he/she creates art, the state in which he/she conceives creative ideas.

I am moving my arms and legs very rhythmically to the music in my CD player. This is my usual work out session at the gym; I feel like dancing to the music I am listening to. This is my favorite piece by A. R. Rahman. I love the consistent, melodious beats in the song. They make me want to jive. I am working out on the stepper, but I feel like dancing instead. I move to the dance studio in the gym and experiment with dancing.

I feel the music is moving through me like a wave and showing in me as a dance. Dance happens to me. I feel no inhibitions and I feel rejuvenated with my choreography. My inner feeling transforms itself into art. I am expressing various emotions and postures as I dance to the words in the song; I feel like I am expanding in my existence. I am not trapped in my body anymore, and I feel like I have moved outside my identity and ego. This feeling of losing myself is very energizing and I am receiving a rush of creative ideas to write about. This state is exhilarating, and I call it a state of *flow [114]*.

What is it about art that intrigues us and connects us deeply to joy? If you have attended a live symphony or a concert by a famous musician, then you will understand the electric nature of such an experience. The energy, the passion, the vibrations of an artist's creativity, are truly infectious. Art fills our whole being with a sense of harmony and makes us feel renewed.

A dancer or a musician expresses and emotes feelings like love, passion, peace, power, and anxiety through their dance or music. In doing so, they are expanding not only their horizons but also the horizons of their audience in perceiving newer dimensions of life. I experienced such an awakening when I witnessed a dance drama by the renowned Indian artist Mallika Sarabhai. The performance revolved around the story of Ahalya from the Ramayana, one of the great Indian epics. Sarabhai was playing the role of Ahalya, a woman who is cursed to turn into a rock for her infidelity. In the solo act, Sarabhai's Ahalya emoted the injustice of a society that punished a woman for her infidelity, but let the man who was equally guilty go unpunished.

I had grown up listening to this story and watching it enacted in many plays on various occasions. However, Sarabhai's portrayal of the characters was simply unique. She took me into the heart of the woman who was accused, and also the passer-by who simply laughs at the injustice done to the woman. Sarabhai's entire persona was very powerful when she expressed the emotion of the injustice done to Ahalya. This was a dimension of the play I had never experienced before. Sarabhai had raised a very important question about the social structure that is partial to men and the powerful economic strata in society. To me, Sarabhai is the epitome of a voice that can bring about social change by way of art. Her performance invoked an awakening in the audience who applauded and acknowledged the angst of the cursed woman.

Artists like Sarabhai use their imagination to help us explore our hidden intelligence and abilities to sense subtle emotions. We need more artists and creative people in our society. A society that appreciates art and promotes it is a haven for love, peace, harmony, and creativity. Let us create more art within us and around us. Art in its different forms is life lived newly every time. A complete submission to any form of art is a momentary catharsis of the ego. The momentary catharsis of the ego is so sublimely and infinitely powerful! Imagine a life led in the state of a dissolved state of ego, in the service of people. It will be a deeply blissful life indeed!

What if humans were viewed as physical, physiological, and spiritual processes in flux? Imagine our universe as evolving in a process. If we were to imagine ourselves as a part of our surrounding universe, we would be the smaller components or sub-processes of a much bigger process called as the universe, in this context. If we look at ourselves this way, we can treat every passing moment as new, because it is a phase in the evolving process of the universe. Life becomes rid of the burden of the past and the pressures of the future, and it becomes very easy to exist in a vertical state of here and now. As processes evolve, so do we.

This next blog entry helps us understand how to maximise our potential in the current moment by accepting ourselves as a process in flux, a flux that is inherent to the nature of life.

BLOG POST NAME: FLUX

Image courtesy: Mausam Hazarika

My heart says: I should write to know if there is a way to live life afresh every single moment. If there is a way, then I should bring this approach to life, by finding examples in nature, to convince myself and others to live life afresh, in-the-moment.

Today, I am a particle of a rock on a cliff and I feel rock sturdy. As the waves of the ocean keep splashing on me, I break down, bit by bit and become a part of the ocean and flow into it; I become part of a fluid particle and I have movement.

As a particle, I vaporise with a droplet, I feel like a part of the cloud, so high and above the world. I feel like I am the cloud itself and everything below me looks small and insignificant

Because I have been so many things in the past, I really don't know who I am. My life has been in a flux, however small it may be. How childish of me to believe that I actually am any one of the solid, vapor, or fluid forms from the past. I have only been evolving from the past. All I am, is what I feel here and now . . .

Such is the true nature of life: we are changing every moment, and if we cling to our past, the power in our current actions is affected. We can only be very humble in assuming the knowledge from the past, in the present situation. There is death and rebirth of reality, in every passing moment. By looking at life this way, we develop tremendous resilience and in regenerating ourselves, physiologically and psychologically, from setbacks.

Human beings adapt faster physically to a given set of surroundings than psychologically, as per ideas shared by spiritual teachers Eckhert Toelle and Osho in their philosophy of ego. Psychological adaptation involves a lot of reprogramming of older concepts, embracing the present completely, loving unconditionally, caring deeply, and most importantly, forgiving and forgetting. It is harder for humans to evolve and adapt psychologically when they are set in mental and emotional pathways ('ego' patterns).

To be young is to live and embrace the present moment completely. To be old is to cling to ideas and thoughts of the past. It is not wrong to be connected to the past, but it is a sign of aging when people refuse to move out of the past and embrace the present moment in its totality. Carrying mental conditionings like hatred and resentment can only blind us from the way life is evolving in the current moment. Great leaders like Mahatma Gandhi, Nelson Mandela, and Benjamin Franklin understood this truth very well. In fact, they relied on deconditioning their ideas about the very people who threatened their survival. All these freedom fighters learned to collaborate and negotiate terms with the colonial forces that were out to destroy them. They did so by letting go of the bitter experiences they had with colonial forces. In philosophical terms, these great leaders understood the transient nature of life and tried to be flexible in their mental conditionings and collaborate with the very people who tried to harm them. Such thinking comes from great mental resilience, and that is why Gandhi, Franklin, and Mandela were successful in becoming game changers in history.

Even the **values** of scientific constants and parameters **are** subject to change with **time. For example,** the axis and rotation of the earth, **and** the value of acceleration due to gravity, are scientific constants **that are** subject to change due to external factors. They are called constants and retain a constant value under specific sets of conditions only, and their value is subject to change. The only certainty about life is that it changes all the time, and it is imperative for us to embrace this change if we are to adapt and grow with life.

We have to understand this aspect about ourselves: human beings are alive and adaptable; we are emotionally and psychologically growing and flexible as living beings. We are capable of changing ourselves by getting rid of a fixed mindset and opening ourselves up to newer ideas and newer thinking. This is also the core idea of **vertical living** as a lifestyle. When we embrace creative perspectives to life, we are better able to view problems due to change of framework. Evolving with changes in life becomes much easier. Such an ability to look at life with many different and creative perspectives is the essence of this chapter. I hope you can benefit from your own creative perspectives in life, to build strength and supersede yourself **by entering** into realms of supra-human **abilities, surpass** your fixed mindset and **aim** towards the next frontier of **thinking. Call it** moonshot thinking, if you will!

- *End Chapter* –

Chapter 10: A Future to Think About

'Humanity is now entering a period of radical
transformation in which technology has the potential
to significantly raise the basic standards of living for
every man, woman and child on the planet.'
-Peter Diamandis
Author of Abundance: The Future is Better Than You Think

-Chapter begins–

Although this is a concluding chapter, it is a great starting point for embracing the life style *vertical living that I have introduced by way of this book*; it is a great step in awakening your senses and perception of life. Such a lifestyle has been adopted by game changers and overachievers throughout history. Individuals who wish to awaken their inner potential and find maximum expression for their creative instincts will benefit from this lifestyle.

What does it mean to find maximum expression of your creative instincts? Did you know that some of the greatest sci-fi novels were meant to be scientific research publications? But due to the inability of the academia to embrace forward-thinking ideas, they remained as fictional novels. Ironically, these novels have now become guidelines for game changers who are envisioning inter-planetary space travel and the harnessing of clean energy and magnetic fields for transportation and communication. These great thinkers found avenues to express their ideas creatively around the existing rigid structure of academia. I quote this example specifically to encourage my readers to persist in their creative undertakings and to not give up at the first sight of resistance. There will always be an avenue open to help you showcase your talent and creation. All you need to do is persist in your approach to finding those opportunities.

Creative thinkers, have time and again, faced resistance because the society they live in are unable to relate to them. However, creative thinkers who have found fruitful end to their efforts seem to have retained a growth mindset to allow for their talents to find realization. Both Steve Jobs and Elon Musk have faced many trials in their career trying to realise a vision, which seemed highly unpractical to the common eye. However, these game changers retained a mindset of constant learning and growth that allowed them to make their visions a reality. Such a mindset of growth can be better understood by using the concepts referred to in the following paragraph, in addition to the ideas of free thinking expressed in Chapter 4 - *Free To Realise Your Dream*.

At this point, I would like to introduce *the idea of a growth mindset* by Carol Dweck, Lewis and Virginia Eaton Professor of Psychology at Stanford University, on how to develop and raise your intrinsic human potential with an optimistic and growth mindset. In her book *Mindset: The New Psychology of Success*, she compares people with fixed and growth mindsets. She brings out how, in a fixed mindset, people believe their basic qualities—like their intelligence or talent—are simply fixed, and their time is wasted in quantifying their intelligence or talent versus developing them. People with fixed mindset are said to believe in genuine talent versus effort. In my book, I call this mindset as being governed by the 'ego' in Chapter 4. In a growth mindset, however, people believe that their most basic abilities can be developed through dedication and hard work, and a love of learning and a resilience that is essential for great accomplishment. I call this as an ability to dissolve the ego in Chapter 4.

Virtually, all great visionaries and thinkers of our time have displayed a growth mindset indeed. Take Leonardo da Vinci or Benjamin Franklin for instance. They were known for their insatiable appetite for experimenting with new ideas in art, physics, and many domains constantly crossing over between disconnected domains like science and art, and gaining creative perspectives. We need a growth mindset to boost our creative skills in maximizing our individual talents, as we realise our true inner calling. Such a growth mindset that has been adopted by game changers in history, is an essential trait of level 5 in vertical living as well.

What can be done differently or better, to facilitate and encourage creative, thinkers, and grand visionaries?

Albert Einstein's revolutionary general theory of relativity faced a lot of resistance and was overlooked by the Nobel Prize committee; Nikola Tesla and his best inventions on Wi-Fi and laser technology never went into production and commoditization. Such a treatment of the greatest thinkers in science and many other disciplines, have slowed down the collective progress of human race by several centuries.

Academia and corporate world, today, need to rework their traditional and slow approach to forward-thinking ideas. They need to adapt to the resources which a fast paced digital world has endowed us, so they can better facilitate and encourage moonshot thinking. For instance, Google has brought about such an unprecedented change in culture of creativity and innovation. The unprecedented work culture at Google served as a model for several companies across the globe in creating a work culture where creativity and play are encouraged alongside innovation. We need such an approach to be embraced by academia to advance research and development, and support emerging technologies.

We are in the age of exponential technologies. It is imperative to move from linear thinking towards exponential thinking. Let me explain how and why with the following examples.

In their book, *Bold: How to Go Big, Create Wealth and Impact the World*, Steven Kotler and Peter H. Diamandis mention that grand visionary businessmen such as Jeff Bezos, Larry Page, Elon Musk and Richard Branson, display certain tenets of exponential entrepreneurship. The important tenets of exponential entrepreneurship, which the book upholds, are an adoption of exponentially growing technology, utilizing advanced and awakened mental states (such as flow [114] states), tapping into 'crowd-power tools' or crowd sourcing tools that allow companies to organise and communicate with their target audiences effectively. Being able to think big and getting into advanced mental states are inherent traits of existing in states of vertical living.

Vivek Wadhwa, a Fellow at the Arthur & Toni Rembe Rock Center for Corporate Governance, Stanford University, and Faculty and Advisor at Singularity University, explained this in a presentation at the World of Business Ideas. He talks about the difference between 30 linear steps and 30 exponential steps. If 30 linear steps measure 30 meters, 30 exponential steps would measure 1 billion meters or 26 times around the earth! This, he calls is the analogy for a leap from linear to exponential thinking. He talks about the exponential evolution of computing power that can provide the combined networked intelligence of human beings for less than $1000 by 2050. Imagine the power that technology is offering us in terms of personal growth and development! Wadhwa, in his talk on entrepreneurship at INK India, emphasises the idea of how humanity needs a shift in thinking from linear to exponential, to keep up with exponential trends in advancements in computing power.

We are looking at a breed of creative individuals who will be well-versed in technology and heading towards individual enterprise, with an abundance of resources at their desktops and palm tops! I refer to this as the entrepreneurial approach to self-realization, which is an approach to adopting vertical living as a lifestyle.

For instance, the IBM Watson computer has provided the ability to make fairly accurate collective assessment about the progression of cancer, and also make quick and accurate clinical decisions to cure many such diseases. What would require in a linear world, a team of doctors and many days of number crunching and deliberation, would require in future only a few minutes due to the unmatched computing power of IBM Watson. Watson will soon be widely used by many more corporations in IT and healthcare. There is a huge wave of innovation waiting to change our entire perspective of health care, as it is today—slow and linear! Human genome will soon be available for free and personalised genomic medicine, which will take over traditional and invasive methods of treatment.

The reason I talk about these examples is that, today, more than ever, <u>we need exponential thinkers, people who can weave grand visions and help landscape a safe and progressive future.</u> As we try to keep up with technology, it is more essential than any other time in human history to develop a deep sense of self, by being in touch with human nature, understanding one's true calling, and feeling compassion for a fellow being.

When I started writing the book, I was seeking answers to the following questions:

1. What makes people dare to dream big and realise those dreams?
2. How can we achieve big goals and yet maintain a healthy and balanced approach to life?
3. What does it take to be creative? Do we realise that creativity by leveraging our awakened human potential in high performing teams?
4. Is there a lifestyle that delivers all of the above results consistently?

Countless realizations came to light during the course of this book. I will have to write another book to showcase even a fraction of these findings! I will try to incorporate the information that I have discovered in an upcoming series of talks and blogs on my website, YouTube, and podcasts. However, here are *key observations* that came to me as I wrote this book:

a. Human potential is the ability to find health, happiness, wealth, and fulfillment in life. It is maximised when you are connected to your inner calling. This is when life starts making sense to you; you feel positively charged and gain mastery over the trade or occupation that suits you best. All the interviews and biographies which contributed to the book, upheld this central theme on finding your true calling to best express your talent and abilities.

b. You can raise your intrinsic human potential, rewire your brain with newer pathways, and maximise your human potential. Human DNA is evolving constantly and you can help express positive changes in your DNA with persistent efforts [1002, 1003]. In order to rewire specific pathways in the brain, you must have powerful motivating factors that will drive you to practice mastering these pathways and build stamina. Such motivation is unleashed in finding your true inner calling, or following a career or lifestyle that enhances your creative thinking and ability to actualise your human potential.

Maximizing your human potential is a continuous, iterative, and incremental process. I say this because there is an entire field dedicated to the study of how genes evolve throughout a lifetime and can even be programmed to cure cancer [1005]. In other words, you can program your body to raise its innate human potential and develop new traits, consciously.

c. You can leverage your inner calling and intuition for building teams and setting goals. You can leverage your inner calling to set reasonable, incremental goals. You can create high performing teams with whom you can match your emotional and intellectual frequencies, intuitively. Let us say you are working on acquiring skills in an area that resonates with your purpose or calling in life. Do this every day, and master the specific skills by working on them regularly and intensely. Leverage your goal setting skills and intuitive abilities adequately in helping you prioritise your goals, and resolving constraints that get in the way of realizing them.

d. You can use an entrepreneurial approach to self-realization. When it comes to using an *entrepreneurial approach to developing human potential*, our inner potential should be considered as our product. It has gone through a lot of molding, training, and experiences and is rich in its ability to sustain creativity. Now it is up to us to present our inner potential to the outside world, and showcase our inner talents in a marketplace where they can be of service. Great inventors and creators made use of the circumstances in their lives and were able to think like entrepreneurs in expressing and marketing their creative ideas, thereby being of service to humanity.

Tina Seelig, Executive Director of the Stanford Technology Ventures Program, mentions in her book, *Insight Out*, that most children have the innate abilities to be entrepreneurs. She encourages parents to promote entrepreneurial thinking in children by fostering open-ended imagination and by allowing children to ask endless questions and find solutions to problems by themselves. I believe it is possible to retain childlike thinking all through our lives. Most inventors and game changers in history kept that inner child alive. They remained curious about life and did not shy away from questioning the nature of things by first principles. Children are also free of biases and are open-minded toward problems and solutions; this is exactly the kind of thinking required for problem solving in any entrepreneurial venture. **So let us try our best, in all our capacities, to leverage that child in us.** In doing so, let us polish our entrepreneurial skills and realise the purpose of our lives.

In the next section, I will share with you my ideas of a future, as I see it coming. These ideas are a culmination of many moments of realization that dawned on me, through the journey of writing this book.

A Future to Think About

➤ <u>Following inner calling or vertical living will become a way of life</u>

Following the calling of the heart will be the norm. Just like luminaries of the past and present—Napoleon Bonaparte, Johann Wolfgang von Goethe, Albert Einstein, Steve Jobs, Sundar Pichai—followed the calling of their hearts in choosing a career, more people in the future will listen to their inner calling when making career choices.

Shravan Kumaran,14, and Sanjay Kumaran,12, are the president and the CEO of Go Dimensions, an application development company that the brothers founded two years ago from their home in Chennai, India. They are the youngest entrepreneurs in India today [1006]. Such young entrepreneurs will become a norm across the globe. They are self-educated and are able to sense opportunities because they have been encouraged to take risks and pursue their creative thinking.

➢ <u>Children will cultivate entrepreneurial skills as part of early schooling.</u>

The future generation will spawn entrepreneurs at a much younger age than in any other generation until now. Formal schooling may blend with vocational training. The next generations will be trained very early on to absorb varied bodies of knowledge related to future professional requirements. These young people will pick up a variety of skills along the way as they start translating their calling into viable products and services.

➢ <u>The education system will be based on advanced tools that are centered on experience and experimentation.</u>

The current system of education, which is mostly information-centric and fact-centered, will slowly transform itself into a system based on self-education by problem-solving, experimentation, and freethinking. Alan Kay, a visionary computer scientist, one of the earliest pioneers of object-oriented programming, personal computing, and graphical user interfaces, talks about the idea behind the next generation of teaching methodologies using effective experiences and user interfaces.

Kay explores the way concepts are taught to children and adults, and calls for radical approaches in perceiving concepts in science. Kay continues to question the deeper purpose of computing, struggling to create the machine that will not only recapitulate patterns in the world as we know it, but also teach both children and adults to think, to see what otherwise is beyond them.

We will be seeing many more such game changers in the domain of education who will provide learning by way of experiences that culminate into formulae or principles, instead of the current method of learning only by theories, equations, and prose.

Learning will be made accessible through virtual classrooms. Networking platforms like Uber, Facebook, and Khan Academy will emerge in the education space and make resources and infrastructure for teaching and education accessible anytime, anywhere.

People who question the norms of the society in first principles, <u>using Socratic thinking (and there are bound to be many)</u> will revolutionise art and science, and even humanity itself. An urge to search for fundamental truths, be it in pure sciences or art or language, will emerge. The new era of knowledge workers will spawn many polyglots and polymaths. In the future, qualifications of a person will not drive the pursuit of truths or a career, instead the pursuits of truths will determine what qualifications a person will need. Else, why would school dropouts and corporate misfits, landscape the face of technology and society as it is today?

➤ <u>Founder dating is already rampant. It will set the stage for a culture of entrepreneurship</u> that will require freethinking and problem solving as prime skills.

➤ <u>We will truly arrive at a state of global thinking and global citizenship.</u>

Traveling as part of seeking newer experiences will become commonplace; living in many countries, with exposure to cultural diversity in food and lifestyle, will become the norm. I have definitely seen these trends emerging among my peers, family, and friends in recent years.

➤ <u>People will learn to make their skill an art</u>

Dr Devi Shetty is a famous cardiac surgeon, philanthropist and a game changer in the field of an affordable health care initiative in India; his initiative is slowly spreading across the world and has caught the attention of the governing bodies in many nations worldwide. Dr Shetty recalls being an average student at school, but he knew his calling all along and did not like being pushed into doing something he did not love. He talks about surgery not just in terms of technique; he calls heart surgery an art! And I agree with him. If you have not mastered something until you feel it is an art, you have probably not experienced your skill in the higher dimensions of vertical living. You still have the room and scope to heighten your senses and polish the creative aspects of your skill or trade. Discovering how to heighten your skills to the level of an art is the next frontier of education. This approach can be mapped back to level 5 in vertical living.

➢ <u>Touching lives as part of your profession will become a way of life.</u>

Our future generations will understand and connect with a higher purpose in their lives much better than we did. Many young people I know are quitting their day jobs to work for social causes, and choosing a lifestyle that is not centered on money. The power of the Information Age will allow the future generations to deeply examine the failures in social infrastructure and go on to create smarter alternatives.

➢ <u>People will use painful experiences in their life as vehicles of social change.</u>

T. N. Seetharam is a renowned media person in India and a game changer who strives to give the common man a voice against corruption. He is one of the most powerful voices in the medium of art and cinema in the South Indian television industry, and has a huge fan base. He has given confidence to the common man in voicing concerns about corruption in governing bodies. His programs have been applauded by eminent people in all walks of life and have garnered him the highest TRP ratings for his TV shows. He has been unafraid to voice criticism about legislation and politics.

When I asked him what gave him such courage and determination to create this game-changing TV and media work, he said that this courage was instigated by pain early on in his life when he lost his father and his beloved sister to poverty and immutable circumstances. He credited his success to his apprenticeship under great moviemakers, journalists, and playwrights. He said that after so many years in serving the public and seeing the highs and lows of success and its fickleness, he has reached a stage of selflessness in his approach. He derives pleasure in serving the public and in doing his best, but he is detached about the results of his efforts. Such an attitude of selflessness is a takeaway for future generations.

You can direct your painful experiences, positively, to effect social change and improve the ecosystem around you. With the freedom and power offered by the social media, you can transform painful experiences in your life into vehicles of positive social change. It is going to get much easier to use digital media and networking platforms to target a much larger audience and awaken them to reality. Our current generation is much more aware and conscious of the effects of genetically modified food, about embracing clean energy technology, about issues related to basic human rights, and such awareness will spread faster with cost-effective infrastructure, helping connect people across geographical and cultural diversities.

> ➢ <u>People will enhance their personal power and creative potential by engaging more often in activities that they love.</u>

I had the pleasure and opportunity of interviewing **Jayalaxmi Patil,** a renowned TV actress, theater professional, poet, writer, and activist. She has authored many books in Kannada, a regional language in South India, and initiated an independent support group to fight the abuse of women. She has portrayed very complex and dark characters in her career as a prominent actress in many popular television series on social issues, mainly corruption and rape. She talks about entering a state of non-thinking when acting her toughest roles.

Such successful and powerful performances are preceded by a bout of rapid heartbeats, after which she is ruled by the character and completely forgets what happens during the performance on stage. She is highly intuitive about the way a performance should go, and is known to be so involved with the character that she sometimes sounds like her character even when she returns home to her family.

I have experienced such states of intuition and high energy myself, followed by rapid heartbeats and memory blackouts during a performance. I believe it is due to a state of the body and mind where I transcend my intrinsic human potential. I have experienced this during solo dance performances, and during talks on topics that I care about deeply. I have been known to deliver many impromptu insights I never knew existed in my capacity or memory.

I believe that when you engage in tasks that you love, and give yourself completely—mind, body, and soul—to that cause, you will enter realms of being where you will raise your intrinsic human potential. This is a domain of great human will, of human submission to a higher cause, and a state where the stream of individual human potential is powerfully focused on one act.

Future generations will engage in such forms of art, sport, and spiritual experiences more often than we did. This is a visible and emerging trend, and will help channel human potential away from crime and negative thinking.

> ➤ <u>Art will emerge as a medium of social change.</u>

Such inner states in maximizing human potential have made artists extremely courageous and effective in their ability to lead political parties, influence government policies, etc. **Jayalaxmi Patil** mentions that the power that energises her during her performances as an artist, coupled with the compassion she feels for the characters whose roles she plays, has caused her to lead many initiatives in real life to fight political corruption and crimes against women.

> ➤ <u>More people will break free of corrupt governing bodies and be the change they wish to see in the world.</u>

Patil proudly mentioned to me that she is part of a breed of thinkers who have been able to influence the society by working outside the corrupt frameworks of a governing body. This is another takeaway for future generations. If you are not able to tolerate the negativity and oppression of a corrupt governing body at any level, you should find freedom by looking past that framework; seek support from networking groups outside your current social structure, and lead the way in effecting social change.

Dr Adler, the inventor of CyberKnife, started his medical publishing company Cureus.com to provide a platform to publish articles that would otherwise get lost in the traditional and slow process-oriented world of medical publishing. Cureus.com aims to develop better solutions to problems in healthcare through crowd sourcing and collaboration. Dr Adler is creating hope for talented and emerging medical and biotechnology professionals by providing a platform for them to speak freely through Cureus.com. He is a classic example of emerging entrepreneurs who have become the change they would like to see in the world. In the future, the public will feel accountable for bringing about social change and will stop blaming the government for inadequacies in society. The age of free information will empower the individual to become the change he or she would like to see in the world.

> ➤ <u>There will be increased awareness about food and lifestyle in general.</u>

Another change that I have been observing over the past few years is a strong sense of awareness about food among my peers and many youngsters. Many have turned into health junkies and are embracing an organic, genetically unmodified, self-cultivated, vegan diet. I see such awareness in Internet and media savvy teenagers who are extremely well informed about conserving natural resources and are volunteering to simplify their lifestyles, use fewer resources to leave a smaller ecological footprint on the planet. Do not be surprised to see a future generation that believes in such a culture of awareness, sharing, equality, and compassion toward fellow human beings by harnessing the genius of technological breakthroughs.

As I conclude this chapter, I am excited to welcome a generation of moonshot thinkers who will stand on the shoulders of eminent scientists, writers, journalists, artists, and politicians who have landscaped our world as it is today. Advancements in social media have scaled the ability to share and brainstorm ideas like never before. Such abundance in enterprise will spawn independent thinkers and game changers galore. Solving massive challenges to humanity like making clean energy affordable and sustainable, and making necessary resources available to all parts of the world, will become a purpose for our generation, and the future as well. The problems in society are massive, but the opportunities to do something about them are endless. Which opportunity draws you as part of your inner calling? What do you plan to do about it? Return to this book often for tips on maximizing your human potential through vertical living. I wish you much luck in helping to create this future filled with prosperity and good will.

- End Chapter –

Glossary

Agile methodology. A project management approach that deals with change using incremental, iterative work processes.

Alan Kay. (Born 1940) An American computer scientist and visionary who imagined the concepts of the personal computer and graphical interfaces decades before they were realised.

Albert Einstein. (1879-1955) Illustrious German-born physicist and Nobel Prize winner whose contributions to theoretical physics include the general theory of relativity, discovery of the law of the photoelectric effect, and the famous mass-energy equivalence formula to mention a few.

Alcatraz. A small island off the coast of San Francisco, California, United States protected by the National Parks Service and the site of the infamous Alcatraz federal prison that functioned from 1934-1963.

Amit Rathore. Founder and CEO of Quintype Inc., serial entrepreneur, and the author of *Clojure in Action*.

Amitabh Bachchan. (Born 1942) One of most influential actors in Indian cinema who has acted in more than 200 movies in a career spanning more than four decades.

Archimedes. A famous ancient Greek mathematician, physicist, inventor, and astronomer who lived circa 287 BC to 212 BC.

Aristotle. A renowned ancient Greek philosopher, polymath, and student of Plato who lived from 384 BC to 322 BC.

Arthur C. Clarke. (1917-2008) An internationally renowned British author, scientist, and futurist most popular for his sci-fi novel *2001: A Space Odyssey*.

Axilum Robotics. A company that developed and commercialises the first robot specifically designed for Transcranial Magnetic Stimulation.

Ayahuasca Retreat in Peru. A traditional shamanic retreat in the Amazon rainforest of Peru.

Beginner's mind. Implies having an attitude of openness and a lack of predetermined notions when learning a subject.

Bengaluru. The capital of Karnataka state in Southern India, and the center of India's high-tech industry. It is also known as the Garden City of India.

Benjamin Franklin. (1706-1790) One of the Founding Fathers of the United States and a renowned polymath, author, printer, scientist, inventor, statesman, and ambassador.

Bhakti yoga. A path to self-realization centered on love and devotion toward God. It is one of the four paths of yoga.

Bharat Chandra. A reputed Indian behavioral therapist, success coach, founder of the Institute of Human Potential and Development, Bangalore, and a sought-after speaker and trainer in human potential development.

Bill Gates. (Born 1955) An American business magnate, philanthropist, investor, computer programmer, author, and co-founder of Microsoft, the world's largest PC software company.

Bollywood. Nickname for the Indian movie or Hindi language film industry, based in Mumbai (Bombay) India.

Brahmakumari Spiritual University. A spiritual organization founded in India in the 1930s, which now has centers in over 110 countries.

Brian Weiss. (Born 1944) An American psychiatrist, hypnotherapist, author, and reincarnation researcher who specialises in past-life regression.

Bruce Lee. (1940-1973) An internationally acclaimed martial artist and actor, creator of the Jeet Kune Do martial arts technique, and author of *Chinese Gung-Fu: The Philosophical Art of Self-Defense*.

Buddhist. A follower of the teachings of Gautama Buddha who believes that suffering is inherent in life, and that one can be liberated from the cycle of suffering and rebirth by attaining enlightenment through right conduct and wisdom.

Carl Jung. (1875-1961) A Swiss psychologist and psychiatrist who founded Analytic Psychology. Jung proposed and developed the concepts of personality archetypes and the collective unconscious.

Chanakya. An Indian statesman and philosopher, who lived from 350 BC to 275 BC; pioneer of the field of political science and economics in India, and author of Indian political treatise *Arthashastra*.

Claudius Ptolemy. A Greco-Egyptian writer, mathematician, astronomer, geographer, astrologer, and poet who lived from 90 AD to 168 AD, and is most famous for his work *The Almagest*.

Clojure in Action. A book written by Amit Rathore and Francis Avila that offers a hands-on tutorial in Clojure language for the working programmer.

Deepak Chopra. (Born 1947) An internationally acclaimed Indian American physician, advocate of alternative medicine, and bestselling author and speaker.

Distinguished Toastmaster. The highest honor given to a Toastmaster that recognises an excellent level of achievement in both communication and leadership.

Don Quixote. The Spanish novel by Miguel de Cervantes Saavedra, which is considered as one of the greatest works of fiction ever published.

Eckhart Tolle. (Born 1948) An internationally renowned writer and public speaker most well-known for his books *The Power of Now* and *A New Earth: Awakening to your Life's Purpose*.

Edgar Cayce. (1877-1945) An American mystic who prophesied on a wide range of topics—healing, reincarnation, wars, Atlantis, and future events.

Ego. Any image you have of yourself that gives you a sense of identity. This sense of identity derives from your own thinking and the impressions other people impose on you that you choose to accept as truth.

Elon Musk. (Born 1971) The founder, CEO and CTO of SpaceX; co-founder, CEO and product architect of Tesla Motors; chairman of SolarCity; co-chairman of OpenAI; co-founder of Zip2; and co-founder of PayPal.

Energy-healing. A branch of alternative medicine that is founded on the belief that an expert practitioner can direct healing energy to patients, and achieve positive results.

Flipkart. An Indian e-commerce company founded in 2007 that proved to be a game changer in India's online shopping business.

Flow. An ideal state of motivation, where the doer is fully absorbed in what he/ she is doing, unbothered by the restrictions of time, food, ego, etc.

Fritjof Capra. (Born 1939) An Austrian-born American physicist and author of *The Tao of Physics: An Exploration of the Parallels Between Modern Physics and Eastern Mysticism.*

Galileo Galilei. (1564-1642) A famed Italian polymath who played a pivotal role in the development of science during the Renaissance era.

Goddess of Namagiri. An Indian deity who supposedly appeared in legendary Indian mathematician Srinivasa Ramanujan's visions and proposed mathematical formulae, which Ramanujan then proceeded to confirm.

H. G. Wells. (1866-1946) A prolific English writer most well known for his science fiction works like *The Time Machine* and *The War of the Worlds.*

Hatha yoga. Refers to a set of physical exercises or postures, created to align your skin, muscles, and bones to enhance the nerve centers in the spine and energise the body.

Henry Ford. (1863-1947) An American industrialist, founder of the Ford Motor Company, and the promoter of the assembly line method of mass production.

Higher intelligence. Refers to attaining higher levels of intelligence by sharpening the five senses, and being compassionate about one's ecosystem and fellow humans. Compassion-centric intelligence aids greater utilization of the brain.

Human potential. Refers to human ability that is collectively represented by human intelligence, skill, and talent expressed through creativity, independence, spontaneity, and a grasp of the real world.

Icebreaker. Refers to opening up to your fears and overcoming them. In common parlance, it refers to an opening remark, action, activity, game, or event that is used to welcome and warm up the conversation among participants in a meeting, training class, or team building session.

Inner Engineering Program by Isha Foundation. A human potential development program developed by Isha Foundation, an international nonprofit organization based in Southern India.

Institute of Human Potential and Development. See Bharat Chandra.

Isaac Newton. (1643-1727) One of the most influential physicists and mathematicians of all time, and a pivotal figure in the scientific revolution of the 17th century most famous for his laws of motion and the law of universal gravitation.

Jeet Kun Do. A style of martial art created by martial artist Bruce Lee. JKD uses minimal movements with maximum effects and extreme speed. The techniques are not fixed or patterned, but more spontaneous.

Jiddu Krishnamurti. (1895-1986) An Indian speaker and writer on psychological revolution, the nature of the mind, meditation, inquiry, human relationships, and effecting radical change in society.

Jung and Briggs-Myers Personality test. A personality type indicator that classified people into 16 different types based on four dichotomies: Extroverted/ Introverted, Sensing/Intuition, Thinking/Feeling, Judging/Perceiving.

Kapalabhathi. A yogic cleansing technique involving short, strong, forceful exhalations and automatic inhalation intended chiefly for cleaning the cranial sinuses, but also has other health benefits.

Karma yoga. The yoga of action that teaches the doer to act selflessly, without thought of gain or reward. It is one of the four paths of yoga.

Katha Upanishad. One of more than 200 important Sanskrit spiritual texts— the Upanishads. Katha Upanishad contains some of the key philosophical concepts of Hinduism such as the nature of soul and liberation.

Khadi. A versatile hand-spun and hand-woven Indian fabric woven primarily from cotton that became a symbol of patriotism during India's struggle for independence from British rule.

Kinsey Institute. A research institute at Indiana University, Indiana, USA, for interdisciplinary research and scholarship in the fields of human sexuality, gender, and reproduction.

Lean philosophy of management. A management approach that believes in continuous improvement, and in systematically striving to achieve small, incremental changes in processes to improve efficiency and quality.

Leonardo da Vinci. (1452-1519) An Italian Renaissance painter, sculptor, architect, scientist, musician, mathematician, engineer, and writer whose most popular works include the *Mona Lisa* and *The Last Supper*.

Lumosity. An online program designed by the neuroscientists at Lumos Labs. It uses games that claim to train the brain and improve cognitive abilities.

Mahatma Gandhi. *(1869-1948) The foremost leader of the Indian independence movement and proponent of the idea of nonviolent civil disobedience that inspired movements for civil rights and freedom across the world.*

Mallika Sarabhai. (Born 1954) An activist and Indian classical dancer who is famous for using arts to deliver social commentary and effect social change.

Mark Zuckerberg. (Born 1984) An American computer programmer, entrepreneur, philanthropist, co-founder and CEO of the social networking website Facebook.

Marten Mickos. (Born 1962) Silicon Valley entrepreneur and the CEO of HackerOne, a company that makes security vulnerabilities tracking software. Previously, he held senior positions at Hewlett-Packard, Eucalyptus Systems, and Nokia.

Morihei Ueshiba. (1883-1969) The founder of the Japanese martial art of aikido, which emphasises not only martial techniques, but also self-development through spiritual and physical training.

Mother Teresa. (1910-1997) Renowned humanitarian and founder of the Missionaries of Charity, a Roman Catholic religious congregation that runs hospices and homes in more than 130 countries.

Nachiketa. The central character in an ancient Hindu fable. Yama, the Hindu god of death, teaches Nachiketa self-knowledge and how the soul can attain moksha or emancipation from the cycle of rebirth.

Napoleon Hill. (1883-1970) An American author who made a lasting contribution to the genre of personal-success literature through his best known book *Think and Grow Rich*.

Narayana Hrudayalaya. A group of low-cost, high-quality health centers based in Southern India that include the world's largest, most prolific cardiac hospital.

Nelson Mandela. *(1918-2013) The South African anti-apartheid revolutionary, politician, and philanthropist, who served as the country's president and first black chief executive from 1994 to 1999.*

Nikola Tesla. (1856-1943) An inventor, engineer, physicist and futurist whose most prominent contributions include the design of the alternating current (AC) power system, Tesla coil, and the rotating magnetic field.

Osho Rajneesh. (1931-1990) An Indian mystic, guru, spiritual teacher, professor of philosophy, and public speaker who had an international presence in the 1960s, 1970s, and 1980s.

Patanjali. Considered the father of modern yoga and the author of the celebrated Yoga Sutras or yoga rules, and the Mahābhāṣya, an advanced treatise on Sanskrit grammar and linguistics.

Paulo Coelho. (Born 1947) A Brazilian lyricist and novelist most famous for his novel *The Alchemist*, which has been translated into 80 languages.

Pilgrim's Progress. John Bunyan's lasting work of Christian literature and spiritual allegory that portrays the life and struggles of a believer.

Positive arrow. An act of kindness during a stressful situation that can turn things around and create positive vibes.

Pranic healing. An energy healing system that claims that illnesses of the body can be cured by manipulating or treating the body's energy field.

Pratyahara. Is the fifth limb in the eight-limbed yoga system described in the Yoga Sutra of Patanjali. Pratyahara is defined as the conscious withdrawal of energy from the senses.

Pritish Nandy. (Born 1951) An Indian poet, journalist, media and television personality, film producer, animal activist, and politician.

Puja. A Sanskrit term for the act of showing respect to the divine through chants, prayers, songs, and rituals.

Pythagoras. A great Greek philosopher, scientist, and mathematician, who lived from 570 BC to 495 BC, and is best known for the Pythagorean theorem named after him.

Quintype. A cloud-based, data-driven publishing platform that can be customised for use by modern media companies.

Rabindranath Tagore. (1861-1941) India's first Nobel laureate and renowned Bengali poet, philosopher, artist, playwright, composer, and novelist.

Ramakrishna Mission. A religious, philanthropic, volunteer organization founded by Swami Vivekananda, who was a disciple of the nineteenth century Indian saint Ramakrishna Paramahamsa.

Reiki. A Japanese energy-healing technique that uses hands to help relax and relieve stress. It associates illness and health with the levels of life force energy present in individuals.

Richard Branson. (Born 1950) An English business magnate, investor, and philanthropist, most famous as the founder of Virgin Group, a conglomerate of more than 400 enterprises.

Richard Lewis. (Born 1930) A British polyglot, cross-cultural communication expert, and author with international readership.

Robert Franklin Stroud. (1890-1963) An American criminal and self-taught ornithologist who reared and sold birds during his time at Leavenworth Penitentiary. He authored the 60,000-word book *Diseases of Canaries*.

Robert Greene. (Born 1959) An American author who has penned many international bestsellers including *The 48 Laws of Power*, *The Art of Seduction*, *The 33 Strategies of War*, *The 50th Law*, and *Mastery*.

Robert Noyce. (1927-1990) Co-founder of Fairchild Semiconductor and Intel Corporation, and co-inventor of the integrated circuit that powered the personal computer revolution, and gave Silicon Valley its name. Noyce is referred to as 'The Mayor of Silicon Valley'.

Rock Star Chapter. Refers to a Toastmasters leadership and public speaking club that meets its club goals in record-breaking times.

Sadhguru Jaggi Vasudev. (Born 1957) An Indian yogi, mystic, philanthropist, author, and founder of the Isha Foundation, an international nonprofit organization based in Southern India.

Samyama. A Sanskrit term for binding or integration. The yogic state of samyama is the simultaneous combination of the states of Dhāraṇā (concentration), Dhyāna (meditation) and Samādhi (union).

Satyagraha. A form of nonviolent or civil resistance and a strategy of passive political resistance promoted by Mahatma Gandhi against British rule in India.

School of Herring. Marten Mickos's blog on leadership for present-day organizations that function using collaborative models.

Self-realization. The act of achieving the full development of your abilities and talents.

Siddha Samadhi Yoga. An Indian organization that instructs individuals on techniques of the ancient Vedic science of effortless joyful living. Its flagship program is also called *Siddha Samadhi Yoga* or the science of silence yoga.

Singularity. Refers to an imaginary event in which artificial intelligence becomes capable of repeated self-improvement until machines create more intelligence that will be beyond human control.

Srinivasa Ramanujan. (1887-1920). A self-taught Indian mathematical genius who made outstanding contributions to mathematical analysis, number theory, infinite series, and continued fractions.

Stephen Covey. (1932-2012) An American educator, author, businessman, and keynote speaker who is most well known for his bestseller *The 7 Habits of Highly Effective People*.

Steve Jobs. (1955-2011) An American information technology entrepreneur and inventor; co-founder, chairman, and CEO of Apple Inc.; and pioneer of the personal computer revolution.

StrengthsFinder2.0. Gallup's online assessment tool that claims to help individuals identify their top five talents and offers strategies for applying those strengths.

Sudarshan kriya. A breathing technique that uses the breath to influence emotions or the way an individual feels.

Suprahuman. Refers to having powers that are above and beyond that of a normal human.

Swami Chinmayananda. (1916-1993) A Hindu spiritual leader, author, and inspiration behind the Chinmaya Mission—a spiritual, educational, charitable, global nonprofit organization.

Swami Vivekananda. (1863-1902) An Indian monk whose speeches at the 1893 Parliament of World's Religions in Chicago were pivotal in the introduction of the Hindu philosophies of Vedanta and Yoga to the Western world.

The Discovery of India. A book by India's first Prime Minister Jawaharlal Nehru that pays tribute to the rich traditions, culture, history, and philosophy of India and is considered an Indian classic.

The Story of My Experiments with Truth. The autobiography of Mahatma Gandhi, which is considered one of the most important spiritual and inspirational literary works of the twentieth century.

Timelessness. Refers to a state of not being bound by time, in the context of this book.

Toastmasters International. A worldwide nonprofit educational organization that helps its members improve their communication, public speaking, and leadership skills through its member clubs.

Tony Robbins. (Born 1960) An American entrepreneur, motivational speaker, and best-selling author of books such as *Unlimited Power*, *Unleash the Power Within*, and *Awaken the Giant Within*.

TRP ratings. Stands for television rating point ratings, a calculation conducted to assess viewership of a television channel.

Upanishads. A collection of Sanskrit texts that contain the cardinal philosophical principles of Hinduism. There are more than 200 known Upanishads.

Vedanta. One of the six systems of Indian philosophy. The three important Vedanta texts are the Upanishads, the Brahmasutras, and the Bhagavadgita.

Vedas. Sanskrit term for knowledge. Vedas are the oldest known examples of Sanskrit literature and consist of hymns and religious texts. The four Vedas are the Rig-Veda, Sama-Veda, Yajur-Veda, and Atharva-Veda.

Veena. An ancient Indian stringed instrument used mainly in Carnatic and Hindustani classical music.

Vertical Living. Is a lifestyle of awakened living that emphasises that the present is the only truth to think about—a simple formula used by many game changers and successful high performers.

Vertical states. Refers to states of heightened overall awareness, compassion, and creativity.

Vipassana. A meditation technique that teaches one to see things as they really are. It is often taught as a ten-day course during which participants are trained in mindfulness of breathing, thoughts, feelings, and actions to understand the true nature of reality.

Yama. The Hindu god of death.

Yoga. A Hindu discipline or practice that includes breath control, meditation, and the adoption of particular physical postures for health and relaxation.

Bibliography

PREFACE

[1] Vishen Lakhiani's transformational course, 'Consciousness Engineering'
http://www.finerminds.com/mind-power/brain-waves

[2] 'Additional ABCs about PLM', accessed 2/25/2016,
http://www.thefreelibrary.com/Additional+ABCs+about+PLM.-a0140194934

[3] Definition of entrepreneur. http://dictionary.reference.com/browse/entrepreneur

[4] Natalie Sisson, 'Suitcase Entrepreneur' http://suitcaseentrepreneur.com/

[5] Pichler, Roman. *Agile Product Management with Scrum: Creating Products That Customers Love.* Upper Saddle River, NJ: Addison-Wesley, 2010

[6] 'Vipassana Fellowship' http://www.vipassana.com/

[7] Bundzen PV, Korotkov KG, Unestahl LE (April 2002). *Altered States of Consciousness: Review of Experimental Data Obtained With a Multiple Techniques Approach.* The Journal of Alternative and Complementary Medicine, Vol 8, 153-165. doi:10.1089/107555302317371442. PMID 12006123.

[8] 'Debiasing the Mind Through Meditation: Mindfulness and the Sunk-Cost Bias'
http://pss.sagepub.com/content/early/2013/12/06/0956797613503853

[9] Quotes from Steve Jobs http://www.goodreads.com/
quotes/445286-have-the-courage-to-follow-your-heart-and-intuition-they

[10] 'Learn How to Meditate and Trust Your Intuition'
http://jackcanfield.com/learn-how-to-meditate-and-trust-your-intuition/

[11] The Complete Works of Swami Vivekananda, Volume 6/Lectures and Discourses

[12] 'Theory Of Constraints'
http://www.leanproduction.com/theory-of-constraints.html

Chapter 1

[100] Doidge, Norman. *The Brain That Changes Itself: Stories of Personal Triumph from the Frontiers of Brain Science*. New York: Viking, 2007.

[101] Kotler, Steven. *The Rise of Superman: Decoding the Science of Ultimate Human Performance*. Chapter 3, Page 44, New Harvest, 2014.

[102] Lee, Bruce. *Chinese Gung Fu: The Philosophical Art of Self Defense*. Burbank, CA: Ohara Publications, 1988.

[103] Quotes from Bruce Lee
http://www.goodreads.com/quotes/204903-if-you-always-put-limits-on-everything-you-do-physical

[104] 'Calligraphic Meditation: The Mindful art of Thich Nhat Hanh'
http://www.thichnhathanhcalligraphy.org/newyork/

[105] Isaacson, Walter. *Steve Jobs*. New York: Simon & Schuster, 2011.

[106] Gage, Randy. 'Be Like Water.' *RandyGage.Com: Success and Prosperity Blog* (blog). http://www.randygage.com/like-water/.

[107] Grau C, Ginhoux R, Riera A, Nguyen TL, Chauvat H, Berg M, et al. (2014) Conscious Brain-to-Brain Communication in Humans Using Non-Invasive Technologies. PLoS ONE 9(8): e105225. doi:10.1371/journal.pone.0105225

[108] Gregoire, Carolyn. '10 Things Highly Intuitive People Do Differently.' The Huffington Post. http://www.huffingtonpost.com/2014/03/19/the-habits-of-highly-intu_n_4958778.html.

[109] Gonda, Jan. *The Indian Mantra*. Vol 16, Pages 244-297, Leiden: Brill, 1963.

[110] Rajvanshi, Anil K. 'Decoding Subconscious Mind: How Dreams Can Be Guided by Yoga - NewsGram.' NewsGram. April 08, 2015. http://www.newsgram.com/decoding-subconscious-mind-how-dreams-can-be-guided-by-yoga/.

[111] 'Albert Einstein's Certificate of Qualification for University Matriculation.' Albert Einstein's Certificate of Qualification for University Matriculation. http://www.einstein-website.de/z_kids/certificatekids.html.

[112] 'Vipassana.' Meditation. https://www.dhamma.org/en/about/art.

[113] 'How to Develop Your Sixth Sense.' WikiHow. http://www.wikihow.com/Develop-Your-Sixth-Sense.

[114] Csikszentmihalyi, Mihaly. *Flow: The Psychology of Optimal Experience*. New York: Harper & Row, 1990.

Chapter 2

[200] Fisher Jr, W. 'Galileo and Scientific Method.' Galileo and Scientific Method. http://www.rasch.org/rmt/rmt64g.htm.

[201] Galilei, Galileo. *Galileo on the World Systems: A New Abridged Translation and Guide*. Page 47, Edited &Translated by Maurice A. Finocchiaro. Berkeley: University of California Press, 1997.

[202] Hilliam, Rachel. *Galileo Galilei: Father of Modern Science*. Page 96, New York: Rosen Pub. Group, 2005.

[203] 'Learn How to Meditate and Trust Your Intuition' http://jackcanfield.com/learn-how-to-meditate-and-trust-your-intuition/

[204] 'Develop Your Intuition through Meditation - EOC Institute.' EOC Institute. 2013. http://eocinstitute.org/meditation/develop-your-intuition-through-meditation/.

[205] Fripp, Patricia. 'Public Speaking: How Did Patricia Fripp Get Started? - Patricia Fripp.' 2010. http://www.fripp.com/public-speaking-how-did-patricia-fripp-get-started/.

[206] 'Join, or Die,' by Benjamin Franklin, Pennsylvania Gazette Philadelphia, PA), May 9, 1754. Courtesy, Library of Congress http://www.history.org/history/teaching/enewsletter/volume5/november06/primsource.cfm

[207] 'Benjamin Franklin's Inventions.' Ushistory.org. http://www.ushistory.org/franklin/info/inventions.htm.

[208] '9 Powerful Success Lessons from Bill Gates.' Life Optimizer RSS. http://www.lifeoptimizer.org/2015/01/20/success-lessons-bill-gates/.

Vidyangi

[209] 'Baidu CEO Robin Li Interviews Bill Gates and Elon Musk at the Boao Forum.' Futurism Baidu CEO Robin Li Interviews Bill Gates and Elon Musk at the Boao Forum Comments. 2015. http://futurism.com/videos/baidu-ceo-robin-li-interviews-bill-gates-and-elon-musk-at-the-boao-forum/.

[210] Suzuki, Shunryu, and Trudy Dixon. Zen Mind, Beginner's Mind. Page 21, Boston: Weatherhill, 1999.

[211] Baer, Drake. 'Elon Musk Uses This Ancient Critical-Thinking Strategy To Outsmart Everybody Else.' Business Insider. 2015. http://www.businessinsider.com/elon-musk-first-principles-2015-1.

[212] Geocentric Model, Wikipedia. https://en.wikipedia.org/wiki/Geocentric_model.

[213] Two New Sciences, Wikipedia. https://en.wikipedia.org/wiki/Two_New_Sciences.

[214] 'Albert Einstein.' Albert Einstein Biography and Quotes. http://www.sourcedquotes.com/Albert-Einstein-biography-and-quotes.

[215] Strozzi-Heckler, Richard. 'Clairsentience: A Somatic Approach to Intuition.' Strozzi Institute. December 2011. http://www.strozziinstitute.com/node/475.

[216] Clucas, Joan Graff. Mother Teresa. Page 35, New York: Chelsea House, 1988.

[217] Katz, Michael. Tibetan Dream Yoga- The Royal Road to Enlightenment. Kindle Edition. Edited by Ed Levy. Bodhi Tree Publications, 2011.

[218] Hardy, G. H. 'Obituary: S. Ramanujan, F.R.S.' Nature.com. DOI 10.1038/105494a0,
http://www.nature.com/nature/journal/v105/n2642/abs/105494a0.html.

[219] 'The Neuropsychological Connection Between Creativity and Meditation.' Taylor & Francis. http://www.tandfonline.com/doi/abs/10.1080/10400410902858691.

[220] Rajvanshi, Anil K. 'Decoding Subconscious Mind: How Dreams Can Be Guided by Yoga - NewsGram.' NewsGram. April 08, 2015. http://www.newsgram.com/decoding-subconscious-mind-how-dreams-can-be-guided-by-yoga/.

[221] 'Leonardo Da Vinci.' Wikipedia. https://en.wikipedia.org/wiki/Leonardo_da_Vinci.

[222] Pearson, Craig. 'Plato – "And This State Of The Soul Is Called Wisdom".' TM Blog (blog), March 20, 2011. http://www.tm.org/blog/enlightenment/plato-and-this-state-of-the-soul-is-called-wisdom/.

[223] Plato. *The Collected Dialogues of Plato: Including the Letters*. Edited by Edith Hamilton and Huntington Cairns. Princeton, NJ: Princeton University Press, 1973.

[224] Plato. *The Dialogues of Plato: In Five Volumes*. Translated by Benjamin Jowett. Page 222, Oxford: Clarendon Press, 1892.

[225] West, John Anthony. 'Theosophical Society in America.' The Wisdom of Ancient Egypt -. https://www.theosophical.org/publications/quest-magazine/42-publications/quest-magazine/1278-the-wisdom-of-ancient-egypt.

[226] Childress, David Hatcher. *Technology of the Gods: The Incredible Sciences of the Ancients*. Kempton, IL: Adventures Unlimited Press, 2000.

[227] 'Gellman, Jerome, "Mysticism", The Stanford Encyclopedia of Philosophy (Summer 2011 Edition), Edward N. Zalta (ed.)'. Plato.stanford.edu. Retrieved 2013-11-06.

[228] 'Fritjof Capra.' http://www.fritjofcapra.net/.

[229] Yang, Fenggang; Tamney, Joseph (2011). Confucianism and Spiritual Traditions in Modern China and Beyond. BRILL. p. 132. ISBN 978-90-04-21569-6.

[230] Fisk, Peter. *Creative Genius: An Innovation Guide for Business Leaders, Border Crossers and Game Changers* ISBN: 978-1-84112-789-7 400 pages, March 2011, Capstone
http://thinkers50.com/blog/innovation-leonardo-da-vinci/

[231] McMahan, David L. *The Making of Buddhist Modernism*. Oxford: Oxford University Press, 2008.

[232] Elon Musk: Tesla, SpaceX, and the Quest for a Fantastic Future is Ashlee Vance's biography of Elon Musk, published in 2015.

Chapter 3

[300] 'Sudha Murthy.' Wikipedia. https://en.wikipedia.org/wiki/Sudha_Murthy.

[301] 'A Philanthropist Speaks: "Lessons from Life"' YouTube. https://www.youtube.com/watch?v=x1Cp4qta4bU.

[302] Chopra, Deepak. 'The Health Benefits of Practicing Compassion.' The Huffington Post. http://www.huffingtonpost.com/deepak-chopra/the-health-benefits-of-pr_b_7586440.html.

[303] 'Scientific Insights from the Greater Good Gratitude Summit.' Greater Good. http://greatergood.berkeley.edu/article/item/new_insights_from_the_gratitude_summit.

[304] Keller, Gary, and Jay Papasan. *The One Thing: The Surprisingly Simple Truth behind Extraordinary Results*. Austin, TX: Bard Press, 2012.

Chapter 4

[400] Lutz, Antoine, Heleen A. Slagter, John D. Dunne, and Richard J. Davidson. 'Attention Regulation and Monitoring in Meditation.' *Trends in Cognitive Sciences* 12, no. 4 (2008): 163-69.

[401] Watts, Alan. '11 _10-4-1 Meditation.' Eastern Wisdom: Zen in the West & Meditations. The Alan Watts Foundation. 2009. MP3 CD. @4:45].

[402] 'An Intimate Interview with Dr Brian Weiss – Brian L. Weiss.' Hay House Australias Blog. 2011. https://hayhouseoz.wordpress.com/2011/02/07/an-intimate-interview-with-dr-brian-weiss-brian-l-weiss/.

[403] http://www.swamivivekanandaquotes.org/2013/12/swami-vivekananda-arise-awake-and-stop-not-till-the-goal-is-reached.html.

[404] Swami Vivekananda, Wikipedia. https://en.wikipedia.org/wiki/Swami_Vivekananda.

Chapter 6

[600] Goleman, Daniel. *Emotional Intelligence: Why It Can Matter More than IQ*. London: Bloomsbury, 1996.

[601] Lubin, Gus. 'The Lewis Model Explains Every Culture In The World.' Business Insider. 2013. http://www.businessinsider.com/the-lewis-model-2013-9.

[602] Deborah Rozman. 'Let Your Heart Talk to Your Brain.' The Huffington Post. http://www.huffingtonpost.com/heartmath-llc/heart-wisdom_b_2615857.html.

Chapter 7

[700] Robinson, Lynn A. *Divine Intuition: Your Inner Guide to Purpose, Peace, and Prosperity.* San Francisco: Jossey-Bass, 2013.

[701] 'Dr Helen Fisher - Biological Anthropologist - Home Page.' Dr Helen Fisher - Biological Anthropologist - Home Page. http://www.helenfisher.com/.

[702] 'The Science of Love.' The Science of Love. http://www.youramazingbrain. org/lovesex/sciencelove.htm.

[703] 'Strategic Intuition: The Creative Spark in Human Achievement.' Strategic Intuition: The Creative Spark in Human Achievement. http://cupola. columbia.edu/978-0-231-14268-7/.

Link to my blogs:

http://vidyaangi.blogspot.com/

http://voxtmsj.blogspot.com/

https://headhearthead.wordpress.com/author/vphhh/

https://www.facebook.com/vidyangi/notes

Acknowledgements

I am nobody and nothing without the blessings and guidance of my mother (Amma) who bore me for nine months, loved me, educated me, and nourished me in every possible way a mother would. Thank you!

I am very grateful to my personal friend, philosopher, coach, counselor and guide. I dedicate this book to my mentor.

I offer the book to my father, Dr S. N. Patil and husband Devjit N. Gopalpur. They have been the pillars and support structures of my life. It is one thing for me to be able to write a book; but to accept me for who I am, and to believe in what I do, can come only from very giving and generous souls, as my father and husband have always been in my life. Their calm and collective approach, and wisdom in perceiving life has only humbled me in my efforts. Much of my inspiration in public speaking has come from my father, who I wish to emulate. Devjit has been a role model to me in all walks of life. I owe every success in my speaking and writing career to Devjit. As a loving husband, he wears many hats to strike a work-life balance in our family. He sacrificed his comforts, many a time, to make my efforts in writing and speaking happen.

I dedicate the book to my sister Sumathi. She has time and again, in action and words, shown me the actual art of giving and loving. Hats off to you, you are no less than a part of my heart and soul. I would like to thank my brother-in-law,

Dr Ashwini Kumar Kudari, for instilling confidence in me to proceed boldly with my enterprise.

I would like to thank my mother-in-law, Dr Renukarani Nagendrappa (Amma), and father-in-law Dr G. Nagendrappa, for serving as my role models in the realm of writing, communication and publication. My father-in-law has been an ardent critic and source of support as well, for my efforts in writing and publishing. Dearest Amma, I am so lucky to feel your love and blessings. Your guidance and love are unmatched. I thank Suchit Gopalpur for lending his critical eye in molding the content of the book.

I would like to thank Dr John R. Adler for being a huge motivation and support to me through this endeavor. He not only helped shape the objectives for the book but also genuinely stood for the message in the book. He knew the challenges I was facing at every step and helped me through each one of them with utmost care. I would like to express my in-depth gratitude to John for sharing his ideas in the book.

I would like to thank Dr Devi Shetty for his valuable time and guidance which he has provided for the book. I thank Suhas Gopinath for sharing his ideas and inspiration. I am immensely thankful to Mekin Maheshwari for taking me through his experiences in building Flipkart. I thank Amit Rathore for sharing his ideas on art, writing, entrepreneurship and being such a dear friend and guide.

If there is a community of helpful souls representing excellence in communication and leadership, they call themselves Toastmasters! Have you been to a Toastmaster meeting yet? Well, then maybe it's time to make some cool friends. Let me name a few Toastmasters who taught me what leadership and communication is all about. They lead the by example and excelled in verbal communication skills. Thank you Deep Kakkar, Elaine Lung, Dilip Kikla, Kavitha Badhri, Karthik Kalpat, Michael Chojnaki, Joseph Fernandez, Vicky Iu, Hla Minh, Katherine Pratt, Mythili S. Prabhu. All my friends at Vox, Lee Emerson Bassett and other Toastmaster clubs, I can't name every one of you as the list would be endless, but I would like to acknowledge your undying support.

My sincere thanks to veteran and accomplished Toastmasters Michael Chojnaki, PK, Joseph Fernandez, Karthik Kalpat and Vicky Iu for agreeing to interview with me for the book. They are not only mentors to the Toastmasters community, but also to all people out there who aspire to be great communicators and leaders.

I can't thank enough my friends Shruti Murthy and Spoorthy Murali for the undying support and love they have shown me through ups and downs in my life. They have painstakingly read every sentence of this book three years ago, in its initial draft and given me an honest feedback about what they have felt. I love you so much for your unconditional support! Megha Manohar, you have been a source of strength and support in so many ways. Thank you for being you. What would I do without friends like you?

Thank you Megha Vishwanath and Swetha Dixit, for shaking me up and showing me the path to the world of publishing. Every time I write, I hear your voices at the back of my mind.

I would like to thank all the artists and photographers who have contributed to the depth and personality of the book. I would like to thank Erwin D'Souza and Mausam Hazarika for their photographs which transport us to a space defined by divinity and creativity. I am immensely thankful to Nivedita Gouda, Spoorthy Murali, Ashwini Bharadwaj and Megha Vishwanath for their art work. Each of them has worked hard to realise a vision for the message in the book.

I thank Arya Hebbar for being such a great editor and consultant on the book. She has been a sturdy support in so many ways in seeing the book take its final shape.

I would like to thank my editor, Linda Jay. She has been a great guide and support to me in voicing my message. I thank Jyoti Paintel who is the light in my life in so many ways. She has contributed a lot in terms of developing the content in the book.

Thank you, Gaurav, and your team at The Random Lines. You are not only good at building websites, but great guides in helping people to manage their careers and lives.

Last but not the least, to all people who have been reading my articles, listening to my talks and encouraging me to write and speak: I would like to thank you from the bottom of my heart.

Printed in the United States
By Bookmasters